DATE DUE

3/16			

DEMCO 38-296

A WORLD IGNITED

Also by the Authors

Glass Houses: Congressional Ethics and the Politics of Venom
Selling Our Security: The Erosion of America's Assets
Buying Into America: How Foreign Money Is Changing the Face of Our Nation
Dismantling America: The Rush to Deregulate
Clout: Womanpower and Politics
To the Victor: Political Patronage from the Clubhouse to the White House
The Angry American: How Voter Rage Is Changing the Nation

A WORLD IGNITED

How Apostles of Ethnic, Religious, and Racial Hatred Torch the Globe

Martin and Susan J. Tolchin

ROWMAN & LITTLEFIELD PUBLISHERS, INC.
Lanham • Boulder • New York • Toronto • Oxford

ROWMAN & LITTLEFIELD PUBLISHERS, INC.

Published in the United States of America
by Rowman & Littlefield Publishers, Inc.
A wholly owned subsidary of The Rowman & Littlefield Publishing Group, Inc.
4501 Forbes Boulevard, Suite 200, Lanham, Maryland 20706
www.rowmanlittlefield.com

PO Box 317
Oxford
OX2 9RU, UK

British Library Cataloguing in Publication Information Available

Library of Congress Cataloging-in-Publication Data

Tolchin, Martin.
  A world ignited : how apostles of ethnic, religious, and racial hatred torch the
globe / Martin Tolchin and Susan J. Tolchin.
    p.   cm.
  Includes bibliographical references and index.
  ISBN-13: 978-0-7425-3656-2 (cloth : alk. paper)
  ISBN-10: 0-7425-3656-4 (cloth : alk. paper)
    1. Political violence.   2. Culture conflict—Religious aspects.   3. Ethnic
relations—Political aspects.   4. Hate speech.   5. Anti-Semitism.   I. Tolchin,
Susan J.   II. Title.
JC328.6.T645   2006
303.6—dc22   2006003147

Printed in the United States of America

♾ ™ The paper used in this publication meets the minimum requirements of American
National Standard for Information Sciences—Permanence of Paper for Printed Library
Materials, ANSI/NISO Z39.48-1992.

To the memory of our beloved son
Charles Peter Tolchin
(1968–2003)

"Brave of spirit,
Pure in heart."

CONTENTS

ACKNOWLEDGMENTS

According to legend, the collaboration between Beatrice and Sidney Webb was so exhilarating that the couple would work for two hours and then make mad, passionate love before returning to their manuscripts. As in all apocryphal stories, this one is probably untrue, and after seven books, we now know why. Exhilarating, yes. But an aphrodisiac?

It is the first question everyone asks us: how can you collaborate on a book with your spouse? "I can't even boil an egg with my wife; how can you write a book together?" is one variation. We try to comfort people with the fact that we can't play golf together, that we each write chapters separately and edit each other, and that the whole enterprise is kind of like the old saw about porcupines making love: very carefully.

Martin comes from the long and honorable tradition of print journalism, where words aren't minced and the criticisms come in the form of ripped-up manuscript pages lobbed into the trash. Susan, honed by the academic world, tended to scrawl voluminous notes in the margins as "suggestions for revision."

But it had to work. Unlike the Webbs, no independent income sustained us, and neither of us had chosen professions known for their high salaries. Our collaboration began at an inauspicious moment: we were broke, Susan was seven months pregnant and unemployed, and we needed a larger place to live. When our first publisher beckoned with a small advance, we promptly seized the opportunity to put a down payment on a house, despite the fact that we had never so much as written a thank-you note together. When our son was born, there was no longer any excuse not to start writing. We deposited him on an infant seat in the middle of a long table, set our typewriters (remember them?) at either end, and in a reversal of roles we squalled at each other as he rolled his head from side to side. Three books and another child later, our babysitter timidly asked if we planned to use our royalties for marriage counseling!

We finally realized the advantages of marrying journalism and academe. Journalism brings an approach to inquiry that isolates themes and establishes the necessity of interviewing sources directly. The academic approach offers the advantage of reflection, unburdened as it is by the pressures of the daily deadline or a limited word count.

Lest the reader think that love conquers all problems, we suggest a short story by Somerset Maugham about a mystery writer whose fame and fortune rested on her use of the semicolon—a source of great conflict between us—and whose despairing husband eventually abandoned her to run away with the cook. I guess it is just fortunate that Susan happens to be the cook!

All of our books have benefited from the help and advice of our friends and colleagues, and this book is no exception. We especially offer our thanks to all the people who helped us understand global anger, a subject that encompasses many disciplines, and who so generously shared their insights, knowledge, time, and experience. The study focuses on data compiled from a variety of primary and secondary sources, including interviews with journalists, scholars, public officials, and advocates who are all deeply involved in the subject. All direct quotes in the text that are not cited in the chapters' endnotes are drawn from these interviews, including Ali H. J. Al-Marri, Samar Al-Rayyis, Amr Abdalla, Nabeel Abdrabalnabi, Daniel Alter, Andrew Baker, Tim Baker, Adel Bashatah, John Becker, Randolph Bell, E. Brearley, Milica Chernick, Phyllis Chesler, Agastin Comejo, Robert Dallek, Tom DeMarchi, Desmond Dinan, Dmytro Dobovolosky, Marian Douglas, Rick Eaton, Stuart Eizenstat, Amitai Etzioni, Nadia Fam, Eugene Fidell, Mistik Halici, Hussain Haqqani, Elyette Levy Heisbourg, Jess Hordes, Phan Hong, Norma Joseph, Nfagie Kabba, Kitty Kelley, Harriet Kelman, Rami Khouri, Tom Korologos, Barba Koroma, Robyn Krauthammer, Jean David Levitte, Roxana Loaiza, Brian Marcus, Edward Martin, Michael McClintock, Dinah McDougall, Myra Mendible, Robert Merry, Nzigamye Nahayo, Mary Rose Oakar, Taqwa Omer, Mustafa Ozkaya, Solomon Passy, Gonzalo Paz, Benedicta Pésceli, Mark Potok, Alan Riding, Elaine Sciolino, Natalie Sequeira, David Shipler, Cathy Sulzberger, Henry Vega, Shirley Williams, Robin Wright, and Ali Yurtsever.

Many of our friends, colleagues, and outside experts read selected chapters as well as the entire manuscript and were especially helpful in sharing their criticisms. They are Kenneth Beldon, Linda Cashdan, Michael Catlett, Pat Choate, Dave Davis, Jane Dixon, Fred Dobbs, George Driesen, Albert Eisele, Abraham Foxman, Yahya Hendi, Jack High, John L. Hirsch, Martha Kessler, Kenneth Kessler, Barry Kosmin, Robert Lifton, Peter Mandaville, Jeremy Mayer, Janice O'Connell, Mark Rozell, Stephen Ruth, Minna Morse Scherlinder, Sid Schwarz, Richard Shmaruk, Karen Tolchin, Janine Wedel, Harold White, and Christopher Wolf.

Susan's professional home at George Mason University has been consistently supportive of her research efforts. Her students, particularly those from abroad, have provided many ideas and critical perspectives to the subject. Grants from the Office of the Provost and the School of Public Policy paid for both travel and research assistance. Many thanks to Dean Kingsley Haynes, Provost Peter Stearns, Senior Associate Dean James Finkelstein, and Vice Provost Christopher Hill for making these resources possible. Thanks, also, to Dean Rita Carty for her help and advice.

Also at George Mason University, Susan's research assistants provided stellar skills at checking facts, tracking down leads, editing the manuscript, constructing charts, and navigating the complexities of research and writing on the computer. In alphabetical order, they are Aaron Arnold, Pritam Banerjee, Sarasin Boopanan, Brandon Powell, and Carol Whitney. Jennifer Stone, administrative assistant at the School of Public Policy, worked cheerfully throughout the research and the writing periods. Martin's *New York Times* colleagues also were helpful, especially Barclay Walsh, research librarian in the Washington bureau.

We are also grateful to our editor, Christopher Anzalone, for his close attention to detail and incisive editing. He inherited the book but was an enthusiastic supporter from the start. His assistant, Claire Rojstaczer, also offered valuable suggestions. We would also like to thank the original editor of the book, Jennifer Knerr, for her thoughtful comments, and for sticking with us even after she had left the company. Thanks also to the members of the Rowman & Littlefield family who guided the book to publication: Lea Gift, Jenni Brewer, and Jen Linck.

Our daughter, Karen Tolchin, gave generously of her time and energy, to edit the manuscript at various stages of its development. We are proud that her first book, *Part Blood, Part Ketchup: Coming of Age in American Literature and Film*, was just published by Lexington Books, an imprint of Rowman & Littlefield.

Our beloved son Charlie, to whom this book is dedicated, remains an inspiration. He lost his life two weeks short of his thirty-fifth birthday after a lifelong struggle with cystic fibrosis. Although we will always miss him, we are truly grateful for the time we had with him.

Susan J. Tolchin and Martin Tolchin
Washington, D.C., and Warren, Vermont

PREFACE

This book is about the surge of anger that has swept the world in the last decade, its myriad causes, its toll in lives and human misery, and what can be done to halt, and even reverse, this cacophony of hate.

From the end of the Cold War, to tyrants who translate their lust for power and profits into the death and destruction of their own people, there is no dearth of causes of this surge. The anger is amplified by modern communications technology, especially television and the Internet, and made more lethal by modern weaponry, including AK-47s and rocket launchers.

Today's apostles of hate have fine-tuned a long tradition. Genocide and other mass murders—in Russia, China, Western Europe, Africa, and Asia—killed more people in the twentieth century than all the wars combined, according to the International Campaign to End Genocide.

This book is a sequel to *The Angry American: How Voter Rage Has Changed the Nation*, which described how voter anger (nonviolent, to be sure) affected the political landscape of the 1990s. Anger was a key factor in the defeat of George H. W. Bush in 1992, who violated his campaign pledge, "Read my lips: no new taxes." It also was central to the Republican takeover of the House of Representatives in 1994, after forty years of Democratic rule, as well as the GOP victory in the Senate. The continued disaffection of American voters led Republicans to recapture the White House in 2000.

This escalation of anger in the United States was underscored by the decline of civility in the political arena, especially in Congress and state legislatures, and in increasingly corrosive political campaigns marked by the defamation of candidates rather than by substantive discussions of issues.

The ousting of California's Democratic governor Gray Davis in a recall vote shortly after he was elected, accompanied by the national proliferation of referenda, also suggests Americans' declining trust in their elected officials.

The escalation of anger is not just an American problem but has increasingly become a global phenomenon. From the genocide in Kosovo, Rwanda, and the Congo to the suicide bombings of three hotels in Amman, Jordan, and the weeks of riots in France in the autumn of 2005, uncontrolled rage has taken over the world's streets, cities, and villages.

This violence is fed by political power struggles, economic disparities, and religious and cultural wars that sometimes go back centuries, as well as by deep-seated feelings of defeat and humiliation. Much of it is directed against the United States. Indeed, 9/11 and previous attacks on U.S. targets—including the USS *Cole* off the coast of Yemen, the Khobar Towers in Saudi Arabia, and embassies in Kenya and Tanzania—unfortunately represent only the tip of the iceberg. Enormous worldwide anger also is directed at Israel, most recently because of its policies toward Palestinians, although most of the world resented the very existence of this nation from its very start in 1948, and still does. Some leaders are more candid than others. In November 2005, President Mahmoud Ahmadinejad of Iran told a rally that Israel "must be wiped off the map." Anger erupts from almost every nation, sometimes between rival nations, such as India and Pakistan; at other times, internal anger takes hold, as in Kosovo and Rwanda.

A World Ignited: How Apostles of Ethnic, Religious, and Racial Hatred Torch the Globe seeks to explore the roots of this rage and why it seems to have reached a fever pitch. The end of the Cold War was a major factor. Without the Soviet Union to tamp down internal dissension in its own regions as well as in Eastern European countries, ancient rivalries erupted anew. The end of colonialism brought more conflict, as tribal chieftains displayed a lust for power and profits that matched, and at times exceeded, the hated colonialists. The rise of worldwide fundamentalism, and the emergence of religious fanatics who regard nonbelievers as instruments of Satan, looms large on the global landscape as yet another troublesome factor. Modern communications technology has also contributed to mounting global anger, as has the tendency of leaders—as they always have—to demonize their opponents in order to escalate the violence.

Alas, since there are thousands of examples of the eruption of global anger, the book chose to be selective, not comprehensive. Some of the worst examples occur in Africa, the Middle East, Asia, and South America, where authoritarianism is the rule. Despots need scapegoats, as their citizens, unable to protest against governments armed with secret police and corrupt leaders, are whipped into a frenzy against traditional ethnic, religious, and racial foes. But at times, the citizens need no prodding to install hatred on the political agenda.

To be sure, political anger can have a positive effect. It gave birth to the American and French revolutions and jettisoned royalists, colonialists, and despots the world over. Anger has driven the civil rights revolution in this country and led to enactment of laws that ended child labor and provided protection against impure food and drugs and the hazards of the workplace. *A World Ignited* focuses on the negative effects of global anger and on how that anger has changed the world's political landscape, often for the worse. It also discusses how some politicians foment and manipulate that anger, and how responsible leaders can overcome past patterns of conflict that seem inexorable.

This book also discusses the affliction of anti-Semitism, the oldest of ethnic and religious hatreds, with roots in both the Old and New Testaments. Anti-Semitism has been nurtured by demagogues through the centuries to distract citizens from their real problems of powerlessness, poverty, hunger, and disease. It delves into the psychological roots of ethnic, religious, and racial hatreds, focusing on the central role of defeat and humiliation on the collective psyches of people in the world's worst trouble spots. Before he took his dramatic trip to extend the olive branch of peace to Israel, President Anwar Sadat convinced his fellow Egyptians that the 1973 War—a stalemate in the eyes of the rest of the world—was a military victory for Egypt. This temporarily erased the feeling of defeat that had pervaded Egypt since the Crusades and colonialism, and it set the stage for Sadat's dramatic peace overture to the Knesset.

The economic roots of anger also play a substantial role in these human tragedies, as the real villains, leaders who plunder for profit and power, victimize those who languish in poverty and despair, often benefiting from the complicity of the rest of the world. U.S. foreign policy, including the nation's recent foray into Iraq, has exacerbated worldwide anger toward the United States to the surprise of its leaders. A chapter on technology analyzes how the Internet promotes the organization, communication, and financing of hate groups around the world.

Finally, although anger and hatred seem to be as much a staple of the human condition as love and kindness, some victims' groups have resorted to unusual strategies that offer forgiveness and reconciliation. Although some of these strategies are centuries old, they have much to offer in ending the downward spiral of hate.

Note: This book relies on a wide variety of primary and secondary sources, including interviews with scholars, journalists, government officials, political advocates, and clergy. All direct quotes in the text that are not cited in the endnotes are drawn from these interviews.

1

ANCIENT HATREDS, MODERN WARS

Why do the nations rage, and the peoples plot a vain thing?

—Psalms 2:1

A distinguished physician and research scientist at the National Institutes of Health, Dr. Milica Chernick, was born and raised in Macedonia but has lived in the United States for over thirty years. She recently spoke movingly about the Croatian assaults on Skopje, the village where she was born and raised. She angrily related the mass executions of her countrymen and the rape and murder of the women, speaking with great emotional intensity in a manner that more than suggested a desire for revenge. When had these outrages occurred? she was asked. In the fifteenth century, she answered, in a voice still tinged with a Slavic accent. But to her, it was as though it had happened yesterday.

Inflamed by politicians who manipulate ancient religious, ethnic, racial, and national hatreds, the world has seen a surge of violence by those who carry the banner of revenge, often for acts that occurred centuries ago. In India, Hindus and Muslims have discarded the teachings of both Gandhi and Muhammad in their murderous assaults upon one another. In Kosovo, Serbs and Croats continued to exact revenge on each other for outrages that occurred centuries ago. In Sierra Leone, a onetime corporal led a group of rebels in a genocidal conflict over diamonds, amputating the arms and legs of those who dared to vote in a national election. In the Middle East, Shiites, Kurds, and Sunnis in Iraq are engaged in life-and-death struggles, as they have been for centuries, as are Muslims and Jews in Israel and the Palestinian territories. In Darfur, the Sudan, ancient tribal hatreds have become a way of death.

Genocide has taken millions of lives. "Genocides and other mass

1

murders killed more people in the twentieth century than all the wars combined," said the International Campaign to End Genocide, which compiled these horrifying statistics.[1] In the Congo alone, an estimated 3.8 million people were slaughtered by "an amalgam of rebel insurgencies, tribal rivalries, competition for resources and just plain butchery, . . . making it the deadliest conflict since World War II."[2]

In addition to those intentionally slaughtered, millions of others were killed because of the disruption of services and resources in the wake of these ragtag armies. "The first killer is flight" as "desperately poor people are driven from their subsistence existence into even more hostile environments." Hospitals are emptied and looted. Fields lie fallow. Livestock die, and "the thin fibers that knit lives together for survival may have been torn beyond repair." The International Rescue Committee estimates that 31,000 Congolese die every month from causes related to the conflict, most of them from disease.[3]

Although these mass slaughters were rationalized by some leaders as a means to restore religious, ethnic, racial, or national honor, their real purpose was to acquire power and wealth in the form of land, oil, gold, diamonds, bank deposits, and other property. In Rwanda, where the lengthy genocidal war between Hutus and Tutsis claimed three million lives, the major difference between the groups was clearly economic rather than ethnic. The Tutsis, cattle herders, were far richer than the Hutus, who were farmers. The Tutsis ran the government, although they were in the minority. "If you were close to the king, you owned wealth, you owned a lot of cattle, you were a Tutsi. If you are far away from the king, you are a (soil) cultivator, you don't own cattle, you are a Hutu."[4] The Belgians, who colonized Rwanda and Burundi, exacerbated the differences by requiring Hutus and Tutsis to carry identity cards, and by allowing only Tutsis to attain higher education and hold positions of power. It was the classic strategy of divide and conquer, sowing seeds of hatred that eventually claimed millions of lives. Ironically, most genocidal slaughters, including the Hutu-Tutsi conflict, occurred shortly after the collapse of repressive colonial regimes, with native leaders assuming the role of their former masters.

SEEDS OF HATRED

It is almost as if the world had a genocide quota, and if the fascists, communists, and colonialists weren't up to the job, the locals would take care of it.

Just as Tito kept the lid on in the former Yugoslavia, the former Soviet Union dominated Eastern Europe, as did old-line colonialists who ruled Africa and the Middle East. The collapse and ouster of these former oppressors gave rise to local leaders who fanned ancient hatreds in their desire to consolidate power and wealth. The recent proliferation of associations and international conferences dedicated to combating the rise of xenophobia is an indication of the alarming spread and virulence of these hatreds.

Anger is at least as old as the Bible. The writers of the Psalms asked, "Why do the nations rage, and the peoples plot a vain thing?" The "vain thing" refers to the elevation of local leaders above God, and the fulfillment of immediate desires over godliness. Modern hatreds are magnified by all the communication tools provided by modern technology: television, videos, and the Internet. The anti-Semitic Egyptian television series based on the fictitious *Protocols of the Elders of Zion*, the Hindu propaganda machine against Muslims, and the Muslim crusade against Christians and Jews are all promoted on television, videos, and the Internet, in addition to the more traditional outlets—newspaper articles, radio broadcasts, and comic books. These hatreds now have a new handmaiden: global terrorism. Invoking Allah, murderous representatives of Al Qaeda and other terrorist groups stalk the Western world in search of targets that will yield the most destruction. Young men and women, many of them jobless and uprooted, are brainwashed into becoming suicide bombers with the promise that a multitude of virgins await them in heaven. They now threaten civilian populations the world over, wedded to violent strategies that most Muslims consider a perversion of their faith. In November 2005, thousands of unemployed Muslim youths vented their anger by rioting in more than three hundred French cities, including the Paris suburbs; setting fire to hundreds of buildings and more than three thousand automobiles; and injuring hundreds of civilians and police officers.[5] The riots touched off not only fires and physical assaults, but also a wave of Islamophobia, which is rapidly spreading throughout Europe.

But anger has been used for good as well as evil. It has fueled progressive revolutions that have brought democracy to vast regions of the world, and it has also brokered less sweeping political change. In 2005, the angry mass demonstrations in the Ukraine after a Moscow puppet stole an election, and the demonstrations in Mexico City as the ruling party sought to disqualify (and threatened to imprison) its leading political opponent, served to strengthen democracy in those countries, even as the Boston Tea Party helped usher in the founding of the United States.

AMERICA'S HERITAGE

Fortunately for the United States, few religious and ethnic feuds go back hundreds of years, although the nation's westward expansion still breeds smoldering resentments on the part of Native Americans. A nation of immigrants, the country is scarcely two centuries old. Even its great divisive wars—the Civil War and the Vietnam War—produced no lasting ethnic or religious vendettas. America's character and culture are forward looking, not regressive. Americans do not long for ancient days of conquest; they were few, and relatively short lived. The U.S. acquisition of the Philippines, Cuba, and Pacific islands after the Spanish-American War does not compare with the empires ruled by the British, French, Dutch, Spaniards, and Belgians. Nor do Americans harbor smoldering resentments against foreign satraps who ruled with an iron hand. Geography has been kind. Protected by two oceans, the nation has not had to cope with invading armies, except in the early days of the Republic. After the westward expansion, Americans focused on a future of an ever-expanding democracy, not expanding borders. And the United States always had a way of getting rid of homegrown despots via the ballot box, a remedy not available to most people around the world. Americans are a can-do people who believe they can rise to any challenge and control their destiny. The flip side of that philosophy is that Americans have always found it difficult to appreciate the ancient ethnic, religious, and national hatreds that roil other parts of the world.

Until now. America's vision of its impregnability has been severely challenged by the tragedy of 9/11. For the first time, Americans can empathize with those who have lived in constant fear of being victimized by religious fanatics and suicide bombers. The nation's two great oceans now offer little protection against nuclear and biochemical weapons of mass destruction. Also challenged is the nation's vision of democracy and civil liberties, which have been seriously eroded since 9/11. Immediately after the horrors of the attack on the Pentagon and World Trade Center, the United States reaped sympathy from around the world. People grieved for the thousands of Americans who died in the World Trade Center, as well as for the ensuing loss of confidence and stability among its citizens.

But sadly, world opinion changed drastically. The invasion of Iraq and the mistreatment of prisoners, along with the nation's steadfast support of Israel, made the United States the object of palpable hatred. "The sheer velocity of the change from worldwide sympathy to worldwide antipathy is . . . incredible," noted former national security adviser Zbigniew Brzezinski.[6]

A survey by the Pew Center in 2005 concluded that "anti-Americanism is deeper and broader now than at any time in modern history . . . and while much of the animus is aimed directly at President Bush . . . especially the war in Iraq, the new global hardening of attitudes amounts to something larger than a thumbs down on the current occupant of the White House."[7] The Pew survey, which canvassed forty-four countries and thirty-eight thousand people, also revealed that the war in Iraq "frayed international unity" and caused the plummeting of America's "global image." Outside Western Europe, there was a "widespread sense that U.S. policies were a major cause of the 9/11 attacks."[8]

The Pew survey delved deeply into the specific reasons for anti-Americanism, which are complex and alarming. A vast majority of people in many countries regard the United States as responsible for increasing poverty, and specifically, for increasing the gap between rich and poor: 74 percent of Bolivians, 69 percent of Japanese, 73 percent of Lebanese, and 69 percent of French.[9] While anti-American views were expected in Middle Eastern countries, Pew researchers were surprised to find those ratings substantially down in Europe as well: from 75 to 58 percent in Great Britain; 63 to 37 percent in France; and 61 to 38 percent in Germany.[10] Even in friendly Middle Eastern countries like Morocco, the favorable image of Americans had eroded from 54 percent in 2003 to 37 percent in less than a year. America's allies also resented the fact that the United States failed to take their views into account when making foreign policy decisions.[11] Unimpressed by this data, one U.S. military official said, "If we had listened to our European allies at the outset of World War II, Hitler would have won."

But anti-Americanism is not a new phenomenon. Much of the world long regarded the United States as the center of capitalism—an oppressive, rich nation that promoted a materialistic lifestyle that included rampant greed and sexual excesses. Nor was America's image bolstered by its intervention in foreign governments, its overthrow of the elected leaders of Iran and Chile, its installation of puppet governments, and its longtime support of dictators. America's recent emphasis on globalism is often viewed abroad as merely a mask for the type of colonialism that had shackled the Third World for centuries.

As the world's staunchest protector of Israel, the United States also finds itself a target of the new wave of anti-Semitism that has surged in Europe, the Middle East, and parts of East Asia. Anti-immigrant sentiments, which translated into restrictive quotas in the last century, have recently surged in the United States—as undocumented workers tax the diminished resources of America's cities and compete with poor Americans for low-level jobs. Anti-immigrant sentiments are also rife in many other industrialized nations, exploited by demagogues such as France's Jean-Marie Le Pen, who charge that these resident aliens are taking jobs formerly held by citizens, and placing increasing demands, and costs, on government health and welfare services.

Americans aren't the only ones under attack. Politicians everywhere are branded as corrupt and as more interested in furthering their political careers than in advancing their nation's interests. Similarly, the world's media are attacked for being biased, unreliable, tawdry, sensational, and unfairly critical of government, or not critical enough.

THE PSYCHOLOGY OF DEFEAT

A few years ago, after a speech about American politics to a group of officers at a military academy in Madrid, the questions grew hostile. How about the U.S. role in the Spanish–American War? Most Americans dimly recall the conflict as an event that occurred nearly a hundred years ago and had something to do with President William McKinley. They might also "remember" the battleship *Maine*.

But unlike most Americans, the Spanish officers in their starched, well-tailored uniforms still cared, and cared deeply. To them, it occurred only yesterday. The Spanish–American War was the last great war their country had "fought," said the officers, who seemed to have conveniently forgotten the bloody Spanish Civil War from 1936 to 1939. Spanish–American War battles were still being taught as bitter defeats in their military academies. What was important was that even though the Spanish–American War was fought more than a century ago, Spaniards still felt humiliated by their nation's defeat and remained hostile to the nation that had vanquished them.

A very thin layer down from all the conflicts that are rooted in anger—whether they are called "clashes of civilization," "tribal wars," or the residue of "colonialism"—lies a profound feeling of defeat. This defeat runs the gamut: military, political, territorial, cultural, religious, and economic.

Each major global crisis confronting us today is rooted in defeat, either a recent defeat or defeats that go back centuries. These defeats fester into anger, and anger often leads to violence. One example is the inexorable

Israeli-Palestinian conflict. Looking at both sides in terms of past defeats offers a sad perspective.

For their part, the Israelis, who live in the Middle East's only mature democracy, cling closely to their tiny country, slightly smaller in size than the state of New Jersey. Their experience in the Holocaust has led them to resolve "Never again," a theme that infuses Israeli life and explains the nation's militaristic approach to external threats. Israelis work hard to overcome past images of European Jews walking meekly to the Nazi gas chambers; they would rather look back to a past that glorifies Masada, the mountain fortress where Jews chose to die rather than succumb to Roman rule. Yet the memories of murdered relatives in World War II color the current worldview of many Israelis, making their small piece of land in a sea of hostile Arab nations even more valuable: a matchbook on a football field, is how some describe the territory won in their war of independence in 1948.

The Palestinian psyche parallels the Israelis in revealing profound anger over past humiliations. Many Palestinians were summarily ejected from their homes after Israel achieved independence; refugee camps today house the third generation of Palestinians. Yet most of the fifty-three countries with large Muslim populations refuse to accept Palestinian refugees, although many of those nations send their leaders arms and money. The Jordanians, for example, were so threatened by the Palestinians living in their midst that they massacred ten thousand of them in the early 1970s and evicted most of the rest. Today, Palestinians feel like prisoners in their own land: rebuffed by their fellow Arab nations, too poor to leave their villages, their freedom to travel stifled by Israeli checkpoints.

Defeat is a recurrent theme throughout the Middle East. Bernard Lewis has written eloquently about Islam and "what went wrong" in the West's relationship with Muslim countries. Lewis argues that for a thousand years before the Crusades, Islam was the dominant culture. It was then replaced by the West, which surpassed Islam in terms of technology, invention, the arts, and the sciences. Colonialism only added to the feeling of defeat, particularly in Egypt and Syria.[12]

Defeat plays a large role in politics everywhere. In 1968, a large student demonstration against Egyptian President Gamal Abdel Nasser accused him of too much leniency against those who lost the 1967 war with Israel. It was reminiscent of the previous decade in the United States, where the question of "Who lost China?" ushered in a period of political instability and anti-Communist fervor capped by the McCarthy era.

Defeat, and its partner, humiliation, remain strong components of political anger. Psychohistorian Robert Jay Lifton has linked the psychology of defeat to an ingrained concept of "the Other," defined as pinning responsibility for one's condition on another nation, culture, tribe, religion, or region. Modern communications technology has fueled resentments by making it easier for the "have-nots" to see how the Other lives.

ANWAR SADAT AND THE JAWS OF PEACE

The themes of defeat and victory played important roles in Sadat's famous pursuit of peace with Israel. In Cairo, a bridge and statues are among the symbols that celebrate the "October 6 victory." What was that victory? It turned out to be what the rest of the world called the "Yom Kippur War," the war between Egypt and Israel in 1973. The reason that no one else referred to the war as a "victory" was that most historians regarded it as a stalemate rather than a clear triumph for either side.

Was Anwar Sadat, then president of Egypt, "spinning" the story? Conjuring up a victory from a military stalemate? Manipulating the public? Perhaps. But Egyptians felt very defeated at that time, from the failure of Pan-Arabism to take hold; from the acute reminders of English, French, and Russian colonialism; and from the 1967 war, when the Israelis trounced the Egyptians and other Arab nations and captured a large hunk of land including Jerusalem in the process.

Ultimately, Sadat was so successful in convincing the Egyptians that the Yom Kippur War represented victory that military academies throughout Egypt still teach the battles of that war as models for victory. But most important, this "victory" enabled Sadat to make his dramatic trip to Jerusalem to forge a peace treaty with Prime Minister Menachem Begin of Israel, something unthinkable if the Egyptians had remained in a defeatist mode. Sadat had shrewdly prepared the Egyptian people for their separate peace. He had also risked a great deal, eventually paying with his life for his peace efforts.

DEFEAT, THE COLD WAR, AND
U.S. FOREIGN POLICY

Americans are not immune from face-saving solipsisms; the Vietnam War was also sold to Americans as a "stalemate." The reality, however, was evident to anyone who watched the television shots of South Vietnamese clinging to the wings of U.S. aircraft. Few Americans doubted that the Communist North Vietnamese were the clear victors in that devastating ten-year war. As a result, the United States has been wary of committing troops anywhere in the world. Today, South and North Vietnam are united under Communist rule; even the name of the South Vietnamese city Saigon has been changed to Ho Chi Minh City. And the victors, the Vietnamese, remain one of the few Asian countries still outwardly friendly to the United States. This demonstrates once again that a belief in "victory" remains an important element in the establishment of peaceful bilateral relations.

America was chastened by its defeat in Vietnam. President Jimmy Carter identified a "malaise" that he said had afflicted the American people, whose pride was further buffeted by the taking of American hostages in Iran. This set the stage for Ronald Reagan, who promised voters that America would "stand tall" again. Few challenged the new president when he mobilized Americans' fear of the "Evil Empire," as he called the Soviet Union, and doubled the defense budget, nearly bankrupting the nation.

TARGET: AMERICA

With the end of the Cold War, the United States assumed the role of the world's policeman, and nobody loves a cop. This marked a change in U.S. foreign policy from reactive to proactive, touching off a maelstrom of world criticism. The recent foray into Iraq is a case in point. The United States mounted the war in Iraq to remove Saddam Hussein, a dictator who had ignored the United Nations, had engaged in some of the worst human rights abuses in recent history, and was considered a threat to a wide range of U.S. interests. Saddam was accused of harboring weapons of mass destruction and of aiding Al Qaeda, the terrorist group responsible for the tragedy of 9/11. Americans were assured that they would be welcomed by the Iraqi people.

Waging the war proved easy; winning the peace was not.

The mistakes were legion. No "weapons of mass destruction" or links to Al Qaeda were found. Americans, far from being welcomed as liberators, were seen as old-fashioned colonialists who had their eyes on Iraq's large oil reserves, reviving resentments that had smoldered for most of the twentieth century. The result was a determined insurgency that took thousands of American and Iraqi lives. Further evidence of America's imperialist designs was seen in the Pentagon's mismanagement of prisons in Iraq. This included the army's sadistic abuses of Iraqi prisoners held in Abu Ghraib prison, which brought worldwide condemnation. Nor did the United States have an exit strategy for a long time.

But America's worst mistake was more general: the United States put the military in charge of imposing democracy on Iraq, even though there was a civilian figurehead at the helm. The military proved successful at winning the war, but ill-equipped to organize the country after its military task was completed. The military thought more in terms of victory and defeat than in terms of promoting policies that would enable Iraq to govern itself. Once again, Iraq's defeat and humiliation laid the groundwork for an insurgency likely to plague U.S. and moderate Middle East leaders for years to come. The insurgency also sapped Americans' enthusiasm for the war. By the fall of 2005, polls revealed that most Americans thought the war was a mistake.

The Pentagon also made lucrative deals with American multinational corporations, namely Halliburton and Bechtel, to rebuild Iraq rather than seeking out (or even creating) indigenous Iraqi companies. This became a source of anger among Iraqi businessmen, who allegedly retaliated by financing a large part of the Sunni resistance movement.

Anti-Americanism is only part of the anger that seethes around the world. And for all its mistakes, the Bush administration has taken concrete steps to combat worldwide xenophobia, racism, and anti-Semitism. This has largely resulted from the efforts of the president himself, a born-again Christian, and two African-American secretaries of state, Colin Powell and Condoleezza Rice. They directed U.S. embassies to report all hate crimes and hate speech in their countries, and American officials have expressed their disapproval of specific incidents to appropriate officials, including heads of state. These officials have encouraged their counterparts to come up with concrete proposals to combat these outrages. And the United States was instrumental in convening several international conferences on xenophobia, racism, and anti-Semitism in spite of considerable opposition from abroad.

Many nations have banned hate speech, with varying degrees of success. In the United States such speech is constitutionally protected, but not the violence that flows from it. Singapore has achieved extraordinary ethnic harmony by severely punishing hate speech, and promoting diversity, but at the expense of individual liberty.

This, then, is the new challenge of our times: not to minimize the problems of these venomous ethnic and religious hatreds, but to look at them squarely and understand their roots—defeat, humiliation, and alienation—and, most daunting of all, to come to grips with these strong, destructive emotions in a positive, democratic, and effective way.

NOTES

1. Genocide Watch, *The International Campaign to End Genocide*, 2004, www.genocidewatch.org/internationalcampaign.htm (accessed February 13, 2006). See appendix B.

2. Marc Lacey, "Africa, Beyond the Bullets and Blades," *New York Times*, April 25, 2005, 4.

3. Ibid.

4. *NPR Online Newshour*, "Background Report: The Hutu-Tutsi Conflict," 1999.

5. Molly Moore, "France Beefs Up Response to Riots," *Washington Post*, November 8, 2005.

6. James Traub, "The Things They Carry," *New York Times Magazine*, January 4, 2004, 30.

7. Pew Research Center for the People and the Press, "Global Opinion: The Spread of Anti-Americanism," *Global Trends*, 2005.

8. Ibid., 109.

9. Ibid., 113.

10. Ibid., 107. From the summer of 2002 to March 2004.

11. Ibid., 108. Sixty-one percent of the British, 84 percent of the French, and 69 percent of the Germans felt this way.

12. Bernard Lewis, *What Went Wrong?: Western Impact and Middle Eastern Response* (Oxford: Oxford University Press, 2002).

2

ANTI-SEMITISM: "THAT VERY LIGHT SLEEPER"

Jews rule this world by proxy.

—Mahathir Mohamad, Prime Minister of Malaysia

A nti-Semitism has gone global.

The poison that long infected Europe and the Middle East has spread to the four corners of the world, in the worst outbreak of anti-Semitism since the Holocaust. No longer a cottage industry that relied on word of mouth, or a product of handwritten and mimeographed screeds, anti-Semitism, the oldest ethnic and religious hatred, has escalated with the new communications technology. It is now a constant presence on state-sponsored television and the Internet. Some of the violence can be traced to jobless young Muslims, while the theoretical underpinnings for these hateful acts are often provided by their fundamentalist elders, as well as those on the far left and right of the political spectrum.

Some of today's anti-Semitism has occurred in countries with negligible Jewish populations. In Pakistan, a country virtually without a Jewish community, "widespread" anti-Semitic sentiment has been generated by anti-Semitic articles in the press, reported the U.S. State Department in 2005. In Greece, with five thousand Jews in a population of ten million, "vandalism continued to be a problem in 2004." In Slovenia, with three hundred to four hundred Jews in a population of two million, there was the desecration of graves, and "Jewish community representatives reported widespread prejudice."

Today's anti-Semites are the modern practitioners of a tradition that goes back at least twenty-four centuries. For at least that long, Jews have been the universal scapegoat. They have served through the ages to divert attention from the real problems of the disinherited—hunger, poverty,

13

disease, lack of opportunity, and absence of hope. They have provided an outlet for oppressed peoples who dare not criticize their own governments but can assail Jews with impunity. In its extreme forms, as in Nazi Germany, anti-Semitism has struck terror not only in the Jewish community but also among non-Jews. It served as an object lesson, namely that unbridled brutality awaited those who dared challenge the Third Reich.

Surprisingly, Jews are not the only victims of anti-Semitism. History shows that anti-Semitism is the harbinger of devastation for larger communities as well—Catholic, Protestant, Muslim, even atheists. Hitler's anti-Semitism ended with his nation and much of Europe in ruins. Most recently, the outbreak of worldwide anti-Semitism has been accompanied by terrorist attacks that target the larger community. "Jews are the canaries in the mines," said Rabbi George Driesen.

Jews worldwide are in greater peril than at any time since the Holocaust. Both at home and abroad, Jews are assaulted, their synagogues burned and their cemeteries desecrated. In another ominous development, the Bush administration's strong support of Israel has been a key factor in the surge of anti-American sentiment across the globe. Since 9/11, many Americans empathize with Israel, which has long lived under the threat of suicide bombers. But others blame U.S. support of Israel as the cause of the terrorist attacks.

"I would like to remind you that it is barely 60 years since the Holocaust, and anti-Semitism, that very light sleeper, has again raised its ugly head," Prince Hassan of Jordan told delegates from fifty-five nations at a conference on xenophobia hosted by the Organization for Security and Cooperation in Europe (OSCE) in Brussels in September 2004.

The current rise of global anti-Semitism prompted the concern of the administration of George W. Bush. "The increasing frequency and severity of anti-Semitic incidents since the start of the 21st century, particularly in Europe, has compelled the international community to focus on anti-Semitism with renewed vigor," said a report on global anti-Semitism issued by the State Department on January 5, 2005. "Beginning in 2000, verbal attacks directed against Jews increased while incidents of vandalism (e.g., graffiti, fire bombings of Jewish schools, desecration of synagogues and cemeteries) surged. Physical assaults including beatings, stabbings, and other violence against Jews in Europe increased markedly, resulting in a number of cases in serious injury and even death. Also troubling is a bias that spills over into anti-Semitism in a segment of the left-of-center press and among some intellectuals."[1] The report cited four reasons for this eruption of anti-Semitism:

- Traditional anti-Jewish prejudice that has pervaded Europe and some countries in other parts of the world for centuries. This includes ultranationalists and others who assert that the Jewish community controls governments, the media, international business, and the financial world.
- Strong anti-Israel sentiment that crosses the line between objective criticism of Israeli policies and anti-Semitism.
- Anti-Jewish sentiment expressed by some in Europe's growing Muslim population, based on longstanding antipathy toward both Israel and Jews, as well as Muslim opposition to developments in Israel and the occupied territories, and more recently in Iraq.
- Criticism of both the United States and globalization that spills over to Israel, and to Jews in general, who are identified with both.

The end of the Cold War and the collapse of the Soviet Union also count heavily as factors in the rise of anti-Semitism. Ideological fervor has been replaced by theological fervor, which sometimes descends into fanaticism. Without the Soviets as the enemy, world leaders have turned instead to their various holy books. Fundamentalist regimes have increased in number and have rapidly positioned themselves at center stage. Jimmy Carter was the first "born-again" president, and President George W. Bush claimed he read the Bible from cover to cover every two years.

A COMPLEX PREJUDICE

Anti-Semitism is a complex prejudice, as Phyllis Chesler, the feminist author, has pointed out. "Jews have been persecuted for theological reasons, that is, they presumably killed Christ and refused to accept Christ as their Messiah. Jews have also refused to convert to Islam. They have been persecuted for cultural and racial reasons. They were too Oriental, too Semitic for Europe and too white-European for the Middle East." In addition, she continued, "Jews have been feared and hated for their various cultural and intellectual choices . . . symbolizing modernism, capitalism, free love and free thought . . . but [they are] also seen as symbolizing backwardness, poverty and superstition."[2]

Anti-Semitic prejudices are fraught with contradictions. In the Arabic state-controlled press, derisive cartoons often depict Jews as fat capitalists loaded down with money bags. But they also are reviled as Communists who try to destabilize governments and undermine national cultures. Jews are seen as unprincipled and willing to do anything for self-advancement, while being denounced as a stiff-necked, ornery people who have resisted the opportunity to save their own lives by converting to other religions. "Jews do not submit to the rules of the conqueror the way other subject populations have," noted Dr. Willard Gaylin.[3] "Judaism, unlike most other religions, is not simply a theological credo, but a set of civil laws that prescribe everyday rules for hygiene, morality, managing properties, conditions for worship and sacrifice. Obedience to these laws is not a choice, but demanded by God. To maintain religious identity, the Jew must remain secularly isolated and distinguishably different, in conduct as well as appearance, from those around him or her." (But today, only a small number of orthodox Jews feel they must remain secularly isolated. In fact, Jewish law commands that Jews obey the laws of the land unless those laws jeopardize religious practice.) Then, too, non-Jews who chafe under the rule of dictatorial regimes, where even modest criticism is punishable by death, can always divert their resentment and assail Jews with impunity.

Modern anti-Semitism is more political than religious. The Nazis didn't care whether an individual was an observant Jew, went to synagogue, or conducted a Seder. If a person had a Jewish ancestor, no matter how far back the lineage, that was sufficient to send him to the gas chamber, and not coincidentally, to acquire his land and property in the process. Jews made perfect scapegoats because, although some had been close to power, as a group they were politically weak. Abraham Foxman, national director of the B'nai B'rith Anti-Defamation League (ADL), observed, "If anti-Semitism had one cause, maybe we could eliminate it." Ironically, some scholars wonder whether anti-Semitism is the glue that has kept the Jewish people together. According to this theory, the persecution of Jews has kept them a tight-knit community, while acceptance of Jews and the absence of anti-Semitism has led to secularism and intermarriage. "Has anti-Semitism played a role in preserving the Jewish people?" asked Professor Jacques Berlinerblau of Hofstra University, a scholar of anti-Semitism, at a forum at Georgetown University. "The Jews of China and India didn't suffer much anti-Semitism, and basically disappeared," he noted.

GLOBAL ANTI-SEMITISM

The intensifying global anti-Semitism was manifest in Malaysia, whose prime minister, Mahathir Mohamad, received a standing ovation from leaders of fifty-seven Islamic countries in 2003 when he said that "Jews rule this world by proxy" and called upon his listeners to destroy this Jewish conspiracy.[4] According to this myth, Jews not only run the media, Hollywood, and the financial centers, but they also control Bush, Blair, Putin, and other world leaders. (Of course, if Jews really ran the world, they would have long since eliminated anti-Semitism.) Even in Pakistan with its tiny Jewish population, anti-Semitic articles frequently appear in the press, where the nation's archenemy, India, has been referred to as the "Zionist threat on our borders." In Australia, anti-Semitic slogans were burned into the lawn of the Parliament House in the state of Tasmania in January 2004, and a synagogue in Perth was firebombed. In New Zealand, headstones of Jewish graves were smashed. It has also infected Japan by way of Christian missionaries, the American occupation, and seventh graders learning English by reading about the Jewish stereotyped moneylender Shylock in Shakespeare's *The Merchant of Venice*. In the Middle East, anti-Semitism is taught more directly in the Muslim madrasses, or schools. In Russia, nineteen members of the legislature called for banning all Jewish organizations in January 2005.[5]

Jews are the eternal outsiders, it seems, no matter how long or loyally they have lived in a country. Raymond Barre, then prime minister of France, said after a bomb attack on a French synagogue in 1980, "Jews and innocent French were wounded."[6] Barre apparently regarded French Jews as neither French nor innocent.

Although criticism of Israel does not in and of itself constitute anti-Semitism—few are as critical of Israeli policies as Israelis themselves—there is undoubtedly some spillover. Those who fanatically oppose Israeli policies often oppose the concept of the Israeli state and hold Israel to far higher standards than they hold other nations. That's why Jews around the world were offended by the remark at a London dinner party by Daniel Bernard, the French ambassador to Great Britain, who described Israel as "a shitty little country" and asked, "Why should the world be in danger of World War III because of those people?"[7]

Indeed, attacks on Israel have gained respectability at the highest levels of the United Nations, where Lakhdar Brahimi, who was Secretary General

Kofi Annan's personal representative in Iraq, singled out the policies of Israel as "the great poison in the region." Indeed, the United Nations has been an unrelenting enemy of Israel, expressed in its "Zionism Is Racism" resolution, adopted in 1975 and repealed in 1991 after a long battle. Nevertheless, it remained a constant theme among Muslim countries, who united at a United Nations conference on racism in Durban, South Africa, in 2001. In a naked display of anti-Israeli and anti-Semitic fervor, they managed to get another resolution adopted asserting once again that "Zionism Is Racism," despite its UN repeal a decade before.

Anti-Israeli fervor at the UN has been manifest. In July 2004, the General Assembly voted 150 to 6 to direct Israel to obey a World Court advisory opinion and remove its separation barrier, a wall constructed as a defense measure against terrorism, but which Palestinians decried as an invasion of their territory. The U.S. ambassador to the UN, former Senator John Danforth (R-MO), explained the U.S. opposition to the resolution: "It follows a long line of one-sided resolutions adopted by the General Assembly, none of which has made any contribution to peace in the Middle East."[8] Ambassador Danforth reflected the United States steadfast support of Israel, which it values as the only democratic nation in the Middle East. Although the resolution decried the barrier, it was silent on the issue of rising Palestinian terrorism. However, in November 2004, the United Nations approved a resolution that called for "Elimination of all forms of religious intolerance," including anti-Semitism. The resolution "recognizes with deep concern the overall rise in instances of intolerance and violence directed against members of many religious communities in various parts of the world, including cases motivated by Islamophobia, anti-Semitism and Christianophobia." The resolution was approved despite the efforts of the Organization of the Islamic Conference to omit the reference to anti-Semitism.[9]

There are other hopeful signs. In March 2005, Kofi Annan attended the opening of the new wing of the Yad Vashem Holocaust Memorial in Jerusalem and was the only foreign dignitary among the visiting heads of state to speak there. And in June 2005, Dan Gillerman, Israel's ambassador to the United States, was selected as a vice president of the UN General Assembly, becoming on September 20 the first Israeli to preside over the assembly in fifty-two years.[10]

There is no question, however, that anti-Semitic remarks by public officials fuel violence and vandalism, committed mostly by bitter, jobless, and disaffected young men. The victims also are mostly young people. Some non-European examples include the following:

- Brazil, with a Jewish population of 110,000 out of 160 million, has the largest number of anti-Semitic websites in South America. Comments including "Hitler was right" and "Germany was right" appeared on websites, while acts of vandalism included the tearing of mezuzahs from two synagogues and the painting of swastikas on a Jewish home in 2001.[11]
- Chile, where human excrement was thrown at a kosher restaurant in Santiago in 2001. Young Jews eating in fast food restaurants were assaulted by a group of Palestinians.
- In Mexico, anti-Semitism is expressed in anonymous mail sent to Jewish households continuously throughout the year.
- Uruguay and Venezuela also reported anti-Semitic acts.
- Australia, with a population of 115,000 Jews out of 18 million people, witnessed 328 acts of anti-Semitic violence in 2001.
- In South Africa, with 85,000 Jews out of a population of 43 million, an elderly Jewish doctor was assaulted in Cape Town. Numerous anti-Israel rallies at which anti-Semitic slogans were shouted also occurred there.

THE ISRAEL FACTOR

The escalating conflict between Israelis and Palestinians has unearthed anti-Semitism that existed more than two millennia before the founding of the Jewish state. Its momentum has carried it around the globe. The televised photos of Israeli soldiers killing Palestinian women and children and destroying their homes have brought understandable cries of outrage around the world. These images have translated into anger against Jews everywhere. The reaction of some Arab and Muslim leaders to the tragedy of 9/11 underscores their hatred of American Jews, whom they charge had prior knowledge of the attacks and were therefore absent from their jobs at the World Trade Center when the bombings occurred.[12] Other spurious charges: Only Israel could benefit from the attack, and Israel and the Jews wanted to drag the United States into a war against Islam.

Mere criticism of Israel should not be interpreted as anti-Semitism. There is much to criticize about Israeli brutality toward the Palestinians. Israelis have found—as the United States did in Iraq—that it is difficult to be both an occupying power and humane at the same time. The world was shocked during the intifada by nightly television broadcasts that showed

Israeli troops destroying Palestinian homes and villages as Palestinian youths threw stones at Israeli tanks. Israeli settlements drew scarce water from Palestinian farms and olive groves to fill the settlers' swimming pools.[13]

Imam Yahya Hendi, Muslim chaplain of Georgetown University, an American citizen who was born in Palestine, described his anger when the Israelis appropriated his family's farm in Nablus, and at Israeli aggression against him as a child. "I was seven or eight years old when I was stopped by Israeli Defense Forces on my way home from school. They started beating me. They said, 'We'll get you F---Muslims out of here.' I said, 'We'll get you F---Jews out of here.' I came home with a bloody nose, and told my mother what happened. My mother came to my bedside at night, and read me passages from the Koran that spoke positively about Jews. 'What you said was offensive to me,' she said."

He said that as an adult, when he tried to return home to visit his dying mother, he was kept naked at the Tel Aviv airport for ten hours and was forbidden to enter the country. Israeli officers threw his American passport on the ground and said, "That means nothing," he recalled.

Nevertheless, it is sometimes difficult to distinguish between those who simply oppose Israeli policies and those who descend into naked anti-Semitism. Amitai Etzioni, university professor at George Washington University, and an Israeli himself, noted that no one is more critical of Israeli policies than the Israelis themselves. "At least half of the Israelis criticize the policies of Ariel Sharon, and they're not anti-Semitic," he said. "But if you believe there's no justification for a Jewish state, then you're anti-Semitic." Just as the Nazis sought to eradicate the Jews, Etzioni said, so do their ideological successors want to eradicate the Jewish state.

The State Department report noted that "the demonization of Israel, or vilification of Israeli leaders, sometimes through comparisons with Nazi leaders, and through the use of Nazi symbols to caricature them, indicates an anti-Semitic bias rather than a valid criticism of policy concerning a controversial issue."[14]

"When someone is railing against Israel," Chesler said, "I wait to see if they are also willing to visit their perfectionism on any other people or nation. For example, do they also rail against the Muslim Turks who genocidally slaughtered the Christian Armenians; the Bosnian Christian Serbs who genocidally slaughtered Albanian and Croatian Muslims; the Indian Hindus and Muslim Pakistanis who slaughtered each other and who continue to do so; the Hutus who genocidally slaughtered the Tutsis in Rwanda; the Iraqis, Iranians, and Turks who genocidally slaughtered the

Kurds; the Christian and Muslim Nigerians who in the last four years have slaughtered 10,000 people in God's name; the Muslims who for centuries have persecuted both Christians and Jews, and continue to do so; and so on?"[15]

Left-wing attacks on Israel have led many of Europe's 2.4 million Jews to abandon their liberal political allies and move toward the right.[16] "Jews say the distinction between anti-Zionism and anti-Semitism has often become difficult to see. Swastikas and anti-Jewish slogans have marked pro-Palestinian marches in some Communist-run municipalities in France. In Britain, many Jews who opposed the war in Iraq stayed away from antiwar rallies because of the strong anti-Israeli element."[17] Barry Kosmin, head of the Institute for Jewish Policy Research in London, said, "Arafat became the leftist pinup boy following Che Guevara." One result: In Britain in the last sixty years, the number of left-of-center Jewish members of Parliament has dropped from more than two dozen to about a dozen, while the number in moderate and right-wing parties has increased from none to half a dozen.

ORIGINS OF ANTI-SEMITISM

It is an old joke: Bicycles and Jews are responsible for most of the world's ills. Why bicycles? one may ask. Why Jews? comes the reply.

Oddly, the first postbiblical expression of anti-Semitism occurred in a secular state. "Anti-Semitism originated in neither Christianity nor Islam," noted Cynthia Ozick. "Its earliest appearance was in Egypt, in the fourth century BCE," during the reign of Ptolemy II.[18] Manetho, an Egyptian priest, in a polemic directed against the biblical account in Genesis and Exodus, described a people who "came from Jerusalem" as the descendants of a mob of lepers. He posited that the Jews were ignominiously expelled from Egypt for having despoiled the country. Judging from the writings of Manetho and his adherents, Egyptians still held a grudge against Jews three thousand years after the "fact," for the boils, locusts, and other plagues inflicted upon them to expedite the Hebrews' exodus from Egypt. To Jews, the plagues were a passport out of bondage; to Egyptians, they were a blight on their country.

The Greeks labeled the Jews lazy atheists who disdained labor once every seven days, on the Sabbath, which Jews believed God created as a day of rest. Greeks also originated the myth of blood libel, in which a Greek captured by Jews was tortured and killed, and his entrails ritually eaten.

Christians altered the libel to Jews killing a child whose blood was needed for the preparation of matzo. Ozick notes that "the blood libel was later adopted by the Muslims." The yellow badge the Nazis forced Jews to wear was initiated by Pope Innocent III, who took the idea from Prince Abu-Yusef Almansur, a Moroccan ruler of the thirteenth century. " 'Hep' was the cry of the Crusaders as they swept through Europe, annihilating one Jewish community after another." Even Martin Luther was infected, asking, "What is to be done with this wicked, accursed race which can no longer be tolerated?" The Nazis' Final Solution was grounded in millennia of Jew hatred.[19]

"For almost 22 centuries . . . the church was the archenemy of the Jews—our most powerful and relentless oppressor and the world's greatest force for the dissemination of anti-Semitic beliefs and the instigation of violent acts of hatred," observed Abraham Foxman in his book *Never Again? The Threat of the New Anti-Semitism*.[20] Church policy, with its origins in the gospels, was reversed in an encyclical, Vatican II, initiated in 1962 under the aegis of Pope John XXIII and concluded in 1965 by Pope Paul VI. The encyclical states that "the Church, mindful of the patrimony she shares with the Jews and moved not by political reasons but by the Gospel's spiritual love, decries hatred, persecutions, displays of anti-Semitism, directed against Jews at any time by anyone." Dr. Gene Fisher, the church's interfaith emissary, claims that because of Vatican II, children who attend parochial schools today are far less prejudiced than those who attend public schools. But in 2004, a movie based on the gospels revived once again the issue of the Jews' complicity in the death of Christ. Mel Gibson's *The Passion of the Christ* tried to convince twenty-first-century viewers of the ancient Catholic view that Jews were responsible for the crucifixion.

THE UNITED STATES

Anti-Semitism arrived in the United States with the colonists. A boatload of the first Jewish settlers landed in New Amsterdam in 1654. The small ship held twenty-three impoverished men, women, and children fleeing from Recife, Brazil. Miraculously, they successfully resisted the efforts of Peter Stuyvesant, who, along with his council and the Calvinist clergy, sought to deport them shortly after their arrival. Anti-Semitism, basically imported from Europe, continued to add strength in the next two centuries, gaining momentum in the 1840s, when waves of central Europeans, mostly

Germans, arrived in the United States. Several leading abolitionists, including William Lloyd Garrison, were violently anti-Semitic. Garrison called New York City sheriff Mordecai Noah, who supported the institution of slavery, "the lineal descendant of the [Jewish] mobsters who nailed Jesus to the cross."

East European Jews, who came to America in waves from 1890 to 1910, encountered virulent anti-Semitism. The lynching of Leo Frank in Atlanta in 1915 for a murder he did not commit represented the nadir of anti-Semitism in the United States: "Never again would anti-Semites in the United States carry out such a violent attack on any Jew, although many anti-Semitic incidents and events would occur during the next ninety years," wrote Michael Grunberger, a historian of Jewish life in America.[21] During the 1920s, Henry Ford's newspaper, the *Dearborn Independent*, published the notorious forgery *The Protocols of the Elders of Zion*, and anti-Semitism continued to flourish. The book, published in tsarist Russia at the end of the nineteenth century, describes a Jewish conspiracy to rule the world. It quickly became a best seller in Europe, fueling growing anti-Semitism, and it is said to have inspired Hitler. During the Great Depression in the 1930s and early 1940s, Rev. Charles Coughlin, a Catholic priest, spewed anti-Semitism on his popular weekly radio program.

In 2000, with the nomination of Senator Joseph Lieberman of Connecticut, an observant Jew, as the Democratic vice presidential nominee, America seemed to have gone a long way toward conquering anti-Semitism. However, anti-Semitism has become a feature of many Internet hate sites, one of which published a lengthy list of "The Jews who Run Bush and the USA" in May 2005.[22] In addition, anti-Semitism today is often manifested in the African-American and Hispanic communities. The ADL estimated that 44 percent of foreign-born Hispanics are anti-Semitic, compared with 26 percent of Hispanics born in the United States.

Anti-Semitism among African Americans has been a growing problem. During his 1988 presidential campaign, Rev. Jesse Jackson referred to New York City as "Hymietown," a derogatory reference to its large Jewish population. Some Jews, mostly of the older generation, reciprocate and refer to blacks as "*shvartzes*," a derogatory term. At a lunch in the 1980s, Supreme Court justice Thurgood Marshall was asked, "What's happened between you blacks and us Jews? We were in the civil rights movement together. We were in the labor movement together. We marched on the picket lines together. Our kids died together in Mississippi. What's happened?" Marshall replied, "It's true that we blacks and you Jews have been going together for a long, long time, but you know and I know that we ain't never going to get married."[23] More recently, Louis Farrakhan, the leader of the Black Muslims, has blamed Jews for much of the world's ills.

In the United States, with 6 million Jews out of a U.S. population of 282 million, the total number of anti-Semitic incidents has been steadily declining. But they still exist. Anti-Semitic acts in 2001 and 2002 included a spray-painted swastika in the driveway of the Reconstructionist synagogue, Congregation Adat Shalom, on the day it opened its doors in suburban Washington. Incidents also included a shooting and a bomb threat directed at a synagogue in Des Moines; a synagogue arson attack in Tacoma, Washington; and a cemetery desecration in Greensburg, Pennsylvania. The Klan and other right-wing extremist groups still disseminate anti-Semitic propaganda, which has unfortunately been emulated by other hate groups in the aftermath of 9/11.

Subtle forms of anti-Semitism also continue. Some country clubs continue to exclude Jews, although they admit a handful of high-profile Jews to counter criticism, and to claim the tax deduction denied to clubs that discriminate. Nor are Jews themselves exempt from this virus; indeed, some Jews are embarrassed by what they consider the crudeness of some of their coreligionists, such as the German Jews, who still disdain those who arrived from Eastern Europe. In fact, a country club founded by German Jews in a New York suburb continues to discriminate against Jews whose ancestors came from Eastern Europe.

WESTERN EUROPE

In Western Europe, "traditional far-right groups still account for a significant proportion of the attacks against Jews and Jewish properties," the U.S. State Department noted, naming "disadvantaged and disaffected Muslim youths . . . responsible for most of the other incidents."[24] Many of these attacks were prompted by Europeans' perception that Israel and the United States constituted the major threat to world peace. A European Union poll of 7,515 randomly selected people in 2003 found that 59 percent of all Europeans considered Israel the greatest threat to world peace, with the United States scoring a close second with 53 percent. By comparison, North Korea, Iran, and Iraq were considered the greatest threat to world peace by 76 percent of Americans.

"While intolerance may not have won the day, it has made progress almost everywhere in Europe during these last few years, relying in particular on an instrument which is at once new and extraordinary, namely the Internet," Michael Barnier, French foreign minister, told the opening session of the OSCE conference in Brussels, in June 2004.[25] Concerned about reports of an increase in anti-Semitism, in 1998 the European Union created a European Monitoring Center on Racism and Xenophobia (EUMC). The purpose was to help member states formulate courses of action to combat these evils. Its first report, *Manifestations of Anti-Semitism in the EU 2002–2003*, was based on in-depth interviews with Jews in eight European countries.

- In Germany, the respondents stated that anti-Semitism was still anchored in German civil society and had become more violent.
- In Austria, the report found the end of a social consensus that in the past had condemned anti-Semitism.
- French Jews said they were suffering the worst anti-Semitic violence since World War II.
- In Belgium, anti-Semitism has become increasingly socially acceptable.
- Italians reported no violent incidents but admitted that the Jewish community was frightened by the public discourse on Israel and the Jews.
- In the United Kingdom, the political climate, previously marked by a high degree of tolerance, was changing for the worse.[26]

Four categories of anti-Semitism dominated the analysis. First, the Christian anti-Jewish tradition led individuals to practice anti-Semitism without being aware of it. Second, anti-Semitism of the far right wing remained a problem. Third, anti-Semitism on the left was driven by those with sympathy for the Palestinians. And, finally, there was Muslim anti-Semitism. Theologically based anti-Semitism was augmented by the ethnocentric nationalism of the nineteenth and twentieth centuries, which regarded Jews as racially inferior and inherently disloyal to the state.

Muslim anti-Semitism is a relatively new phenomenon, according to Akbar S. Ahmed, who occupies the Ibn Khaldun Chair of Islamic Studies at American University's School of Foreign Service. "Islam has no tradition of anti-Semitism," he said. "Osama bin Laden quotes the Koran, 'Fight the Jews and Christians,'" Dr. Ahmed said, "but he doesn't quote the next line, 'Unless they want peace.'"

Muslim anti-Semitism has only recently ratcheted up—on the Internet, from the mosques, and on state-owned television. In 2004, Egyptian state television created a forty-one-part series, *Horseman without a Horse*, which also aired on Arab stations across the Middle East. One episode depicts Jews conspiring to deny that Jews were authors of the *Protocols of the Elders of Zion*. Outside the Middle East, some countries have shown a marked decrease in anti-Semitism, according to an ADL poll based on agreement or disagreement with the following stereotypes:

1. Jews don't care what happens to anyone but their own kind;
2. Jews are more willing than others to use shady practices to get what they want;
3. Jews are more loyal to Israel than to this country;
4. Jews have too much power in the business world; and
5. Jews still talk too much about what happed to them in the Holocaust.

The latest ADL polls convey good news. The 2004 results showed that anti-Semitism in France had declined to 25 percent of the population, compared with 35 percent in 2002. Sweden hosted the Stockholm International Forum on the Holocaust in January 2000 and has since become a model of Holocaust education. Sweden also sponsored a Second International Forum for Combating Intolerance. The poll found that anti-Semitism in Germany was at 36 percent, down from 37 percent. Belgium was 35 percent, down from 39 percent; Denmark was 16 percent, down from 21 percent; Spain was 24 percent, down from 34 percent; Italy was 15 percent, down from 22 percent; and Austria was 17 percent, down from 19 percent. On the other hand, anti-Semitism in the United Kingdom had increased to 25 percent, up from 18 percent in 2002; anti-Semitism in the Netherlands had also increased to 9 percent, up from 7 percent.

Paradoxically, although the number of European anti-Semites had declined, anti-Semitic attacks in Europe have become both more numerous and more violent.[27] Some observers attribute the rise of anti-Semitic incidents in Europe to the end of the Cold War, specifically to the need to find another object of hatred to replace the Soviet Union. Although both antireligious and anti-Semitic, the Soviet Union and the leaders of its puppet states had suppressed much of the overt anti-Semitic extremism during their seventy years of power. After the Soviet Union ceased to exist—in fact, at the first signs of freedom during perestroika and glasnost—anti-

Semitism again reared its ugly head, even though there were few Jews left to scapegoat.

In France, although anti-Semitism has decreased among the general population, anti-Semitic incidents continue to plague the nation. "In France we are confronted with a rise of anti-Semitic acts," said Jean David Levitte, French ambassador to United Nations.[28] With only 600,000 Jews out of a French population of 60 million, a record number of more than four hundred violent attacks occurred from the fall of 2000 to the spring of 2002. These included numerous acts of arson and vandalism against Jewish property and several violent attacks on Jewish individuals. Two Jews were knifed, in separate incidents, by youths of North African or Middle Eastern origin in Strasbourg in January 2001. The rabbi of Rouen was assaulted by a man of Moroccan origin as he was leaving his synagogue, and the blind rabbi of Cannes was cursed and threatened with a knifing. Among the many arson and other attacks on synagogues and Jewish schools, clubs, and cemeteries in 2001 and 2002, the Tiferet Israel school in Sarcelles was burned down, and the Gan Pardes school in Marseilles was set aflame and the slogans "Death to the Jews" and "bin Laden will conquer" were spray painted on the walls. Several acts of desecration were recorded at Jewish cemeteries and Holocaust memorials, including at Cronenbourg and Schiltigheim, near Strasbourg, and the Holocaust memorial at Reims.

"Jews are being persecuted every day in France," wrote Nidra Poller, a Jewish expatriate from the United States.[29] "Some are insulted, pelted with stones, spat upon; some are beaten or threatened with knives or guns. Synagogues are torched, schools burned to the ground. A little over a month ago, at least one Jew was savagely murdered, his throat slit, his face gouged with a carving knife. Did it create an uproar? No. The incident was stifled, and by common consent—not just by the authorities, but by the Jews." She wondered if it was time to heed the warnings and return to the United States, or remain and risk the fate of the six million who died in the Holocaust. "I feel it here," said a woman at the Synagogue de Tournelles in Paris, pounding her chest. "People forget what it was like. How anti-Semitism started. We think this is the beginning of World War III or IV. We're afraid." She asked, "Is there anyone in the U.S. like [Jean-Marie] Le Pen?" referring to the anti-Semitic, anti-immigrant political leader whose numbers rise with every election.

Much of this violence is the work of young Muslims who have become virtually unemployable. Unable to find jobs because of the French bias against Muslims, they attack the all-purpose scapegoat, the Jews.

"Unemployment generates anger and xenophobia," said Elyette Levy-Heisbourg, a member of the Foreign Affairs Committee of the French National Assembly. The influx of six million Arabs, a considerable voting bloc, has muted the response of the French government.

Despite all these devastating incidents, there are some hopeful signs. Although Jean-Marie Le Pen, the far-right politician, gained 15 percent of the vote in the last general election, his party failed to win a single seat in the General Assembly. And the late Simone Veil, an Auschwitz survivor, was elected president of the European Parliament. French President Jacques Chirac has been quick to condemn all acts of anti-Semitism. "He has to," explained Elaine Sciolino, the *New York Times* bureau chief in Paris. "He has to calm down the hatreds in this country."

The hysteria can be contagious. In 2004, an account of an anti-Semitic attack against a young French mother and child on a suburban commuter train turned out to be a hoax. The six attackers were described as being of North African origin. The mother turned out to be what one observer called a chronic "mythomaniac." President Chirac, in a comment similar to that of Mr. Barre in 1980, condemned both the reported assault and the hoax, saying, "We are going through a period of displays of racism in which our compatriots, Jews, Muslim or even others, sometimes even simply French people, are the object of aggression with the only motive that they don't belong or are not from such and such a community."[30]

The rise in anti-Semitic attacks has nevertheless led thousands of French Jews to emigrate to Israel and buy property there.[31] Two thousand French Jews left France for Israel in 2002, compared with one thousand in each of the previous three years. In addition, French Jews have purchased more than one thousand apartments in Israel in the last two years, compared with one hundred a year in prior years.

In July 2004, Israeli prime minister Ariel Sharon touched off a verbal melee by urging France's Jews to flee immediately to Israel to escape anti-Semitism at home. "If I have to advise our brothers in France, I'll tell them one thing: Move to Israel, as soon as possible," Sharon said.[32] "The reaction was swift, angry and unified," Sciolino wrote. "French officials, lawmakers, commentators and Jewish leaders all told Mr. Sharon that he was out of line."

France finally began to deal with the resurgence of anti-Semitic attacks in 2003. French authorities reported 298 judicial procedures related to attacks that occurred in the first eight months of 2004. A total of 162 incidents involved damage to property, such as arson and graffiti; 69 involved anti-Semitic images or articles; and 67 were attacks on people, ranging from insults to physical attacks.[33] France adopted the LeHouche Act in 2003, providing stiffer penalties for racist, anti-Semitic, and xenophobic offenses. First-degree murder in a hate crime now carries a punishment of life imprisonment rather than thirty years. Perpetrators of torture and barbaric acts now face twenty years' imprisonment rather than fifteen. Those who damage private property now risk three years' imprisonment instead of two, and five years' imprisonment when the site is a place of worship. And damage to property using dangerous means, such as explosives and incendiary devices, now carries sentences of twenty years' imprisonment rather than ten. Another law, the Perben II Act, adopted in 2004, expanded the list of crimes that could be considered racist or anti-Semitic, and it extended the deadline for filing a complaint from three months to one year.

The criminal court in Strasbourg gave prison sentences ranging from eighteen months to three years to six individuals who had tried to destroy the synagogue at Cronenbourg. The following year, in 2004, the criminal court in Dijon imposed a two-month prison sentence on a man who had struck French transit agents and had used anti-Semitic language. The head of the French media watchdog, Conseil Supérieur de l'Audiovisuel, asked the highest administrative court to ban a European satellite operator from broadcasting programs from Al-Manar, which carried anti-Semitic broadcasts.

France is also trying to use quiet persuasion. Ambassador Levitte recalled an incident involving an anti-Semitic film made in Lebanon and Syria that was being shown on French television. French officials went to Damascus and Beirut accompanied by officials of the television network and warned of public action if the film was not withdrawn. The diplomacy worked, Ambassador Levitte said, and the film is no longer shown in France.

- In Belgium, with 35,000 Jews out of a population of 10 million, there were seventeen violent acts of anti-Semitism in 2001 and twenty-five in the first five months of 2002.
- In Germany, the Jewish population has more than tripled since 1989 and is now estimated at 100,000. There were 1,424 anti-Semitic crimes recorded in 2001, including the desecration of synagogues and cemeteries. However, Germany also has done more to welcome Jews in the postwar period than any other European nation, providing subsidies and other opportunities for them. As a result, in 2003,

more Jews from the former Soviet Union immigrated to Germany than to Israel—19,000 to Germany compared with 12,000 to Israel. "No other country in Europe has done so much to deal with the past," said Dagmar Wiler, an official with the Bridge of Understanding, a group that promotes empathy and cooperation between Germans and Jews in Munich. Gregory Caplan, former associate director of the American Jewish Committee's Berlin office, noted, "Today the state stands against anti-Semitism, in contrast with state-sponsored anti-Semitism."

- In the United Kingdom, with 280,000 Jews out of a population of 58 million, there were 310 anti-Semitic incidents reported in 2001. In February 2002, the cover of the *New Statesman*, a left-wing weekly magazine, showed a Magen David piercing a Union Jack under the headline, "A Kosher Conspiracy?"

EASTERN EUROPE

"In Eastern Europe, with a much smaller Muslim population, skinheads and other members of the radical political fringe were responsible for most anti-Semitic incidents," the State Department reported. "Anti-Semitism remained a serious problem in Russia and Belarus, and elsewhere in the former Soviet Union, with most incidents carried out by ultra-nationalist and other far-right elements. The stereotype of Jews as manipulators of the global economy continues to provide fertile ground for anti-Semitic aggression."[34]

The Eastern European countries are the least anti-Semitic in Europe. "They have learned," said Abraham Foxman. "They know the road to NATO and the European Union was paved by the U.S. through support of the Jewish community." In fact, the Bush administration insisted that these nations take steps to address anti-Semitism as a prerequisite for joining the North Atlantic Treaty Organization (NATO).

"No country of the former Soviet Union includes anti-Semitism in its official policy or state ideology," noted Anti-Semitism Worldwide. "Jews continue to be prominent in economic, cultural and political life, some serving in leadership positions in Jewish organizations as well."[35]

Ten visiting Ukrainian journalists, interviewed during a visit to American University in Washington, noted that 100,000 Jews had emigrated from the Ukraine, and there were very few Jews left in the former Soviet Union.

Although anti-Semitism remained endemic, they said, it was no longer state sponsored. In fact, the government has restored synagogues, including one in the town of Kharkov. Even so, fifty youths marched two miles in 2003 to attack a synagogue in Kiev, where they beat the principal of the Lubavitch yeshiva and the son of the chief rabbi.[36]

About half a million Jews remain in the former Soviet Union, of whom 445,000 live in Russia, Ukraine, or Belarus. This population has been diminished by about 1.8 million since 1989. About 930,000 emigrated to Israel, 570,000 to Western countries, and the negative birth rate accounted for the loss of about 290,000.

- Hungary, with 80,000 Jews out of a population of 10.5 million, constitutes the largest Jewish community in Eastern Europe outside the former Soviet Union. The decidedly racist Hungarian Justice and Life Party failed to pass the electoral threshold in the May 2002 elections, despite its effort to raise the "Judeo-Bolshevik" theme portraying the Jews as the source of all Hungary's misfortunes. Anti-Semitic slogans, such as "The train is leaving for Auschwitz," have marred soccer matches. In 2003, more than one hundred skinheads interrupted a Hanukkah candlelighting ceremony in downtown Budapest for over an hour with shouts of "Hungary is for Hungarians, and it is better that those who are not Hungarians leave."[37]
- Poland, with 5,000 to 10,000 Jews out of a population of 40 million, is also home to right-wing extremists who blare out and draw posters with anti-Semitic slogans. Nevertheless, there has been a revival of interest in things Jewish. About 25,000 young people, mostly non-Jews, attend an annual Jewish festival in Warsaw, while in Krakow, young people now gather to drink beer and listen to klezmer music.
- Romania, with 6,000 Jews out of a population of 21.5 million, had a serious incidence of vandalism in 2001, when twenty gravestones were smashed in a Jewish cemetery. Slovakia, with 3,000 Jews out of a population of 5.35 million, had several incidents of vandalism in 2001 and 2002.

THE MIDDLE EAST

In many ways, the Middle East is the mother lode of anti-Semitism and the violence it spawns. Children are taught anti-Semitism in the madrasses, state-sponsored, religiously oriented schools in Egypt, Saudi Arabia, and other Middle Eastern countries. Leaders of these countries made the mistake of handing education over to the mullahs in the hope of co-opting religious leaders; instead, many of the madrasses became training grounds for fundamentalist insurgents.

Hitler's notorious book, *Mein Kampf*, is printed and sold in several Arab countries. *The Protocols of the Elders of Zion*, the notorious anti-Semitic forgery, has been serialized on state-owned television in Egypt, while the chief cleric of the Grand Mosque in Mecca describes Jews as "the killers of prophets and grandsons of monkeys and pigs." On the positive side, France revoked a broadcasting license for a Lebanese television station, Al-Manar, owned by the terrorist organization Hezbollah, because of its anti-Semitic propaganda.

The Israeli-Palestinian conflict has aggravated anti-Semitic violence in the Middle East. "Anti-Semitism remains deeply ingrained in Egyptian society, finding expression in the mass media, popular literature and public statements, while remaining virtually unchallenged by government leaders."[38] Articles and caricatures in the Egyptian media—which are widely distributed throughout the Middle East—regularly feature anti-Semitic depictions of Jews as stooped, hook nosed, money hungry, and conspiratorial. Israeli leaders are depicted as Nazis, while other articles deny or diminish the Holocaust.

A Jewish-American couple visiting Jordan with their two children in 1979 could not obtain exit visas because the husband had given the wrong answer to the fifth and final question on the visa application: religion. His planned response, "secular humanist," didn't seem right; he refused to deny his heritage and answered "Jewish." It didn't seem to matter to the Jordanian immigration officials that they were Americans, not Israelis. After a day's detention, the issue was resolved by the intervention of the U.S. embassy.[39]

Al-Jazeera, a television network based in Qatar but viewed throughout the world, has become a major engine of both anti-Israel and anti-Semitic propaganda. Its round-the-clock broadcasts of Israeli violence against Palestinians is unmatched by similarly graphic reports of Palestinian violence against Israelis. Secretary of State Colin Powell raised this issue at a meeting with Sheik Hamad bin Jassim bin Jabir-al-Thani, Qatar's foreign minister, in April 2004. "We have deep concerns about Al Jazeera's broadcasts because, again and again, we find inaccurate, false, wrong reports that are, we think, designed to be inflammatory that appear on this network," said

State Department spokesman Richard A. Boucher.[40] A senior American officer added, "All people are seeing is the minaret hit by American fire and falling. They're not seeing the pictures of the fighters shooting at us from those mosques and minarets." Defense Secretary Donald Rumsfeld told a news conference, "We are dealing with people who are willing to lie to the world to make their case."[41]

ASIA

As previously noted, Pakistan and Malaysia, both Muslim nations, have been infected with the virus of anti-Semitism. "In Pakistan, a country without a Jewish community, anti-Semitic sentiment fanned by anti-Semitic articles in the press is widespread. . . . This reflects the more recent phenomenon of anti-Semitism appearing in countries where historically there have been few, or even no Jews."[42]

In China, however, with a small but long-standing Jewish community, there is little anti-Semitism; on the contrary, the country welcomes Jewish business executives from the United States and other countries. In contrast, Japan is infected with anti-Semitism, as is Korea.

CANADA

Canada, with a Jewish population of 364,000 out of 31 million, had 857 anti-Semitic incidents in 2004, a jump of 47 percent over 2003 and 295 percent since 1994. The Jewish community suffered bomb threats, anthrax scares, physical assaults on individuals, vandalism of synagogues, cemetery desecrations, harassment, and hate propaganda. White supremacist and neo-Nazi activity has decreased in Canada, but racist groups from the United States such as William Pierce's white-supremacist National Alliance, have reportedly been active in Canada.

University campuses continue to be a source of anti-Semitic propaganda. One incident involved a speech by former Israeli prime minister Benjamin Netanyahu at Concordia University in Montreal on September 9, 2002. He had been invited by a Jewish student group. Norma Joseph, an assistant professor and chair of the Department of Religion, sought to attend the speech with her husband, Rabbi Howard Joseph. Professor Joseph described what happened:

I was a victim of the new anti-Semitism. I was assaulted by rioting students on my own campus. I was punched, while others kicked my husband. We had arrived early. Demonstrators had circled the building, and 100 Quebec riot police were on duty. It was impossible to get into the building. Pro-Palestinians told me to move back. I refused. Then the riot police pushed me back. They [the protesters] started shouting "Down with Israel." I turned around and saw my husband being kicked. A modestly dressed Muslim woman wearing a head scarf started punching me in the breasts. I wasn't really hurt. In the middle of the punching I called university security on my cell phone. They put me on hold. Netanyahu's security people wouldn't let him in the building. Instead he spoke on TV. He said, "I was going to talk to a few hundred students. The rioters gave me an audience of millions."

We finally got into the building for protection. We were tear-gassed, and couldn't get out. The university suspended three students, out of the hundreds who were breaking windows. There was one Jewish student among the pro-Palestinian demonstrators, and many outsiders. On this campus, student apathy is the norm, not student activism. That was the problem. A small group of activists took over. Most students just wanted to get their degrees. But you only have to take one course a year to qualify as a full-time student, and some students have been here 12 years. The student newspaper said the riot was the Jewish students' fault, a classic case of blaming the victims. They editorially condemned the Jewish students for inviting Netanyahu, saying that the Jewish students knew they would outrage the Muslims, and that would lead to violence.

THE BUSH ADMINISTRATION

President George W. Bush has played a heroic, unsung role in combating worldwide anti-Semitism. The White House was instrumental in keeping three European conferences on anti-Semitism on track, pushing heavily and nearly alone for the first conference and allying with Germany for the second. The United States also strongly urged Eastern European nations seeking entry into NATO to take steps to combat anti-Semitism. Several nations were edgy about the conferences on anti-Semitism sponsored by the fifty-five-nation Organization for Security and Cooperation in Europe in Vienna in June 2003, in Berlin in April 2004, and in Brussels in September 2004. The organization was created in the 1970s as a trade-off with the Soviets—security and economic prosperity in exchange for guarantees on human rights. "The Bush administration was key in keeping these conferences on track," said Rabbi Andrew Baker, director of International Jewish Affairs at the American Jewish Committee.

The ADL's Abraham Foxman agreed on the importance of Bush's role, formed in the crucible of his belief in born-again Christian fundamentalism. "You'll find denial (of anti-Semitism) wherever you go," he said. "Governments deny it. Perpetrators deny it. Bystanders deny it. Even victims deny it. These conferences mark the end of denial. That is why they are important. They force nations to go on record. Jordanians and Egyptians lobbied against the OSCE conferences. They wanted no mention of Israel, the Middle East, Arabs or Muslims. The Bush administration has bludgeoned the Europeans to deal with it. They made calls before the Vienna conference. (Secretary of State Colin) Powell made calls, he lobbied the foreign ministers. The U.S. wouldn't let go. Powell's presence in Berlin was very important."

President Bush and his aides also urged Eastern European nations to confront their anti-Semitism. "I have to give a lot of credit to the Bush administration," said Rabbi Baker. "A major decision in NATO enlargement has been dealing with Jewish issues. The U.S. has repeatedly raised these issues. There was never a meeting with the Romanian government when anti-Semitism wasn't on the table. George Bush spoke to the Lithuanian president when he visited here, about preserving Judaica, including scrolls and menorahs. Dealing with the unfinished business of the Holocaust era was the litmus test applied to these NATO aspirant countries."

Anti-Semitism occupies an important place on the list of priorities in U.S. embassies around the world. Officials are instructed to report all incidents to Washington. Many credit Bush's strong policies in the area of global anti-Semitism to the presence of two African Americans in his cabinet: secretaries of state Colin Powell and Condoleezza Rice. "Look where they grew up," said a Jewish activist. "Look how they grew up." In 2004, Rice was given a book, published in Egypt, containing anti-Semitic cartoons with French subheads. Two days later, she discussed the book and its contents with an Arab diplomat. "I know what this is all about," Rice told him, according to the Jewish activist. "I grew up in the South. I saw the cartoons that demonized us, and made us vulnerable to lynching. Why don't you stop it?"

As undersecretary of state in the Clinton administration, Stuart Eizenstat created the position of Ambassador and Special Envoy for Holocaust Issues. The position continued and gained momentum in the Bush administration. "The Bush administration deserves a lot of credit," Eizenstat said.

The OSCE conferences marked "the first time that anti-Semitism was an issue" at an international conference. Randolph Bell, the second ambassador and special envoy for Holocaust issues, held the position in the Bush administration. He noted that Jewish groups in the United States had sought conferences on anti-Semitism. "The U.S. delegation pressed that point extremely hard," he said. "It was a politically accepted objective of the administration.

"The Bush administration provided enormous support for this, but there is a history of bipartisan cooperation," Bell continued. The State Department joined nongovernmental organizations (NGOs) in visiting all seven Eastern European nations that sought to join NATO. "We had what we called a road show. We went to all seven countries more than once, and reviewed with them issues including civilian control of the military, fighting corruption and other issues of building a democratic society. We wanted to make sure they came to terms with anti-Semitism in their countries. This is not a Jewish issue. It's a human rights issue." Although there was no explicit requirement that Eastern European nations address their anti-Semitism as a requirement for joining NATO, "it was clear that they had to do something about it, or at least pay lip-service to the problem," said Rabbi Baker.

OTHER HOPEFUL SIGNS

Western Europe also has made progress in combating anti-Semitism. In France, for example, the city of Marseilles has taken the lead. While anti-Semitic incidents have increased in Paris, Lyon, Strasbourg, and other major French cities, "in Marseilles, the animus has fizzled out," noted writer Claire Berlinski.[43] "The city reacted with revulsion to the burning of the Or Aviv synagogue. Citywide protests against anti-Semitism were immediately organized; Arabs participated in the demonstrations. The leaders of Marseilles' Islamic community firmly condemned the attack." The key to Marseilles' success is a program, "Marseilles Espèrance—The Hope of Marseilles," which was inaugurated in 1990, uniting the city's religious leaders and the mayor in regular discussion groups. "As soon as there's a crisis, they calm things, they issue communiqués—they are seen together. It's symbolic, seeing them together, the rabbi, the preacher, the mufti," observed Police Chief Pierre Carton.

On a broader scale, there are hopeful signs that nations are banding together to combat anti-Semitism. At the OSCE conference in 2004 in Berlin—the heart of the Third Reich—fifty-five nations pledged vigilance against resurgent anti-Semitism in Europe.[44] Secretary of State Colin Powell told the conference that anti-Semitism was "not just a fact of history, but a current event." He told the conference that the United States "has its share of anti-Semites and skinheads and other assorted racists, bigots and extremists who feed on fear and ignorance and prey on the vulnerable." Powell also noted that some anti-Israeli attacks were tinged with anti-Semitism. "It is not anti-Semitic to criticize the policies of the state of Israel," he said. "But the line is crossed when Israel or its leaders are demonized or vilified, for example, by the use of Nazi symbols and racist cartoons."[45]

The conference ended with a "Berlin Declaration" in which the fifty-five nations "declare unambiguously that international developments or political issues, including those in Israel or elsewhere in the Middle East, never justify anti-Semitism." The participating states committed themselves to take specific steps to combat anti-Semitism in their countries, including the collection of data on anti-Semitic attacks, initiation of education programs, and assuring that no aspect of their governments, including their legal systems, promotes or tolerates anti-Semitism.

Individuals and business groups also have a role to play. Alarmed by 857 anti-Semitic incidents in Canada in 2004, a 47 percent increase over the previous year, Tony Comper, president and CEO of the Bank of Montreal, and his wife Elizabeth created a coalition of twenty-one Canadian business leaders, called Fighting Anti-Semitism Together. Their recruits included John Hunkin, CEO of Canadian Imperial Bank of Commerce, and Timothy J. Hearn, chairman and president of Imperial Oil Ltd. "This is a crisis that must be resolved by non-Jews," Comper said. "Non-Jews must join the battle against what has been described sadly, but accurately, as the oldest and the longest of hatreds." The group's first project, a four-part DVD series in partnership with the Canadian Jewish Congress, is shown in Ontario's schools. It features three Holocaust survivors, a former white supremacist, a woman who witnessed the 1994 genocide in Rwanda, and a black hockey player who suffered racism—all talking about their experiences. The group hopes to discourage anti-Semitic incidents such as one at a private school in Toronto, in which three tenth graders created an Internet chat room named the "Gas Chamber" and the "Reichstag" on a student site, where they posted old images of Jews being tortured and sent to gas chambers. The three boys, one of whom was Jewish, were expelled. Four others were suspended for knowing about the chat rooms and not revealing them to the school authorities. "We're trying to teach the kids that to witness it and to be silent is not proper," Mrs. Comper said.[46]

That's the good news. Although "that very light sleeper," anti-Semitism, has again raised its ugly head, it is not state sponsored as it was for millennia, except in the Middle East. Men and women of goodwill, as well as governments and business groups, are organizing opposition to this recurring scourge. The U.S. government has taken a strong stand against global anti-Semitism and is encouraging other nations to do the same. And the Europeans, at least, are taking steps to rid themselves of this ancient affliction, a centuries-old blight on their otherwise rich civilizations.

NOTES

1. U.S. State Department, "Report on Global Anti-Semitism," ed. Bureau of Human Rights, Democracy, and Labor (Washington, DC: U.S. State Department, 2005). See also appendix A.

2. Phyllis Chesler, *The New Anti-Semitism: The Current Crisis and What We Must Do About It* (San Francisco: Jossey-Bass, 2003), 80.

3. Willard Gaylin, *Hatred: The Psychological Descent into Violence* (New York: Public Affairs, 2003), 205–6.

4. See appendix A.

5. Douglas Burch, "Russian Jews Say Nationalists Rekindle Anti-Semitism," *Baltimore Sun*, June 29, 2005.

6. Elaine Sciolino, "On Bastille Day, France Buzzes over a Hoax and Racism," *New York Times*, July 15, 2004.

7. Charles Krauthammer, "The Real Mideast 'Poison,'" *Washington Post*, April 30, 2004.

8. Warren Hoge, "Remove Wall, Israel Is Told by the U.N.," *New York Times*, July 20, 2004.

9. Ibid.

10. Warren Hoge, "U.N. Is Gradually Becoming More Hospitable to Israel," *New York Times*, October 11, 2005.

11. Dina Porat and R. Stauber *Anti-Semitism Worldwide, 2001–2002* (Stephen Roth Institute at Tel Aviv University, the Anti-Defamation League, and the World Jewish Congress). The following figures for Chile, Mexico, Uruguay, and Australia also come from the above-mentioned report.

12. Esther Webman, "Al Aqsa Intifada and 11 September: Fertile Ground for Arab Anti-Semitism," in *Anti-Semitism WorldWide*, Anti-Defamation League and the World Jewish Congress, in association with Tel Aviv University, Stephen Roth Institute for the Study of Contemporary Anti-semitism and Racism, 2001–2002 (2003), 52.

13. Jessica Stern, *Terror in the Name of God: Why Religious Militants Kill* (New York: Ecco, 2003), 32.

14. U.S. State Department, "Report on Global Anti-Semitism."

15. Chesler, *The New Anti-Semitism*, 182.

16. Craig S. Smith, "Europe's Jews Seek Solace on the Right," *New York Times*, February 20, 2005.

17. Ibid.

18. Ron Rosenbaum, ed., *Those Who Forget the Past: The Question of Anti-Semitism* (New York: Random House Trade Paperbacks, 2004), 595.

19. Ibid.

20. Abraham H. Foxman, *Never Again?: The Threat of the New Anti-Semitism* (San Francisco: HarperSanFrancisco, 2003), 74.

21. Michael W. Grunberger, *From Haven to Home: 350 Years of Jewish Life in America* (New York: George Braziller, 2004).

22. See chapter 8, "Megabytes of Hate."

23. The lunch was attended by Martin Tolchin, Justice William Brennan, and Judge David Bazelon.

24. U.S. State Department, "Report on Global Anti-Semitism."

25. "Relationship between Racist, Xenophobic and Anti-Semitic Propaganda on the Internet and Hate Crimes" (Paris, France, June 16, 2004).

26. European Monitoring Centre on Racism and Xenophobia, "Manifestations of Anti-Semitism in the EU" (2002–2003), 11–13.

27. Anti-Defamation League, "Attitudes toward Jews, Israel and the Palestinian-Israeli Conflict in Ten European Countries" (New York: Anti-Defamation League, 2004).

28. Jean David Levitte, "Anti-Semitism on the Internet" (U.S. Capitol Building, Hart 902, September 9, 2004).

29. Nidra Poller, "Betrayed by Europe: An Expatriate's Lament," *Commentary*, March 2004, 23.

30. Sciolino, "On Bastille Day, France Buzzes over a Hoax and Racism."

31. Joseph Berger, "Israel Sees a Surge in Immigration by French Jews, But Why?" *New York Times*, July 4, 2004.

32. Elaine Sciolino, "France Wants Sharon to Explain His Call for Jews to Flee," *New York Times*, July 20, 2004.

33. French Embassy, "France's Fight against Anti-Semitism" (Washington, DC: French Embassy, 2004).

34. U.S. State Department, "Report on Global Anti-Semitism."

35. Porat and Stauber, *Anti-Semitism Worldwide, 2001–2002* (2003).

36. Senate Foreign Relations Committee, *Testimony of Daniel S. Mariaschin, Executive Vice President, B'nai B'rith International*, April 8, 2004.

37. Ibid.

38. Anti-Defamation League, "Anti-Semitism in Egypt: Media and Society, July 2003–February 2004" (March 30, 2004).

39. Experience of Martin Tolchin and Susan Tolchin in December 1979.

40. Christopher Marquis, "U.S. Protests Broadcasts by Arab Channels," *New York Times*, April 29, 2004.

41. Jehane Noujaim, "The Control Room" (Magnolia Pictures, 2004).

42. U.S. State Department, "Report on Global Anti-Semitism."

43. Claire Berlinski, "The Hope of Marseilles," *Azure* 19 (2005): 33.

44. Peter Slevin, "Ending a 'Deadly Hate' of Jews," *Washington Post*, April 29, 2004.

45. Noujaim, "The Control Room."

46. Janie Gosselin, "Businessmen Fight Anti-Semitism in Canada," *Barre-Montpelier Times Argus*, Associated Press, August 14, 2005.

3

RELIGION AND THE
RISE OF ANGER

Convictions are more dangerous than lies.

—Friedrich Nietzsche[1]

FUNDAMENTALISM

"There is nothing worse than a religious war," reflected the late George Herman, a former CBS reporter who has covered wars for over four decades, "because people are so convinced that they are right."[2] Lest anyone think that the Crusades and the Thirty-Years War are history, witness the many conflicts that circle the globe today in the name of religion. The "who" and "where" find easy answers in the daily press. But the "why" poses a nagging question: why is fundamentalism so influential at this point in time, especially in a world that has emerged from the Dark Ages more secularized than religious? And why has so much anger been provoked in the name of religion?

Fundamentalists today claim all three "Abrahamic" religions—Islam, Christianity, and Judaism—as their own. Yet mainstream religious leaders deny the legitimacy of fundamentalists, whom they consider religious extremists. All three religions share a long, sad history of disputes with each other, as well as often bloody schisms within themselves. At times, these intrareligious clashes escalated beyond mere differences of opinion into outright wars, such as the religious battles in Lebanon in the 1970s and 1980s; the numerous wars that took place between Catholics and Protestants in Europe over the last four centuries; and the clashes among Kurds, Shiites, and Sunni Muslims in Iraq today.

Their many conflicts mask the commonalities that the Abrahamic religions share: they all worship one God, they follow a strict code of ethics, they recognize each other's prophets, and they claim to have descended from the same man: Abraham. In Islam's Koranic tradition, followers of the other two faiths are supposed in theory to be treated with the greatest respect—since Muslims consider them "People of the Book."

Fundamentalists from all three religions also believe in an apocalypse. The Jews look forward to the coming of the Messiah; fundamentalist Christians wait for the Second Coming of Christ; and one of the Muslim Hadiths prophesies that "the hour [of the world's end] shall not occur until the Euphrates will disclose a mountain of gold over which the people will fight."[3] A perfect metaphor for the war in Iraq: the Euphrates is a river in Iraq, and a mountain of gold is a symbol for oil. Islamic fundamentalists "interpret the U.S. occupation of Iraq as setting the stage for the final battle between good, led by the Mahdi (the rightly guarded), and evil, represented by Dajjal (the deceiver)."[4]

Fundamentalists of each faith also share the conviction that they alone have sole ownership of the "truth": a view of right and wrong that does not tolerate nuances, challenges, or disagreement. While the absence of contradictions serves as a deep source of comfort to those who fear an increasingly uncertain world, it also carries with it a deep-seated intolerance for the views of others. Fundamentalists reserve their most vehement criticism for those who diverge from the fixed points that they alone have arbitrarily established as the truth. That means one book, one code of conduct, one land, and one set of laws.

Compared with the fundamentalists' rigidity, religion itself is more dynamic: it changes with the times, is more flexible than fundamentalists allow, and its holy books each contain many contradictions. "The test of a first-rate intelligence," wrote F. Scott Fitzgerald, "the ability to hold two opposed ideas in the mind at the same time, and still retain the ability to function," doesn't apply in a fundamentalist world.[5]

In the wake of the collapse of the Soviet Union and the end of the Cold War, religious fervor has escalated; in fact, the Soviet collapse signaled the last era in which "political conflicts were animated by secular ideologies"[6]—at least on the surface. After the demise of Soviet rule, where for seventy years atheism functioned virtually as an established state religion, the churches in Russia have lit up once again, energized mostly by the very young and the very old.

The anger unleashed by fundamentalists has had an overwhelming impact on politics. Governments have changed, as in Iran; elections were easily swayed by fear, as in Spain; human rights are widely violated, as in—take your pick. Legal codes also bear their imprint, as in Saudi Arabia, Iran, and Israel; and millions of people have become refugees and victims of widespread government-led genocide, as in Darfur and Afghanistan.

Do religious conflicts signal a "clash of civilizations" among the West, Islam, Sinic, and other civilizations, as Samuel Huntington has predicted?[7] Or are these clashes more localized, between sects of the same religion, as in Iraq? Or are they conflicts between the freedom to practice religion versus the needs of the secular state, as in the head scarf controversies in France, Germany, and Turkey? Or are they simply inexplicable, as the perennial Hindu-Muslim fights over Kashmir, or the dispute between the British and the Irish over Northern Ireland?

The real question is, are these wars geopolitical or religious in nature? Are these fights really over land and water, with religion as an excuse, as in many parts of the Middle East and Africa? Are leaders manipulating their people for political power in the name of religion? Is religion synonymous with culture, and are these battles fought among belief systems, with political power as the goal, as in the Sudan? Or are these battles a potpourri of all of the above?

At the beginning of the twenty-first century, Sudan represented one of the worst mixes of geopolitics, racism, religion, and tribalism ever witnessed—some say ignored—in world history. Government-supported militia, known as Janjaweed, have destroyed villages, killed and injured more than one million people, and have created a refugee population of hundreds of thousands more. Although government officials deny it, this state-sponsored genocide has been identified by observers as a blatantly racist attempt by the ruling group of Muslims to wipe out darker-skinned Muslim communities in a "deliberate attempt to eliminate three tribes in Darfur so Arab [leaders] can take their land."[8]

ISLAM

While transparent grabs for power fool no one, some of the most violent conflicts that plague the globe today are rooted in political anger that originates with religion, specifically with faiths (like Islam) whose adherents feel defeated by history. In the early fall of 2004, the U.S. Federal Bureau of Investigation admitted that the agency had intercepted over one hundred thousand electronic communications that were still not processed because there were not enough Arabic translators. (Arabic also happens to be the lingua franca of Al Qaeda, the international terrorist group responsible for the disaster of 9/11.) Shocking as this was in terms of the nation's security, what this meant was that there was not much interest outside of academe in the United States in Muslim culture and language until the tragedy of 9/11 occurred in 2001. Since that time, a rash of books, articles, and newspaper stories have focused on the Middle East, as Americans still struggle to understand why all of the hijackers were middle-class practicing Muslims linked to the terrorist group Al Qaeda, with fifteen of the nineteen hijackers citizens of one of America's closest allies, Saudi Arabia. Political scientist Richard Pape argues that it was not fundamentalism that created 9/11 or the Madrid and London bombings, but Muslims who did not want a secular power like the United States to take over their countries. His research found that 43 percent of suicide bombers were religious, and 57 percent were secular; in other words, a larger percentage of suicide bombers were motivated by secular, not religious, goals.[9]

Although the vast majority of Muslims condemn terrorist acts like 9/11, there still remains a deep well of anger from the Muslim world toward the West, particularly toward the United States. It began with a succession of defeats that occurred over the last eight to nine hundred years, but that are recalled by Muslims today as if they occurred yesterday. Although these defeats began as military losses, they eventually led to political and cultural losses that spelled the ultimate eclipse of Muslim civilization. Consciously and unconsciously, many Muslims viewed the domination of the West as a rejection of their religion, rationalizing that if they had been more devout, pious Muslims, military defeat and territorial losses would never have occurred.[10]

For almost one thousand years after the prophet Muhammad introduced his religion in Medina in 622 AD, Islam enjoyed a golden age, its culture in "the forefront of human civilization and achievement."[11] At the pinnacle of Muslim power, from the tenth to the thirteenth centuries, Islamic civilization led the world in economic power, military strength, medicine, biology, astronomy, science, and cultural life; in fact, Muslims looked down on other cultures, including and especially Europe, as infidels and barbarians. At its height, Islamic civilization claimed to be the "greatest military power on earth," the "foremost economic power in the world," and to have achieved the "highest level so far in human history in the arts and sciences."[12]

Arab Muslims date the decline of their civilization to the fall of Baghdad in 1258, when Mongol hordes defeated the ruling Arab caliph. This marked the end of the Abbasid dynasty and the passing of Muslim power into non-Arab hands. Until that time, caliphs had ruled that area for five centuries without any serious challenge to their power. Some Islamic theologians still argue today that the reason the city fell to "unbelievers" was that at that time Muslim citizens had embraced tolerance, pluralism, and worldly knowledge and had failed to adhere more strictly to their religion; had they been more devout, they would have retained political power.

The Mongol hordes opened the door to the Crusaders, who undertook to spread Christianity by the sword in eight major campaigns over a period of three hundred years—from the eleventh to the thirteenth century. The Crusaders cut a wide swath from Spain to the Middle East, winning battle after battle against Muslim armies, known as the Saracens. (The Crusaders were victorious except for a brief period, considered a second golden age by Muslims, when their hero, Saladin, drove the Crusaders out of Egypt and Syria in the twelfth century.) The Crusades were propelled by geopolitical goals wrapped in lofty statements by such popes as Urban II, who said he wanted to drive the "infidels" out of Jerusalem and the holy sites. But the Crusades were also a blatant power grab, an attempt to consolidate earthly power in the name of religion. At the beginning of the Crusaders' campaign, Muslims had already conquered a great deal of territory, controlling much of the Persian Empire, Syria, Iraq, Egypt, most of Spain, and the Mediterranean from Sicily to Anatolia (later Turkey). Within a few hundred years, they lost control of their entire empire.

Both sides in the Crusades saw the other as "militant, somewhat barbaric and fanatical in its religious zeal, [and were] determined to conquer, convert, or eradicate the other."[13] In fact, both religions were so similar theologically that their perennial clashes were essentially geopolitical in nature, despite the rhetoric of their leaders. Each regarded the other as heretics; both thought the highest honor of all was to "fall in battle"; and each religion romanticized the battles of the era from its own perspective. And, similar to the suicide bombers that today plague Israel and other countries, both Christian and Muslim warriors thought that the greatest honor was to "die a martyr for the faith and gain immediate access to heaven despite past sins."[14] In fact, the Arabic word "for martyr (*shahid*, sometimes spelled *shaheed*) comes from the same root as the profession of faith (*shahada*). As in Christianity, the reward for martyrdom is paradise."[15] (During the 1967 war against Israel, Palestinian leader Yasir Arafat was heard yelling the word *shaheed* into a mobile phone.)

Muslims today regard the Crusades as the precursor of colonialism, a long and painful experience that still rankles followers of Islam, particularly those from Middle Eastern countries. When President George W. Bush called his antiterrorist wars in Iraq and Afghanistan a "crusade," he unknowingly evoked an unpleasant historical memory held by many Muslims, who quaked at the analogy. "Bush used the word 'crusade' before going into Iraq," charged Mustapha Ozkaya, International Relations Coordinator for the Volunteer Organizations in Turkey. "This was a red flag to Muslims. It reminded them of the Crusades."[16] Even though the United States had nothing to do with the crushing defeats of either the Crusades or imperialism, the wars in Iraq and Afghanistan—as well as Bush's unwitting comments—drew worldwide condemnation.

The years between the Crusades of the eleventh through thirteenth centuries and colonialism in the nineteenth and twentieth centuries left the Arab countries in the Middle East far behind their Western counterparts in culture and economic development. The Renaissance crowned Europe as the center of culture, especially in the arts and the humanities, with the Catholic Church well established in the feudal duchies of the Holy Roman Empire, as well as in the nation-states that eventually followed. Each faith, displaying the intolerance that grew worse with each century, viewed the others as "infidels." When Protestantism split off from the Catholic Church, its chief proponent, Martin Luther, saw Islam "as a movement of violence in the service of the anti-Christ [to be] resisted by the sword."[17]

The periods of the Enlightenment and the Industrial Revolution, which followed the Renaissance, brought spectacular economic and technological development to the Western World. Some nations in the Middle East attempted to catch up to the West economically by building factories in the last half of the twentieth century, but many of these failed because they were unaccompanied by the kind of infrastructure—such as bridges, roads, and banks—necessary for genuine industrial development. In contrast, countries in Asia started from a much lower economic base but soon outstripped their competitors in the Middle East. The real economic failure—inevitably followed by political unrest—of nations like Saudi Arabia, Kuwait, and Iraq was their reliance on oil, a natural resource that the leaders of these countries knew would disappear in time. Instead of investing their considerable profits from oil into diversifying their economies and creating an industrial base, wealthy oil entrepreneurs (and the political leaders who partnered with them) invested abroad, spent their money on conspicuous consumption—Saddam Hussein had at least eleven palaces in Iraq—and were then surprised when growing unemployment led to political unrest. The World Bank estimated that the "total exports of the Arab world other than fossil fuels amount to less than those of Finland, a country of less than five million inhabitants."[18] The lifestyle of many of these oil billionaires, particularly in Saudi Arabia, led to further conflict among their coreligionists, who accused them of debauchery abroad and piety at home.

In trade policy, Americans and their Western counterparts contributed to irresponsible economic behavior by encouraging foreign investment in such instruments as U.S. Treasury notes, and by ignoring rampant breaches in reciprocity between themselves and the Arab nations. Kuwaiti nationals, for example, were allowed to invest in U.S. oil fields, but American investors were prohibited by Kuwaiti law from investing in that nation's lucrative oil industry.[19] Industrialized nations, together with the United States, ignored the hollowing out of the small middle classes in these countries, as investors in Latin America, the Middle East, Africa, and Asia sent their money abroad for safekeeping.

Following a long period of defeats, perceived defeats, and subsequent humiliations came what many Muslims today regard as the worst experience of all: colonialism. At the close of World War I, the map of the world was redrawn in favor of the winners, with the biggest loser being the Ottoman Empire. The French colonized nations in the "North, West and equatorial Africa and the Levant (Lebanon and Syria); the British [were firmly ensconced] in Palestine, Transjordan, Iraq, the Arabian Gulf, and Indian subcontinent; and in Southeast Asia, the British [ruled] Malaya, Singapore, and Brunei, [while] the Dutch [colonized] . . . Indonesia." Where the Muslims held on to power, in Turkey and Iran, "they were constantly on the defensive against the political and economic ambitions of the British, French and Russians."[20] Egypt had been colonized for a short time by the French, and then the British; after independence in 1953 and during Nasser's reign from 1954 to 1970, Egyptians then found themselves resisting further— albeit minor—encroachment by the Soviet Union. Europe turned out to be the "enemy that threatened both the faith of Islam and the political life of the Muslim community. . . . European . . . colonialism would dominate the history and psyche of Muslims," warned John Esposito, who wrote that European colonialism "continues . . . to affect relations between Islam and the West today."[21]

The issue of colonialism also relates to the duplicity and lies that were an inherent feature of this long-term foreign policy. The British, for example, promised Arab leaders sovereignty over the same lands they were simultaneously carving up secretly with the French at the end of World War I. Oppressed people have long memories, recalling these machinations of decades ago as if they occurred yesterday.

Although the Ottomans were the biggest losers, their base, Turkey, evolved into the most secular of all the world's nations with majority Muslim populations. But in 1918, the Ottoman losses were attributed to the same reasons that Baghdad fell in 1258: the loss of faith. Many Turkish citizens were imbued with the idea that their rulers and most of their subjects had approached "religion with tolerance and accommodation rather than viewing civilization as divided between Islam and infidels."[22] As in the Crusades, believers linked the loss of devotion and the absence of piety with military defeat; if believers practiced their religion more faithfully, victory would occur more often than defeat.

Throughout the twentieth century, Muslims suffered a succession of defeats, all interpreted as attacks against them and their faith: the Serbs' "ethnic cleansing" in Kosovo, Bosnia, and Herzegovina; the repression of fundamentalist Muslim groups by leaders in Egypt and Algeria; the Russian suppression of Muslims in Chechnya; and the defeat of the Taliban in Afghanistan. Rich Arab nations like Saudi Arabia failed to come to the rescue of their poorer coreligionists either in the former Yugoslavia or in Chechnya.

Encouraged by their leaders, Muslims also felt defeated by Israel's successive victories in the wars of 1948 and 1967, and to a lesser extent by their experiences in Lebanon with Israel and Syria. Today, "Islamophobia" has become an increasing concern in Europe, where large Muslim populations from the Middle East and Africa find themselves subject to job discrimination and anti-immigrant sentiment.[23] In the post-9/11 era, Muslim citizens in the United States protest blatant discrimination against them, particularly at airport security checkpoints.

The United States also never shared the history of colonialism in the Middle East with Europe and Great Britain, but nevertheless it finds itself today firmly associated with "imperialism" in the minds of many Muslims. One reason was America's unwavering support of Israel since its founding in 1948. American leaders opposed UN resolution 242—equating Zionism with Racism—and fought hard to have it overturned. Another reason involved U.S. Cold War policy of supporting countries, however unsavory, that allied with America against the Soviet Union. In Iran, the CIA/British coup against the popularly elected prime minister Mohammed Mossadegh elevated in his place Mohammed Reza Shah, an unpopular dictator who ruled the country with an iron hand for twenty-six years.

"Why did you Americans do that terrible thing?" asked an Iranian woman at a book party celebrating her memoirs. "To us, America was . . . the country that helped us while other countries were exploiting us. But after that moment [the coup] no one in Iran ever trusted the United States again."[24] She was right: the United States had no tangible interests in Iran but supported the British, who stood to lose the most from Mossadegh's nationalization of the Anglo-Iranian Oil Company. In light of future events, it was a short-sighted policy. The coup strengthened the country's religious leaders and paved the way for the fundamentalists' later seizure of power in 1979 under the leadership of Ayatollah Khomeini. Strongly anti-imperialist, the mullahs proclaimed that "every good Muslim had a sacred duty to support nationalization," with one mullah issuing a "fatwa asserting that from his place in paradise, the Prophet Mohammad himself had condemned [preceding governments] for selling Iran's birthright to infidel foreigners."[25] Through the crafty use of religion, Khomeini mobilized the anger that had been percolating since Mossadegh's overthrow; and although most Iranians did not consider themselves fundamentalists, they preferred Khomeini to the unpopular shah. Several years later, history repeated itself when U.S. support of the insurgents in Afghanistan led to an overthrow of Soviet power and its replacement by the ultrafundamentalist Taliban. To the surprise of U.S. leaders, both the Taliban and Khomeini turned out to be violently anti-American, with Khomeini calling America—not Great Britain—the "Great Satan."

JIHAD AND THE THEME OF DEFEAT

Today, Muslims are preoccupied with the question of why the infidel West remains superior in terms of military power, economic development, standard of living, and general wealth. Originally, the word *jihad* meant "effort," as in effort to convert the "heathen." To students of national security today, *jihad* has two meanings: the terrorist acts committed against the West in the name of Islam, and the splits within Islam that have escalated into war in the Middle East. One recent intrareligious jihad involved the brutal war between Iran and Iraq, which lasted eight years, from 1980 to 1988. Khomeini, a Shiite, called the war with Iraq a "jihad" and encouraged a "campaign of underground terror against the Sunni-dominated Gulf states

. . . [which represented] a third form of 'holy war.' ''[26] Khomeini's use of the word *jihad* masked the real reason for the conflict, which was also a regional struggle for strategic control of territory.

Of the major Islamic sects, the Shiites are the angriest, claiming to have been discriminated against by Sunnis for thirteen centuries. ''Sunni Islam is the doctrine of power and achievement. Shia Islam is the doctrine of the opposition. The starting point of Shi'ism is defeat.'' In fact, the word *assassin* came from the name of a Shia sect, the *hashashin*, ''who [frustrated by early defeats] launched daring raids for one hundred years against both Christian Crusaders and Sunni Muslim opponents.''[27] Many believe that Osama bin Laden hails from the tradition of the ''assassins,'' who went on suicide missions, promised paradise to martyrs, and vigorously protected the secrecy of their operations—although it is important to point out that bin Laden does not claim any linkages with modern Shiites. Founded by Hasan I Sabbah, known as the Old Man of the Mountains, the sect attracted followers through the ''judicious use of *hashish*, hence *hashishin*, and then *assassin*.''[28] The first ''assassins'' have been traced back to 1090 and were written about nearly two centuries later by Marco Polo.[29]

In the final analysis, the mixed messages of *jihad* are left to the interpreter: on the one hand, it means the effort to ''lead a good life, to make society more moral and just''; on the other, it means ''to spread Islam through preaching, teaching, or armed struggle.'' Frustrated with centuries of defeat, jihad today focuses more on armed struggle than on its doctrine of teaching and preaching. It encourages its followers to ''wage war against polytheists, apostates, and People of the Book who refuse Muslim rule, and those who attack Muslim territory.''[30] Moderate Muslims, in contrast, would argue that ''People of the Book'' be treated with respect, which is quite different from submitting them to ''Muslim rule.''

The violent concepts of jihad have influenced militants in Great Britain and Europe, who have escalated their activities in the early twenty-first century. The bombings in the London Underground in the summer of 2005 led Prime Minister Tony Blair to warn alien extremists that they would be expelled if they continued their incendiary speech. Later that summer, the British government followed through by deporting ten foreigners who were deemed threats to national security. Long before the bombings, Sheik Omar Bakri Mohammad threatened that if Europeans continued to ignore bin Laden's demand that all foreign troops leave Iraq, ''all Muslims of the world will be obliged to become his [bin Laden's] sword'' in a new battle. ''Stoking that anger are some of the same fiery Islamic clerics who preached violence and martyrdom before the September 11 attacks," arguing that the West was a "godless society."[31] An Iraqi-American engineer, Abu Hashem, who was taken hostage in Iraq by terrorists, recounted the incident:

> They said, "Are you a Muslim?" and I said "yes." They said, "give us the proof." . . . One gunman told a hostage, "We only want to hurt Westerners and Americans. Can you tell us where we can find them here?" . . . They had one attitude toward Muslims and another toward non-Muslims. Islam does not sanction this.[32]

Mainstream Muslims are outraged by their radical coreligionists, arguing that "the actions of a few are causing [them] to be singled out for surveillance and making the larger population distrustful of them." In London, Muhammad Sulaiman, of the mainstream Central Mosque I led a campaign to "ban radicals from the city's 10 mosques."[33] A group of eighteen Muslim scholars and clerics in North America followed suit after the London bombings in 2005 and issued their own "fatwa" condemning as anti-Islamic the violence against innocent civilians.

Widespread protests were also heard in Africa after Kano, a Muslim city-state in northern Nigeria, banned polio vaccinations for ten months under pressure from Islamic militants who claimed the inoculations were part of a Western plot to spread AIDS and infertility. The World Health Organization protested that the ban had spread polio to ten other African countries as well as to other states in Nigeria that had all previously eradicated the disease. The vaccinations were resumed only after the governor of Kano publicly vaccinated his own young children.[34]

The writer Daniel Pipes interprets anger among Islamists in terms of a split between Islam and "militant Islam." While militant Islam—which looks at jihad as violence—rejects the West, its advocates actually embrace the West's concept of an all-encompassing ideology, turning "the traditional religion of Islam into a twentieth-century-style ideology." The West, he warns, should take militant Islam even more seriously than it now does because of its goal of world domination.[35]

Pipes points out that in differentiating between the two wings of Islam, a "significant minority" of Muslims denounced Ayatollah Khomeini's fatwa against the novelist Salman Rushdie, which accused Rushdie of blaspheming Islam in his novel *The Satanic Verses*. In Iran, 127 intellectuals signed a protest against Khomeini's death edict at considerable risk to their own lives and livelihoods.[36]

Regardless of its varying interpretations, the concept of "jihad" has served as a useful recruitment tool for Islamic fundamentalists, who use the concept of humiliation to mobilize and attract new followers. Yasir Arafat's Fatah movement emerged from the 1967 war with Israel, the crisis in Kashmir erupted following India's military victory over Pakistan in the 1971 war over Bangladesh, and the "jihad" against British rule in India lasted for forty years during the nineteenth century. In the West Bank, recruiters for Palestinian suicide bombers frequently appear after an Israeli incursion, while in Israel the response to terrorism tracks the theme of Masada, when over one thousand Jews died by their own hand rather than capitulate to Roman rule.

The militant version of "jihad" is what occupies Western leaders most. Al Qaeda broadcast its role in the destruction of two U.S. embassies, in Nairobi and Dar Es Salaam, in addition to the four aircraft hijackings of 9/11. And since the U.S. attack on Afghanistan, Al Qaeda has claimed "credit" for a number of operations, including

- the desecration of a synagogue in Djerba, Tunisia;
- the foiled shoe bomber on an American airliner;
- the attack on French soldiers in Pakistan;
- the attack on a [French] oil tanker in Yemen;
- the assassination of U.S. marines in Falayka, Kuwait;
- the destruction of a discotheque in Bali; and
- two operations in Mombasa against Jewish business interests.[37]

JIHAD AND THE KORAN

In the aftermath of 9/11, a debate raged in countries throughout the world over whether Islam encouraged violence or forbade it. Militants who engineered the car bombing in the early fall of 2004 at the Egyptian resort of Taba that killed thirty-two people and wounded many others, mostly Israelis, maintained that they objected to the "decadence" of semiclad women frolicking on the beach in Egypt, which they reminded the world was an Islamic country. Journalist and foreign policy expert Robin Wright asserted that the militants were winning, citing as evidence the examples of recent violence in Lebanon, Kuwait, Bahrain, Saudi Arabia, the Philippines, Turkey, Bangladesh, India, Pakistan, and Egypt.[38]

The ambassador of Bangladesh, As Salaam alai Kum, condemned the bombings of 9/11, specifically contradicting the militants' view of jihad.

Since the Koran prohibited murder and suicide, he said, the terrorist attacks denigrated the "core spirit and essential values of Islam in whose names the criminal acts were perpetrated."[39] The very word Islam was derived from the Arabic word *salaam*, which means "peace, purity, submission and obedience . . . submission to the will of God and obedience to His law."

The Koran explicitly forbids murder and suicide, he continued. In verse 29 of Sura Nisaa, God commands, "(Do not) kill (or destroy) yourselves: for verily Allah hath been to you Most Merciful." Another verse in the Koran sets down the rules of war, enjoining believers not to "kill women or children or an aged, infirm person."[40] In Islam, "war is permissible in self-defense, and under well-defined limits. When undertaken, it must be pushed . . . only to restore peace and freedom for the worship of God." This is a marked contrast to the interpretation of *jihad* as justification for murder and suicide, or as a proselytizing tool to force either nonbelievers or people of other faiths to practice Islam.

On "9/11, the jihadists killed Muslims as well as non-Muslims, which virtually guarantees that their final journey is not to Paradise, but to Hell," Ambassador Kum argued. "The terrorists waged war on Muslims and non-Muslims . . . transgress[ing] the irrefutable law of God. In surah Al-Nisaa, it is unequivocally stated:

> If a man kills a believer intentionally his recompense is Hell to abide therein (forever): and the wrath and the curse of Allah are upon him, and a dreadful penalty is prepared for him.

As for *jihad*, the real meaning according to the Prophet Muhammad involved the "lesser jihad," the armed battle, and the "greater jihad," which represented an inner struggle for true submission to God. The greater jihad was connected to a more traditional view of religion and involved prayers, charity, fasting, the hajj, and faith—all of which were wars of a different kind, wars against passions.[41]

The Koran may be clear to some Muslims, particularly its prohibitions against murder and suicide, but unfortunately many key influential leaders favor the lesser jihad. Ayatollah Khomeini, for example, regarded Islam as a vehicle for world domination: "At the advent of Islam . . . a small . . . number of people, in less than half a century . . . conquered almost all of the world of that time. . . . The weapon of faith was held in their hands. . . . God willing, the Lord will help us Muslims to awaken, . . . to familiarize ourselves with our Islamic and divine duties."[42]

In Iran, as in so many regions, many question whether religion is merely an excuse for ethnic, tribal, and geopolitical conflict. "Ayatollah Khomeini was emphatic in his insistence that the movement he led was an 'Islamic revolution,' not an Iranian revolution," wrote political scientist Richard Falk. But, as "with the BJP in India and Likud in Israel, the religious vision is bound up with strong versions of statist nationalism."[43] The result was that Khomeini met his goal of temporal power as the only way to ensure an Islamic state.

The goals of Osama bin Laden, on the other hand, appear to be very different, although the results are similar. Instead of world domination, bin Laden wants to change U.S. policy and protect Muslim countries from outside invaders. That means stopping U.S. attacks on Muslim countries and ridding Muslim countries of corrupt leaders who are propped up by the United States to guarantee the continued availability of cheap oil. Bin Laden's defenders are quick to point out that he has never attacked to gain land but to defend Muslim interests, although it is hard to see how killing innocents in the Pentagon, in the World Trade Center, and in the hijacked aircraft defended Muslim interests. Bin Laden's rhetoric also spells out his paranoid view that the Christian West plans to wipe out Muslims, which he claims is why the "West" supports Israel against the Palestinians, India against Muslim Kashmir, and Russia against Chechnya.

It is no coincidence that bin Laden dreams of Saladin, the Arab hero who successfully fought off invaders during the Crusades.[44] Regarded as a sort of Robin Hood in the Arab world—"Osama" is a very common boys' name in the Middle East—bin Laden's hatred of America, according to a former CIA agent, Michael Scheuer, who wrote about him, is based on that nation's support of "Muslim leaders [who] are mostly effete kings and princes who preach austere Islam but live in luxuriant debauchery; or murderous family dictatorships, like Iraq's Husseins, Egypt's Mubaraks, Libya's Qadahfis, and Syria's Assads, or coup-installed generals holding countries together after politicians have emptied the till."[45] Yet bin Laden has directed his resources—which are considerable; he is reputed to be a billionaire— exclusively to violent actions; he has never, to anyone's knowledge, attempted to effect the changes he promotes through peaceful means. He remains an example of a leader who is manipulating his followers through rhetoric while his strategies lead to violent outcomes.

Regardless of their differing interpretations of *jihad*, Muslims still retain the advantage of numbers, which makes the threat of terrorism in the name of religion so potent. To begin with, over one billion Muslims live in seventy countries. If one percent of those Muslims "commit themselves to a radical agenda, the recruitment pool for al Qaeda [still] comes to ten million."

What this means is that "religious hard-liners can drive the political agenda in Muslim countries, just as Christian and Jewish fundamentalists have become a force to reckon with in secular nations."[46] President George W. Bush, for example, refused to accede to advocates of federal funding for stem cell research, including the pleas of former first lady Nancy Reagan, since this was a nonnegotiable issue for his supporters among some Catholics as well as evangelical Christian groups. And in Israel, secular political groups have handed over legal power concerning marriage and divorce to orthodox practitioners of Judaism, rendering their country a virtual theocracy in some important matters of civil law.

The outcry of many Muslim clerics over the atrocities committed in the name of Islamic fundamentalism supports the view of the split in the Islamic world over the meaning of jihad. Immediately after 9/11, "leading Muslim clerics in Egypt, Iran, and other parts of the Middle East publicly denounced the September attacks, declaring them to be blatantly incompatible with the Islamic religion."[47] Muslim leaders from many diverse groups condemned the beheading of Nicholas Berg, an American taken hostage in Iraq. Even the head of Hezbollah (also spelled "Hizb Allah"), Hasan Nasr Allah, a fierce anti-U.S. critic, condemned the atrocity as an "ugly crime that flouted the tenets of Islam." The Lebanese Shia groups argued that the act "has done very great harm to Islam and Muslims . . . [by claiming] affiliation to the religion of mercy, compassion and human principles." A less generous interpretation was offered by some observers, who alleged that the murder of Western hostages diverted the "world's gaze from an escalating furor over the abuse of Iraqi prisoners by [U.S.] occupation soldiers."[48]

The height of irony is that jihad—the attempt to spread the faith through violence—repeats the pattern of the hated Crusades, which also believed in spreading the faith through the sword.

VIEWS OF THE STATE

The religious wars plaguing the planet have produced very different views of the relationship between religion and the state: some religions can't survive without political power, while others confine themselves to strictly spiritual pursuits. Speaking of the three Abrahamic faiths, Egyptian-born scholar Amr Abdalla emphasized that of all three leaders—Moses, Jesus, and Muhammad—only Muhammad was able to create and rule over a state. "Moses wandered for forty years, and didn't establish a state," he said. "Jesus transformed the role of the individual. Muhammad did both: he achieved societal transformation *and* individual transformation. To many Muslims, this was a golden era; Muhammad's era extended over 50 years, and he was succeeded by four rulers. Today, Muslims question what went wrong. Extremists are hooked on a 'golden age' idea."

Abdalla also emphasized the different attitudes toward time between Westerners and Muslims. "In Islam, something that happened 50 years ago is important; it was like yesterday. Here in the United States, that is not the case." Perhaps that is why Americans find it so difficult to understand global anger, since so much of it is historical in nature. Muslims recall the Crusades as if they occurred yesterday; with the breakup of Yugoslavia, citizens of Bosnia, Macedonia, Kosovo, and the other nations recalled painful humiliations that occurred four hundred years ago with the same sense of immediacy.

The view of a golden age meant political as well as temporal power; to Muslims, their religion requires a state to survive. If the sharia, the Muslim code of laws, is to be all-encompassing—which it is, in the Muslim faith—then it stands to reason that to control the legal system, Muslims must also be in control of the political process. "In the Muslim perception there is no human legislative power, and there is only one law for the believers—the Holy Law of God, promulgated by believers."[49] In contrast, the other two Abrahamic religions profess not to require a state to practice their religious beliefs, only that they be left free to exercise their beliefs—which in many cases, as with Jews and Israel, requires a state.

Closer to the truth is the reality that fundamentalists of all faiths, and many mainstream believers as well, need a state to practice their religion. Israel has always refused to give Arab citizens full rights of participation in a multicultural state on the grounds that, given the higher birthrate of the Arabs, they would soon overwhelm the Jews, and the country would risk losing its identity as a "Jewish state." Zionism professes that it is the obligation of all Jews to immigrate to Israel, to overcome the effects of the Diaspora (the scattering of Jews after the Babylonian captivity to nations outside of Palestine) and to ensure the perpetuation of the only place that Jews can feel safe, a Jewish state.

Following the reign of Caesar, the Christian religion spread quickly across Western and Eastern Europe. The Catholic Church, which was the only form of Christianity before Martin Luther, quickly became all powerful in secular as well as religious matters, as well as increasingly intolerant of other religions. With a few exceptions, Jews and other minorities lived more peaceably in Muslim countries than they did under Christian rule, where they suffered from the horrific genocides of the Inquisition and the Holocaust. Given the current attitudes of Islamic militants, it is also ironic that over the centuries Islam proved more tolerant than Christianity, even toward Christian minorities.

The idea of the separation of church and state is relatively recent, involving only Europe and the United States. In the United States, the separation of church and state was a founding principle, since the nation was originally founded by groups that were persecuted for their religious beliefs in England, France, Italy, and Spain. But back "home" in those countries, theoretically at least, church and state were supposed to coexist since the time of Caesar, when the oft-quoted "render . . . unto Caesar the things which are Caesar's and unto God the things which are God's" meant that religion and secular power should coexist peacefully. But centuries of power struggles dispelled that theory at least in Europe; in the United States, religion was considered separate from the state for most of its history until recently, when organized religions have begun openly to flex their power in elections and public policy.

Islam played a very different role in the Middle East, where the battles over religion—as in Iraq—took place within one faith, rather than among different faiths. And the range within Islam was very wide, encompassing the Taliban in Afghanistan to adherents in the more secular states, like prewar Iraq and Turkey. Often, their strong religious convictions enabled many believers in Middle Eastern countries with entrenched dictators to weather intolerable political systems, clinging to spiritual rewards in the absence of material security and political freedom. Religion often took the place of the state, particularly in the area of social welfare, where the needs of the poor were taken care of by Islamic-based charities, many of which—as it was later revealed—also had radical political agendas.

Multiculturalism doesn't appear to be a viable option in many places in the Middle East or in Europe. Today, two countries in Europe, France and Germany, and one secular country with an Islamic majority, Turkey, struggle with the separation of church and state in the controversy over the wearing of head scarves in schools and other public buildings by Muslim women.

Symbols abound. Observers charge that the dispute revolves around the widespread panic over Islamic fundamentalism, specifically, the fear that Islam will spread and Europe will become "Eurabia." Turkey's imminent entry into the European Union was abruptly stalled in the fall of 2004 because the Turkish Parliament was about to pass a law outlawing adultery, which many leaders in the European Union felt was a sign of a fundamentalist takeover. But the question that still lurks in the shadows is, is this a sign of Islamophobia, or does it represent a genuine fear that the separation of church and state is threatened? The French "no" vote on the European Constitution in 2005 was attributed in part by some as a fear of Islam.

The struggle between Islam and secularism has come to the fore in France, which has banned the practice of wearing head scarves in lycées, the equivalent of junior and senior high schools; universities are exempt. Fearful of the "benladenization" of the French suburbs, the government claims it is defending the principle of *laicité*, another word for secularism, which represents the nation's hard-won victory against the centuries-old domination of the Catholic Church. "The 1905 law of separation between Church and the state was a victory for the majority of French citizens educated in the Catholic faith," wrote Patrick Weil, a leading French scholar in the field.[50] A majority of Muslim parents and girls—and by last count there are approximately five to six million Muslims in France—do not want to wear the head scarf, Weil contends, and have asked for government protection. The French government declares that it does not discriminate against Muslims; the law also forbids Jews from wearing skullcaps and Christians from wearing large crosses in public schools or government offices. The government stands firm on the point that "religious fundamentalism needs to be fought and contained when it puts at stake basic values of our democracies," particularly the principle of the separation of church and state.[51] The French felt so strongly about the head scarf issue that several months later when two journalists were kidnapped in Iraq, the government refused to give in to the demands of the hijackers to reverse the head scarf law.

In a poignant article in *Vanity Fair* magazine, Marie Bremer wrote of "thousands of French girls wearing the scarf . . . [who are] trapped in strict Muslim families, forced into marriage, and brutalized for seeking the freedoms all around them."[52] On the other hand, many Muslim women consider the veil a badge of Islamic solidarity, as well as a feminist statement which protects them, they say, against sexual harassment in the workplace.

The head scarf controversy also called attention to the treatment of women in Islamic culture, which varies according to region and sect. Women in Afghanistan under Taliban rule, for example, were not permitted to go to school, to work, or to be treated by a physician unless the doctor was female. The worst practices under the Taliban involved stoning prostitutes to death and public executions of both men and women—all in the name of religion. (After the Taliban government was driven from power, it was exciting to see that 40 percent of the voters in the nation's first democratic election in 2004 were women.) In Saudi Arabia, women are not permitted to drive; in many countries, women cannot vote; in some African countries, the practice of genital mutilation defies eradication, remaining an important feature of culture and religion; and in some Middle Eastern countries, "honor killings" (in which young women are killed by members of their own families if they are accused—even falsely—of dishonoring the family) go unpunished by the law. In northern Nigeria, an Islamic court sentenced a woman to death after she had been raped and became pregnant by her brother-in-law, a decision that evoked protests from around the world. Sensitive to the patterns of discrimination against women in Arab countries, U.S. military advisers were careful to include the rights of women in their efforts to influence the drafting of the new Iraqi constitution in 2005.

But what of those who regard wearing head scarves as an essential part of their religion? It all comes down to the very different views of the relationship of the state to religion, even in countries as close as Western Europe and the United States. "For the French, social equality is accomplished not by permitting religious expression . . . but rather by eliminating religion from public life," said Mark McNaught, who concluded that the head scarf controversy in France had become an important human rights issue.[53] In terms of political anger, the head scarf dispute paled next to the long siege of riots and car burnings that France suffered in the fall of 2005. The riots were perpetrated by young Muslim men who were expressing their alienation from French society, and in particular to the overt discrimination against them in employment and housing.

In the United States, church and state are separated, but religions are left relatively free to practice their own customs in public or private as long as those traditions do not violate the law. (The Mormons in Utah, for example, gave up their practice of polygamy to gain entry into the Union.) In the United States, the government often bends over backward to safeguard religious rights, as it did when the Department of Justice tried to intervene on behalf of an eleven-year-old Muslim girl who was suspended twice by her school in Muskogee, Oklahoma, for wearing a head scarf.[54] Ironically, in the first Gulf War, in 1991, practicing Catholic U.S. soldiers were prevented by military decree (and diplomatic expediency) from wearing crosses in Saudi Arabia, for fear of offending the host country.

The head scarf controversy was argued in terms of religious liberty, but some Muslims view it as a cultural relic and not part of the religion at all. "When Arab tribes roamed the desert," explained Mistik Halici, a Muslim from Turkey, "pretty girls would be seized by rival tribal leaders who were attracted to them. That's why women started covering their faces, so that they couldn't be seen and kidnapped against their will."

Headgear remains an important symbol of Islamic culture. In Turkey, when military leaders redesigned uniforms in the late nineteenth century to conform to the more battle-ready Western models, "only the headgear—the fez, the turban, the kefiya—remained, to symbolize their difference from the West." Western-style hats were avoided as "symbols of the infidel."[55] When Mustafa Kemal Ataturk came to power in 1922 and secularized Turkey, the fez was soon replaced by European hats, and many women ceased wearing the veil.

Although the head scarf controversy highlights the differences between the United States and the rest of the Western world, the difference becomes more marked when contrasting Islam with the West. Islam is so all-encompassing that it requires a state to practice its traditions unimpeded by the rest of society, particularly if the rest of society remains in the minority. Notions of freedom and liberty are secondary in Muslim culture to visions of justice, more specifically, social and economic justice. To accomplish their religious goals, observant Muslims argue, they need a state.

FUNDAMENTALIST RELIGION AND U.S. POLITICS

Evangelicals and other religious minorities also feel they need more control of politics to fully practice their beliefs. Howard Fineman, of *Newsweek*, called the George W. Bush presidency a "pastorate-presidency" for the religious themes that permeated his years in the White House. Karl Rove (his major political adviser) and George W. Bush decided early in Bush's career in politics that they would need the support of the evangelical Christian community to win the governorship in Texas as well as the presidential election. Bush's policies reflected their views throughout his presidency: he opposed federal funding for stem cell research, established a faith-based initiative in the White House (through an executive order), advocated a federal constitutional amendment against gay marriage, promised he would appoint judges who supported the "right to life," and remained highly responsive to the ongoing efforts of the evangelical Christian community's leaders to affect public policy. He also emphasized themes of "individual compassion and faith-based strength and, since 9/11, an Armageddon-like struggle between good and evil."[56]

In case they didn't get it, Bush also included phrases in his speeches that were directed toward his religious constituents. He constantly referred to "good and evil" in his speeches and, according to Bruce Lincoln, a scholar who analyzed one of his speeches line by line, inserted code words that conveyed a biblical subtext, including quotes from Revelation, Isaiah, Job, Matthew, and Jeremiah.[57] On Prayer Day, created by Harry S Truman in 1952, Bush addressed evangelical constituents through radio and television networks proclaiming that the United States was "doing God's work by spreading freedom in Afghanistan and Iraq." He moderated his remarks by admitting that "God is not on the side of any nation, yet we know he is on the side of justice." His remarks were made in the East Room, where a Roman Catholic priest, a rabbi, and a Seventh-Day Adventist minister were included.[58]

On the CBS show *60 Minutes*, Bob Woodward recalled how he had asked George W. Bush the question of whether he asked his father, former president George H. W. Bush, for advice. He's the "wrong father to go to, to appeal to in terms of strength," responded the president. "There's a higher Father that I appeal to."[59] The president did not elaborate further on his statement, but his background depicted his deep, personal conversion to "born-again" Christianity. In 1985, he joined a Bible study group in Midland, Texas; was "born again"; talked about how "Jesus Christ has changed my life"; and during the primary campaign in 1999, asserted that Christ was his "favorite" philosopher. According to their spokespersons, the evangelical Christians claimed to know "what he was talking about; the others didn't."[60] Although few questioned the sincerity of his conversion, his advisers must have been mindful of the fact that the president's biological father, George H. W. Bush, lost both the evangelical and the Catholic vote in the 1992 presidential election.

Evangelical groups came as close to endorsing Bush in the 2004 presidential election as they could without losing their tax-exempt status. James C. Dobson, founder of the evangelical group Focus on the Family, sent a "must-read election message" encouraging his followers to recall the Bible's teachings on same-sex marriage, environmental regulations, abortion, and preemptive military action against terrorists.[61] The evangelical Christian groups came through for George W. Bush, just as they had in his gubernatorial races. According to post-election figures, about 76 percent of them voted for Bush, with 23 percent for Kerry. Exit polls and other surveys indicated that "moral issues"—particularly Bush's opposition to gay marriage and abortion—propelled their vote. The mobilization of evangelicals also affected the vote in those eleven states holding referenda on gay marriage; all eleven voted against allowing gay marriage, with one of their leaders, Gary Bauer, warning that gay marriage was only a step ahead of polygamy.

Although evangelical Christians claimed all the credit, Bush owed his victory in 2004 to other religious groups as well, including conservative Catholics, mainline Protestants, Hispanics, orthodox and conservative Jews, and Mormons. The pivotal group may have been Catholics, particularly in the very close electoral vote in Ohio, where Bush increased his margin from 47 percent to 52 percent. But in the general election, 78 percent of the voters who identified themselves as white born-again or evangelical Christians voted for Bush.[62]

Other presidents have also drawn on their religious faith, although not as consistently as Bush. Clinton used it; so did Jimmy Carter, who reported being guided by religion in the Camp David Accords. Religion was also the genesis of Carter's human rights policy, a feature of his presidency he was most proud of. The presidency of George W. Bush, however, is viewed as the culmination of a religious strain in American politics. "He truly believes he's on a mission from God," said former domestic policy adviser Bruce Bartlett in an article by Ron Suskind on the "faith-based presidency."[63]

Christianity and the state were also fused at a meeting of the G-8 members at Sea Island, Georgia, where a local group posted a welcome sign reading, "Jesus Christ is Lord, Ruler of Nations, Welcome G-8," over a picture of the flags of the participating nations. The meeting's purpose was clear: to "chart a long-term strategy to tackle . . . the roots of Islamic extremism." Arab leaders boycotted the summit, "furious at not being consulted . . . and fearful that the United States was about to impose its will on their region once again."[64]

Unfortunately, comments by clerics are not taken too seriously by Americans, who cannot understand how offensive some of their religious leaders are to Muslims and Jews. Reverend Pat Robertson was quoted as saying, "Adolf Hitler is bad, but what the Muslims do to the Jews is worse." The Reverend Franklin Graham, son of the famous evangelist Billy Graham, called Islam a "wicked religion," followed by Reverend Jerry Falwell, who referred to the Prophet Muhammad as a "terrorist."[65] Also inflammatory but well within America's guarantee of free speech were remarks by Lt. General William G. Boykin, deputy undersecretary of defense for intelligence, telling a religious group in Oregon that "Islamic extremists hate the United States 'because we're a Christian nation.'" An equal-opportunity embarrassment, Boykin—in full uniform—also talked of his battle with a warlord in Somalia, adding, "I knew my God was bigger than his. I knew that my God was a real God and his was an idol." He continued to make similar incendiary speeches even though he was advised against including religion in them by military lawyers in the Pentagon.[66] His ill-advised talks—twenty-three of them, according to a Pentagon inquiry—did not cost him his job; on the contrary, he remained responsible for coordinating and overseeing all military intelligence activities in the second Bush administration.

JEWISH FUNDAMENTALISM

Some Jewish scholars argue that there is no such thing as a Jewish fundamentalist, because Judaism is a nonproselytizing religion that prides itself on a philosophy that is based on doubt. Since those who doubt cannot be certain of the true nature of their faith, it stands to reason that Jews cannot subscribe to the kind of fundamentalism associated with Islam or with evangelical Christianity.

Perhaps that was true throughout the Diaspora, but not in Israel, where certain groups have emerged that can only be described as fundamentalist: they believe in one people, one book, and one land. To them, Jews are the chosen people, the result of their covenant with God at Mount Sinai; they follow one book, the Torah—that is, their interpretation of the Torah; and they believe that their relationship with the land of Israel is divinely ordained. And like their fellow fundamentalists, they look forward to redemption through the coming of the Messiah, who will usher in a new age. The most important similarity is that Jewish fundamentalists also need a state to function: to be freed from the persecution that has hounded Jews for centuries, and to convince others of the rightness of their views.

The real significance of Jewish fundamentalism is its political influence. No longer regarded as extremists, "Jewish fundamentalism remains ideologically the single most coherent and vigorous political force [today] in Israel."[67] The Yom Kippur War in 1973 evoked a great deal of anger among

many Israelis and spawned the first politically influential group of fundamentalists, which called itself Gush Emunim (Bloc of the Faithful). The
group and its supporters were eventually instrumental in unseating Israel's
Labor government in 1977, and in influencing the new Likud leadership to
adopt their more "authentic" vision of religion.[68] Ironically, Jews are adamant in their view that Judaism is not a proselytizing faith, but this evidently
does not mean that they cannot proselytize each other.

Many of the followers of the Gush Emunim movement live in the settlements of the West Bank and Gaza, many of which were dismantled by
the summer of 2005. The settlements were originally built as a way of establishing Jewish sovereignty over the biblical land of Israel—Judea, Samaria,
and Gaza. Ultimately, Gush leaders hoped to eliminate "Western-style liberal democracy," rebuild the "Temple in Jerusalem," and prepare the way
for the "divinely ordained . . . messianic Redemption."[69]

Other religious groups, such as the National Religious Party, and the
Haredi and Shas Parties, have grown in influence in recent years and have
amassed considerable political power. Their influence is now an important
part of the Israeli political scene, as their clashes with the more secular elements of society become more pronounced. Viewers throughout the world
witnessed this clash of values as they watched the forcible removal of settlers
from Gaza in the summer of 2005. (Most of the protesters were settlers who
supported religious parties and opposed the government's decision to turn
the land over to the Palestinians.)

At their most extreme, the differences between fundamentalist and secular groups reflect the harsh realities of Israeli politics. One example: fundamentalists consider Israel's connection to the land inviolable and refer to
their nation as a living being. "Territorial concessions and the destruction of
settlements" becomes the "severing of a limb from a living body," said
Rabbi Chaim Druckman, a leading fundamentalist thinker. Abandoning
settlements only postpones ultimate redemption, according to this view. On
a more practical level, the influence of the religious parties impedes the
Israeli-Palestinian peace process, where land in exchange for peace has
become a critical feature of the negotiating strategy.[70] The view of Jews as
the chosen people taken literally by fundamentalists puts a further crimp in
Israel's relationship with its Arab neighbors, since these fundamentalists
refuse to see "Jews and Palestinians in comparable terms," and view their
nation's current battles (with Arabs) as the "latest . . . episode in Israel's
eternal battle to overcome the forces of evil."[71] Like their fellow Islamic
fundamentalists who see the wars of jihad as the only way to accomplish

their goals, Jewish fundamentalists see their latest battle with the Arabs as the "latest . . . episode in Israel's eternal battle to overcome the forces of evil." Indeed, even the Holocaust is characterized "as an example of God's discipline . . . God's way of coercing his chosen people back to the Promised Land."[72] Jewish fundamentalists also perceive their land in biblical terms and regard non-Jews as enemy aliens, referring to these words in the Torah: "But if you do not dispossess the inhabitants of the land, those whom you allow to remain shall be stings in your eyes and thorns in your sides, and they shall harass you in the land in which you live." An addendum explains that was the reason the people of Israel were in such difficulties after their settlement there: "They had not in fact [completely] dispossessed the native peoples."[73]

Fundamentalists have also weighed in on public policies at all levels of government. For example, Haredi (ultra-orthodox Jews) prohibit organ transplantation, even from the corpses of relatives, citing religious prohibitions as their reason for denying this life-saving medical innovation. Only Haredi rabbis can authorize organ transplants—presumably to save lives—but they remain steadfast in their opposition to transplanting organs from Jewish donors into Arab recipients. Perhaps one could argue that those whose religious beliefs prohibited organ transplants could refuse to participate on religious grounds. But since it remains very difficult to arrange organ transplantation in Israel, it is clear that the Haredi have inflicted their views on a much wider circle of people who do not share their philosophy.[74]

The question frequently arises as to whether extreme fundamentalists who resort to murder or suicide are psychopaths or are inspired by their political movements to such horrific behavior. Yigal Amir, who assassinated Prime Minister Yitzhak Rabin, said he was acting according to the dictates of Judaism. Amir was supported by some groups of religious Jews who justified his action on the grounds that he was preparing himself for paradise by killing someone he viewed as a heretic and a religious sinner. Baruch Goldstein, another "messianic" fundamentalist like Amir, entered a Muslim mosque and killed twenty-nine worshippers, including children, and wounded many more. Goldstein believed—as Amir did—that these killings were ordained by God and were therefore "a commandment of Judaism."[75]

Government complicity was later blamed for this dreadful massacre and its aftermath. Goldstein was a physician in the Israeli army who refused to treat Arabs and Gentiles, rationalizing the violation of his Hippocratic oath with the statement that he recognized only two authorities: Maimonides (Moses Maimonides, a thirteenth-century rabbi and philosopher) and

Kahane (Rabbi Meir Kahane, an extremist rabbi from the United States). Not only was he never court-martialed for his refusal to treat non-Jews, but he was allegedly protected from dismissal for many years by high-ranking government officials. The fundamentalists' influence on the secular groups in government was also indicated by the government's avoidance of the terms *murder, massacre,* and *killing* in the cases of Amir and Goldstein, using instead the milder words *deed, event,* and *occurrence.* The reason: according to the Halacha (the interpretation of Jewish law), the killing by a Jew of a non-Jew under any circumstances was not considered murder. Also, in religious neighborhoods of West Jerusalem, the "walls . . . were covered by posters extolling Goldstein's virtues and complaining that he did not manage to kill more Arabs."[76]

Some scholars of Jewish fundamentalism regard the influence of the religious parties in Israel today as a major obstacle to peace. Even Prime Minister Ariel Sharon left the Likud Party in the late fall of 2005 to form his own political coalition, frustrated by the party's fundamentalist leanings and their reluctance to give up land for peace. There is no doubt, however, that the secular power of the religious fundamentalists is growing and that their positions are as rigid as those of the fundamentalists of the other Abrahamic religions.

WHY NOW?

The monarchs of Spain, Ferdinand and Isabella, are best known for financing Columbus's journey to the new world. But they should also be remembered for introducing a culture of intolerance that prevailed for many centuries among successive royals and their subjects across Europe. Although the militancy of the church had been on the rise for decades, Ferdinand and Isabella initiated the Inquisition, which killed and tortured Spaniards who refused to convert to Catholicism, in the belief that "unity and harmony" were preferable to multicultural tolerance. Spanish royalty's view of "political correctness" erased a medieval culture that was rooted in the acceptance of contradictions. And although we usually associate medievalism with barbarism, in religious matters, a high degree of tolerance also created a culture that was rich in its artistic, scientific, and literary diversity: "This was a chapter in Europe's culture when Jews, Christians, and Muslims lived side by side [from 750 to 1492 in Spain] and, despite their intractable

differences and enduring hostilities, nourished a complex culture of tolerance."[77]

It took nearly a hundred years for the Inquisition to complete its
work—to "Christianize" the mosques and expel or convert the Jews—and
the spirit of tolerance disappeared for centuries. Few people today see the
philosophical contradictions inherent in wars in the name of religion. The
word *tolerance* is rarely heard, and when it is, it appears usually in selected
pulpits and at international conferences. "You don't get harmony when
everyone sings the same note," reads a T-shirt from the Unitarian Universalist Fellowship. Jews from the Reconstructionist branch of Judaism (the
smallest of the four branches of Judaism; the others are Orthodox, Conservative, and Reform) have eliminated the notion of Jews as a "chosen people" from their liturgy on the grounds that the idea of "chosenness" is too
exclusionary of other faiths. But aside from these notable exceptions, there
are very few examples of the celebration of diversity in religious dialogue.

Religion plays many parts in the drama of political anger. Karl Marx
believed religion was the refuge of those who could not better their lives:
the "opiate of the masses." Others find religion a useful tool in political
organizing: the Christian evangelicals' involvement in the presidential campaign of George W. Bush in 2004, the Catholic Church in Western and
Eastern Europe, American Jews' involvement in preserving the state of
Israel, and the Southern Baptists in the United States, to name a few examples. Recently religion has become a useful recruiting strategy for terrorist
groups, despite the many injunctions in the Koran as well as the Bible
against murder and suicide.

Further study of Islam doesn't answer the question of why terror in the
name of religion plays such a large role, particularly given the wide schisms
within the Muslim faith, among those who advocate it as a tool to repel
foreign invaders. This is why opinion leaders like Pakistani journalist Husain
Haqqani believe that the best policy for the non-Muslim world is to support
moderate Muslims, those who wish to reform their societies from within.
"No other society has had modernity forced on them as [has] Islam," he
explained. "Evolution is not allowed. It has to be done by an internal, theologically engaged people. Americans tend to forget about the political evolution of their country," which took over two hundred years. Muslims also
view proselytizing foreign missionaries as another form of Western
encroachment. "How would you like 1,000 Saudi mullahs in Iowa?" asked
Haqqani. "Missionaries following the flag is not a good idea." In fact,

missionaries were banned in Libya by Colonel Muammar Qadaffi a few years after he seized power in a military coup in 1969.

Often it is hard to differentiate between wars in the name of religion and conflicts that are based on geopolitical factors. Muslims never attacked the former Soviet Union, for example, even though Muslim minorities have been persecuted for generations in territories under Soviet control. The reason: the Soviet government was too powerful, and Muslims too weak. Now that the Soviet Union is reduced to the Russian Federation and the so-called independent republics in its orbit, rebellions have surfaced in Chechnya—with its large Muslim population—as well as in other republics formerly under Soviet control.

In the final analysis, it is not the practice of religion that produces conflict but rather fundamentalist religion. What fundamentalists from all three Abrahamic faiths share in common is their desire to impose their beliefs on their coreligionists. In fact, one of the primary arguments against the "clash of civilizations" theory is that fundamentalists often act more harshly against their coreligionists than they do against outsiders. Muslims in Saudi Arabia, for example, practice an extreme form of Islam—Wahhabism—which has made them even less tolerant of their fellow citizens than they are toward foreign nationals. Saudi Arabia does not allow any churches, temples, or synagogues to function within its borders; Saudis regard non-Muslims as "infidels" and routinely refer to non-Wahhabis (including Shiites, Sufis, and all other Muslim sects) in derogatory terms. Some analysts believe that the political unrest today in Saudi Arabia originated with that government's decision to absorb the dissident fundamentalists that Egypt, Syria, Jordan, and other Middle Eastern countries had expelled. The fruits of that decision ripened when the unrest finally spread to Saudi Arabia, which until then did little to stem terrorism.[78]

Fundamentalism essentially freezes religion at one point in time and reduces it to one book, one leader or one prophet, and one code of behavior. The Amish can wear buttons but not zippers on their clothing. Some ultra-orthodox rabbis in Israel advised soldiers not to obey the government if they were ordered to dismantle settlements in Gaza and the West Bank. The Taliban in Afghanistan routinely murdered people they believed were insufficiently devout—or whose material goods they coveted—recalling the Puritans in colonial Salem, Massachusetts, who prosecuted "witches" and then (coincidentally?) seized their land.

Thousands of years ago, when the Abrahamic religions were founded, those faiths were dynamic, not rigid and static as their fundamentalist advocates would have others believe. Even the most religious Jews would not adhere to some of the more arcane laws in the Old Testament book of Leviticus, which prohibits wearing a combination of linen and wool in the fields, whatever that means, and recommends killing children who are rude to their parents.

Nations that pride themselves on abiding by the rule of law find themselves trapped by fundamentalism. Practicing the sharia code of laws as interpreted by the fundamentalist mullahs in Iran can make life intolerable even for some of the most devout Muslims. *Reading Lolita in Tehran* is a vivid account by an Iranian professor of English that describes how the fundamentalist theocracy in Iran took control of every sector of civic life, in her case, the university. Similarly, the rule of the Taliban in Afghanistan made mincemeat out of the "rule of law."[79]

The rise of fundamentalism is part of a worldwide resurgence of religion. Some scholars attribute this to an "age of despair [where] the need for a hero who can inspire pan-Islamic victories has become acute."[80] Bin Laden doesn't fit the bill, largely because of his extremist rhetoric and violent activities. The Shiite assassins disappeared after Saladin won some victories, which were hailed by the Arab establishment; and "having found Saladin, Muslims didn't need terrorism" at that time.[81]

The decline of the nation-state set the course of history for the last three centuries, and also contributed to the rise of religion-based anger. In place of nationalism, there are regional and worldwide entities that have proven more successful in promoting economic progress, and to a lesser extent, political reform. For the rest of the world—excluded from the rewards of globalism—religion has rushed in to fill the void.

Religious wars remain the worst forms of political anger because, unlike other conflicts, there is no ready resolution. The demise of the Soviet Union also left a vacuum in its wake that was filled partly by religion, which served as an answer to the mysteries of modernity—its uncertainties, economic inequities, and insecurity about the future. And with its emphasis on the past, fundamentalist religions fill the void left by centuries-old military and cultural defeats.

In their reaction against modernity, fundamentalists miss the major lesson of the Enlightenment: the separation of church and state, and the emphasis on tolerating the views, practices, and beliefs of others. In America, fundamentalists still endorse the verdict in the Scopes trial, which decided against Darwin's theory of evolution, in place of what is now called "creationism." Eighty years after the Scopes trial, more Americans believe in the Virgin birth than in evolution, and the teaching of "creationism" and/or "intelligent design" is still an issue very much alive on the state, local, and school board levels of government.[82]

Although fundamentalists remain a distinct minority everywhere, there is no question that they find tacit sympathy—some call it guilt—from fellow believers who do not otherwise identify themselves as fundamentalists. Perhaps this is why it is so difficult to stop fundamentalists in their tracks before they do real damage to society. The Saudis, for example, didn't put a halt to terrorism from fundamentalists until the siege of Mecca and later events proved that they were not immune from attack. Forty-nine percent of the Saudi people supported bin Laden's ideas, according to a secret government poll, while a vast majority named official corruption as the "number 1 issue on people's minds."[83] The Saudi leaders wrongly believed that they could co-opt the fundamentalists by handing over education, cultural affairs, and the courts to the imams, or religious leaders, not realizing how quickly ideology can transform itself into political power.

At a certain point, it is important to differentiate militant fundamentalism from religion. Although many Westerners lump the two together, at many times in history it was the clergy who affected the course of history—for the better. In Iran, for example, the mullahs organized a "massive protest" in 1891 that forced the shah to cancel a questionable deal he had made with a British tobacco firm to grant the company a monopoly.[84] Bishop Desmond Tutu mobilized South Africans to throw off a century of white minority rule and turn the country into a democracy. And in the United States, the Reverend Martin Luther King Jr. changed the course of civil rights for decades to come. Similar efforts by the clergy throughout the world have brought hope to those who craved political and economic reform in their countries.

A more negative perspective, or a real "clash of civilizations," occurred in late January 2006, when riots erupted in the Middle East and Europe over the publication the previous September of a dozen cartoons in a Danish newspaper. They portrayed the prophet Muhammad in a manner many Muslims considered blasphemous. Mobs burned the Danish embassy in Beirut as well as both the Norwegian and Danish embassy buildings in Damascus, while less violent but still passionate protests occurred throughout the world. Fearful of further outbreaks, European leaders issued public apologies, while the Danish government sent recall notices advising its citizens to leave Indonesia, as well as other countries with volatile Muslim populations. The conflict: free speech in secular societies versus sacrilege in cultures dominated by religion.

"To me it is not a clash of civilizations, as Kofi Annan, the secretary-general of the UN, has said," reflected Benedicta Pésceli, a Danish social scientist and eyewitness to the demonstrations in Copenhagen. "It is a clash of two different kinds of fundamentalism: frustrated, repressed people and a group . . . that believes itself secularized." Referring to the increasing right-wing fervor in her country, Ms. Pésceli continued: "We have had to listen for years to members of the Dansk Folkeparti calling the Muslims bad names. Our borders have been closed to foreigners, and the social help to the new refugees who are allowed into the country has diminished. . . . I hope that the dialogue between people of different understanding remains open."

The final irony is that since the Koran, as well as the Old and New Testaments, are replete with contradictions, how can anyone define what is true religion and what is not? Almost anything can be found in the holy books of all three faiths. Take anger. The Old Testament relegated anger to the loathsome company of the seven deadly sins; in fact, some believers think the Hebrews were denied entry to the Promised Land because Moses lost his temper at God. The Bible also advocates vengeance, which is a particularly virulent form of anger: an eye for an eye, a tooth for a tooth.

Yet on the other hand, the Bible advises the suppression of anger, warning not to let the sun set on anger; anger should be resolved before those embroiled in conflict go to sleep.[85] In the New Testament, Jesus preached in favor of loving one's enemies and turning the other cheek when confronted with aggression. Similarly, the Koran enjoins believers from engaging in murder and suicide, but many believers question how those injunctions square with the various meanings of jihad.

What this all means is that fundamentalists have interpreted religion according to their own beliefs about what constitutes their faith, and anyone who contradicts that view is an "infidel," a "nonbeliever," or a "sinner." No wonder religious wars are often the worst. There are no opportunities for compromise. Religion is what a few people say it is; the "take no prisoners" approach leaves no space for tolerance. And when defeat comes—as it must—the losers embrace their anger, allowing it to fester for centuries to come.

•

NOTES

1. Friedrich Nietzsche, *Human, All Too Human* (Cambridge: Cambridge University Press, 1986).

2. Susan Tolchin, "Mixed Feelings, Happy Trade-Offs," *Earth Times*, August 2, 1993.

3. Husain Haqqani, "The American Mongols," *Foreign Policy*, May–June 2003.

4. Ibid.

5. F. Scott Fitzgerald and Edmund Wilson, *The Crack-Up* (New York: New Directions, 1993); See also Karen Armstrong, *The Battle for God: A History of Fundamentalism* (New York: Alfred A. Knopf, 2000). This is one of the best studies of fundamentalist movements in Christianity, Judaism, and Islam.

6. John Gray, "Global Utopias and Clashing Civilizations: Misunderstanding the Present," *International Affairs* 74, no. 1 (1998).

7. Samuel P. Huntington, *The Clash of Civilizations and the Remaking of World Order* (New York: Simon & Schuster, 1996).

8. Nicholas Kristof, "Bush Points the Way," *New York Times*, May 29, 2004.

9. Richard A. Pape, *Dying to Win—The Strategic Logic of Suicide Terrorism* (New York: Random House, 2005). See also Thomas H. Kean and Lee H. Hamilton, *9/11 Commission Report*, ed. National Commission on Terrorist Attacks Upon the United States (Washington, DC: U.S. Government Printing Office, 2004), 232. It is also important here to point out several distinctions between the Muslim religion and the Arab world. The Islamic world represents the community of all believers in the Islamic faith, who are known as Muslims, and who number approximately 1.5 billion people who live in over seventy countries. Arabs, on the other hand, are members of a "Semitic people originally from the Arabian peninsula and surrounding territories who speak Arabic and who inhabit much of the Middle East and northern Africa" (www.thefreedictionary.com/Arab). The Arab states include twenty-two countries in Asia and Africa, almost all of them with strong identifications with the Islamic religion (www.encyclopediathefree dictionary.com/ArabtStates). Iran, Turkey, and Afghanistan, for example, are Muslim countries in the Middle East, and Pakistan and Bangladesh are Muslim nations in South Asia, but none of these countries is ethnically Arab, and their nationals often resent such characterizations.

10. Bernard Lewis, *What Went Wrong?: Western Impact and Middle Eastern Response* (Oxford: Oxford University Press, 2002).

11. Ibid., 3.

12. Ibid., 6.

13. John L. Esposito, *The Islamic Threat: Myth or Reality?* 2nd ed. (New York: Oxford University Press, 1995), 43.

14. Ibid., 41.

15. Ibid., 32–33.

16. Also, in a letter dated March 3, 2004, sent by the Bush-Cheney Campaign chairman, Marc Racicot, President George W. Bush was praised for leading a global crusade against terrorism. See www.boston.com/news/politics/president/bush/articles/2004/04/18/bus.

17. Maxime Rodinson, "The Western Image and Western Studies of Islam," in *The Legacy of Islam*, ed. Joseph Schacht and C. E. Bosworth (New York: Oxford University Press, 1974). Quoted in Esposito, *The Islamic Threat*, 46.

18. Lewis, *What Went Wrong?* 47.

19. See Susan Tolchin and Martin Tolchin, *Buying into America—How Foreign Money Is Changing the Face of Our Nation* (New York: Times Books, 1988); Martin Tolchin and Susan Tolchin, *Selling Our Security—The Erosion of America's Assets* (New York: Alfred A. Knopf, 1992).

20. Esposito, *The Islamic Threat*, 51.

21. Ibid., 46, 51.

22. Haqqani, "The American Mongols," 70.

23. Islamophobia was one of the major themes at the Organization of Security and Cooperation in Europe (OSCE) conference in Brussels, September 13–14, 2004.

24. Stephen Kinzer, *All the Shah's Men: An American Coup and the Roots of Middle East Terror* (Hoboken, NJ: John Wiley & Sons, 2003), ix.

25. Ibid., 77.

26. Robin B. Wright, *Sacred Rage: The Wrath of Militant Islam*, updated with new chapters (New York: Simon & Schuster, 2001), 55. See also Sam Harris, *The End of Faith: Religion, Terror, and the Future of Reason* (New York: W. W. Norton, 2004).

27. Ibid., 38, 164.

28. M. J. Akbar, *The Shade of Swords: Jihad and the Conflict between Islam and Christianity*, ed. NetLibrary Inc., Taylor & Francis e-Library ed. (London: Routledge, 2002), 195.

29. Ibid.

30. John L. Esposito, *The Islamic Threat*, 32–33.

31. Patrick E. Tyler and Don Van Natta, "Militants in Europe Openly Call for Jihad and the Rule of Islam," *New York Times*, April 26, 2004, A1, A10.

32. Donna Anu-Masr, "Survivors Recount Terror of Campaign," *Dallas Morning News*, May 31, 2004.

33. Tyler and Van Natta, "Militants in Europe Openly Call for Jihad and the Rule of Islam."

34. *New York Times*, August 1, 2004, 2.

35. Daniel Pipes, *Militant Islam Reaches America* (New York: W. W. Norton, 2002), 8.

36. Ibid. See also Salman Rushdie, *The Satanic Verses* (New York: Viking, 1989).

37. Gilles Kepel, *The War for Muslim Minds: Islam and the West* (Cambridge, MA: Belknap Press, 2004), 128–30. Quoting a communiqué from the political bureau of Qaedat al-Jihad, an arm of Al Qaeda, posted on the Internet and on one of the Gulf states' satellite TV channels.

38. Wright, *Sacred Rage*, 269–90.

39. Ambassador As Salaam Alaikum, "Address to Bd-Americans" (paper presented at the Reflecting Pool, Washington, DC, October 14, 2001).

40. Ibid.

41. Wright, *Sacred Rage*, 45.

42. Added Wright, "God willing, and with a big assist from the temporal authorities." Ibid.

43. Richard Falk, "Stage of Siege: Will Globalization Win Out?" *International Affairs* 73, no. 1 (1997).

44. See James Reston, *Warriors of God: Richard the Lionheart and Saladin in the Third Crusade* (New York: Doubleday, 2001).

45. Anonymous, *Imperial Hubris* (Washington, DC: Brassey's, 2004), 18. Anonymous is the nom de plume of former CIA agent Michael Scheuer.

46. Haqqani, "The American Mongols."

47. Fred Dallmayr, "Lessons of September 11," *Theory, Culture and Society* 19, no. 4 (2002): 141.

48. Benjamin Duncan, *US Muslims Condemn Brutality and Bigotry*, Al Jazeera, May 31, 2004, http://english.aljazeera.net/NR/exeres/F273E152-91F8-433C-8DCB-2353FE 9D535F.htm (accessed February 13, 2006).

49. Lewis, *What Went Wrong?* 101. See also Bernard Lewis, "The Roots of Muslim Rage," *Atlantic Monthly* 266, no. 3 (1990): 47–60.

50. Patrick Weil, "Lifting the Veil of Ignorance," *Progressive Politics* 3, no. 1 (2004).

See also Husnu Tuna, "The Scope and the Consequences of the Ban on Headscarf in Turkey" (paper presented at the OSCE Conference on Tolerance and the Fight against Racism, Xenophobia and Discrimination, Brussels, September 13–14, 2004).

51. Weil, "Lifting the Veil of Ignorance."

52. Marie Bremer, "Daughters of France, Daughters of Allah," *Vanity Fair*, April 2004. See also Susan Tolchin and Martin Tolchin, "The Feminist Revolution of Jihan Sadat," *New York Times Magazine*, March 16, 1980.

53. Mark McNaught, "Secularism in France: The Banning of Religious Symbols in Public Schools," *Public Administration Times*, 2004.

54. Steve Barnes, "U.S. May Intervene in Head-Scarf Suit," *New York Times*, April 15, 2004.

55. Lewis, "The Roots of Muslim Rage," 75.

56. Howard Fineman, "Apocalyptic Politics," *Newsweek*, May 24, 2004.

57. Bruce Lincoln, *Holy Terrors: Thinking about Religion after Sept. 11* (Chicago: University of Chicago Press, 2003), appendix B, "George W. Bush, Address to the Nation, October 7, 2001." See also Stephen Mansfield, *The Faith of George W. Bush* (New York: Jeremy P. Tarcher/Penguin, 2003).

58. David D. Kirkpatrick, "Bush Addresses Evangelicals on Prayer Day," *New York Times*, May 7, 2004.

59. Bob Woodward, *Plan of Attack* (New York: Simon & Schuster, 2004).

60. *Frontline*, "The Jesus Factor" (United States: PBS, 2004).

61. David D. Kirkpatrick, "Battle Cry of Faithful Pits Believers and Unbelievers," *New York Times*, October 31, 2004.

62. Laurie Goodstein and William Yardley, "The 2004 Election: Faith Groups; President Benefits from Efforts to Build a Coalition of Religious Voters," *New York Times*, November 5, 2004.

63. Ron Suskind, "Without a Doubt," *New York Times*, October 17, 2004.

64. Guy Dinmore, "Middle East Reform to Top G8 Summit Agenda," *Financial Times*, June 8, 2004.

65. Anonymous, *Imperial Hubris*, 3.

66. *New York Times*, "General Said to Be Faulted over Speeches," August 20, 2004.

67. Ian S. Lustick, "Israel's Dangerous Fundamentalists," *Foreign Policy* 68 (1987): 119. See also Ian S. Lustick, "For the Land and the Lord: Jewish Fundamentalism in Israel" (New York: Council on Foreign Relations, 1988).

68. John Donohue, "Mistranslations of God: Fundamentalism in the Twenty-first Century," *Islam and Christian-Muslim Relations* 15, no. 5 (2004): 436.

69. Lustick, "Israel's Dangerous Fundamentalists," 119.

70. Ibid., 127.

71. Ibid., 123.

72. Ibid., 127–28.

73. W. Gunther Plaut, ed., *The Torah: A Modern Commentary* (New York: Union of American Hebrew Congregations, 1981), 1236.

74. Israel Shahak and Norton Mezvinsky, *Jewish Fundamentalism in Israel* (London: Pluto Press, 2004), 42.

75. Ibid., 113.

76. Ibid.

77. Maria Rosa Menocal, *The Ornament of the World: How Muslims, Jews, and Christians Created a Culture of Tolerance in Medieval Spain* (Boston: Little, Brown, 2002).

78. Fareed Zakaria, "The Saudi Trap," *Newsweek*, June 28, 2004.

79. Azar Nafisi, *Reading Lolita in Tehran: A Memoir in Books* (New York: Random

House, 2003). The dehumanization of life under the Taliban in Afghanistan is eloquently portrayed in Yasmina Khadra and John Cullen, *The Swallows of Kabul: A Novel* (New York: Nan A. Talese/Doubleday, 2004); and Khaled Hosseini, *The Kite Runner* (New York: Riverhead Books, 2003).

80. Akbar, *The Shade of Swords: Jihad and the Conflict between Islam and Christianity*, 195.

81. Ibid., 196.

82. Garry Wills, "The Day the Enlightenment Went Out," *New York Times*, November 4, 2004.

83. Zakaria, "The Saudi Trap."

84. Milton Viorst, *In the Shadow of the Prophet: The Struggle for the Soul of Islam* (New York: Anchor Books/Doubleday, 1998), 185.

85. Susan Tolchin, *The Angry American—How Voter Rage Is Changing the Nation* (Boulder, CO: Westview Press, 1998), 42.

4

THE PSYCHOLOGY OF ANGER:
HUMILIATION AND DEFEAT

Policy can never speak to wrath.

—Fouad Ajami[1]

KABUL

A few years ago, a brilliant novel, *The Swallows of Kabul,* was published in France about life in Afghanistan under the Taliban regime. It was written by an Algerian, who smuggled the book out of his country under the pseudonym Yasmina Khadra, a woman's name, to get it past the censors. The theme of the novel traces the dehumanization of three characters, whose personalities slowly undergo cruel changes under the pressures of daily life in Kabul.

The story centers on an Afghani couple, Moshen and Zunaira, both of whom are highly educated and happily married: she was a judge in the pre-Taliban days, and he was a businessman from a wealthy family. When the story begins, they are both out of work, living in poverty, and forced to sell their furniture piece by piece in order to survive. They live in virtual isolation, fearful of venturing out of doors where unknown terrors await them. One day, when they can no longer stand the solitude, they decide to go for a walk, where they are assaulted by the very indignities they had sought for so long to avoid. Zunaira, the wife, faces a barrage of insults from Taliban policemen, who beat bystanders at will and threaten violence to others. Unable to defend her, Moshen is forced by the police into a mosque to pray, leaving his wife unprotected outside for several hours until he is free to leave. Before leaving on their "excursion," Moshen had confessed to his wife that he had participated in a ghastly public spectacle orchestrated by the governing Taliban: the stoning death of a prostitute. Zunaira is horrified, since nothing in her husband's character or background should have led him to take part in such a barbaric act. He is just as appalled by his own behavior, particularly by how quickly he was swept up in the mob excitement.

When they return home, Zunaira undergoes a drastic change of personality. She turns on Moshen, asks for a divorce, and refuses to explain to her mystified husband her change in attitude toward their marriage. All of a sudden, she becomes violent and commits an act that lands her in prison, where she comes in contact with the book's third character, Atiq, the jailer. Atiq is also dehumanized—but for different reasons. His job as a prison guard requires him to engage in daily cruelties, but he had quickly grown accustomed to them; he displays much more of a hardened attitude to Taliban society than Moshen and Zunaira. At the end of the novel when their lives intersect, Atiq experiences a spell of humanity but eventually goes mad as a result of this brief encounter. The book's message: that humanity in the midst of a dehumanized society will drive otherwise sane individuals mad.[2]

DEFEAT AND HUMILIATION

Although the dehumanization experienced by Moshen and Zunaira was fiction, it was all too realistic in portraying how grim life had become under Taliban rule. Especially vivid was the depiction of how the Taliban leaders exerted power: humiliating people in order to control them. Sadly, the Taliban was not the first government to engage in this behavior under the banner of official policy. History is replete with examples of leaders who wielded brutal power at the expense of their fellow citizens. Organized campaigns of dehumanization all too often precede genocide because "the Other," the target of the killing, must be perceived not only as an object of hate, but as beyond human. Psychopaths like Hitler, Stalin, Pol Pot, and Idi Amin have risen to positions of power by demonizing the Other before engaging in their genocidal campaigns. Hitler and the Nazi government murdered over six million Jews and four million other Europeans; Stalin and the Bolsheviks surpassed the Nazis, killing tens of millions of Russians. The former Serbian leader Slobodan Milosevic engaged in a practice he termed "ethnic cleansing," a euphemism for genocide, to rid his country of the Other—Muslims, Croats, Albanians, or anyone who was not Serbian.

Recently, genocides have occurred without visible leaders, such as the tribal war between the Hutus and the Tutsis in Rwanda, where almost one million people have died and many more have been injured. Similarly, the massacre in Darfur also was conducted by anonymous Sudanese leaders, who hid behind their positions as pillars of government. Anonymity was also important to many of the colonial powers of Europe, who ruled their colonies through policies of humiliation and, occasionally, genocide. Often, the perpetrators of organized violence and their supporters actually look like "normal people," like the Turkish citizens bent on destroying Armenia, and the German burghers who closed their eyes to the Nazi genocide, or the Americans, whose history included shameful chapters in the treatment of Native Americans and African Americans.

"Many of the worst genocidal and human rights excesses of the last century were perpetrated under the guise of creating a more perfect society," wrote Alex Alvarez, a professor of criminal justice at Northern Arizona University. Political leaders found particularly receptive audiences in societies that believed these ideologies that envisioned a perfect world could be grafted on to their own "imperfect political, social and cultural social systems."[3]

The mobilization of popular anger is used by a variety of political leaders to acquire and maintain power. Are the conditions ripe? Have the majority of the people already been humiliated by military or economic defeat? Do they view their situation as hopeless? Is there a convenient scapegoat? Are the leaders responsible? "How do you get a guy to stick a bayonet into another guy's stomach?" asked a history teacher trying to enliven a discussion of World War II before a class of bored high school students. What angers and passions inspire wars, making them such hardy perennials of world history? And what happens to the defeated populations left to survive the ravages of war when the winners go home to bask in their victory and enjoy the "spoils." The losers carry on, but their anger and resentment grow with time, hardening their emotions in preparation for future conflicts.

Lest anyone doubt the long-term impact of defeat, witness the current celebration in China, where a vodka-based drink called "9-3 Beautiful Liquor" commemorates September 3, 1945, the day China was victorious over Japan.[4] Coming after decades of defeat, this victory is now celebrated daily in bars throughout China.

How long anger festers, and what form it will take afterward varies from culture to culture, and also with the conditions accompanying defeat. Germany and Japan, nations that were vanquished in World War II, later became economic powerhouses, in part because of initial help from the

United States in the form of the Marshall Plan and other efforts at postwar reconstruction. In addition to creating markets for themselves, the Allies also sought to prevent the mistakes of the Treaty of Versailles in 1918, which many historians blamed for creating the conditions that led to the Second World War. And, fearful of a recurrence of their inherent militaristic tendencies, both Germany and Japan worked hard to suppress any signs of a resurgence. After World War II, Japan renounced force as a means of settling international disputes and was prohibited (by Article 9 of its own constitution) from allocating funds for military expenditures, except for self-defense. National security never became a paramount issue in either country, thanks also to the U.S. decision to assume the major responsibility for the defense of both nations. Well into the twenty-first century, American military bases remain in both Germany and Japan to the consternation of some political groups in those countries. In the case of Japan, the United States also protected the steady flow of oil imports from the Middle East that proved so necessary to that nation's industrial development.

Both Germany and Japan also fell back on rich cultures that remained separate and distinct from politics. True, the composer Richard Wagner was used by the state to support the Nazis, as was the movie director Leni Riefenstahl, but she was later vilified for crossing the line into Nazi political life. And for a long time after World War II, many people (including Germans themselves) questioned how a culture that produced the poetry of Goethe, the music of Bach, and the philosophy of Kant could also produce the horrors of Nazism. Like the Germans, the Japanese separated their culture from their politics, although a distinct strain of militaristic samurai traditions could be traced back for generations. Martial traditions were also part of the German culture—which helped explain the natural tendency of these two countries to ally with each other in World War II—but in both cases these traditions occupied only a part of the culture.

THEOCRACY

Not so with Islam. Unlike Germany and Japan, the Islamic religion encompasses both culture and politics. Muslims believe they need a state to fully practice their religion, although some are now beginning to question this view. Iran is called "The Islamic Republic of Iran," and Pakistan, "The Islamic Republic of Pakistan." (In fact, Pakistan and Bangladesh were created as refuges for Muslims after Hindu-dominated India achieved independence from Great Britain.) Theocracy remains a way of life for many countries whose populations include a majority of Muslims, who do not understand why Americans feel so strongly about keeping church and state separate. Indeed, the separation of church and state remains a distinctly Western concept, born of centuries of struggle between the Catholic Church and those who preferred secular rule. The French enacted a law in 1905 emphasizing this separation, while other Western European nations similarly guard their independence from church rule.

Some countries are a hybrid of church and state. Israel, for example, functions in part like a theocracy; the nation has abdicated an important part of its marriage and divorce law to the Orthodox rabbis and remains averse to granting citizenship to non-Jews on the grounds that the nation could no longer continue to function as a "Jewish state" if non-Jewish groups could potentially outvote Jewish citizens. This is offered as a major reason for excluding Palestinians from full voting rights in Israel: since the birthrate among Palestinians is so much higher than it is among Israelis, Israeli leaders fear that Jewish voters would be subsumed politically.

Ironically, the Western concept of the separation of church and state also stems from defeat and the fear of future defeat: in that case, the church's defeat of those who prefer a secular state. The struggles to create nation-states were struggles against the church, which in its heyday ruled vast territories encompassed in the Holy Roman Empire. Today, the Catholic Church still wields enormous international influence, but has virtually no land, although the Vatican remains a separate country in a prime, though tiny, piece of real estate in Rome.

Since the culture of Islam is so strongly bound up with the state, military defeats are felt more profoundly than they are in the West. Its collective humiliation goes back centuries. Even though some victories were achieved by Muslim armies, the Crusades changed the map of Spain, the Mediterranean, and the Middle East, leaving many Islamic groups frustrated and bereft of political power. Their collective humiliation was reinforced by the Industrial Revolution in Western Europe, which led to the colonization of many nations with large Muslim populations in the Middle East and Africa. The slow collapse of the Ottoman Empire and the shrinking of its borders only added to the shared humiliation of Muslims, as did the carving up of the region into artificial nation-states with little regard for the nuances of ethnic tensions.[5] Similarly, since Africa was divided up in much the same cavalier way, perhaps it is not entirely coincidental that wars, genocides, and other political horrors have proven to be the rule not the exception on that continent—long considered the cradle of civilization.

The centuries of political and military defeat suffered by followers of Islam built up a collective sense of humiliation, which psychiatrists call "the most painful and indelible of human emotions . . . [involving] feelings of shame and disgrace, as well as helplessness in the face of abuse at the hands of a stronger party."[6] None of this was helped by President George W. Bush's initial rhetoric about a "crusade" in Iraq, since the memory of the Crusades was still fresh in the minds of Muslims nearly a millennium later. Time evidently does not heal all wounds when it comes to historical humiliation; it might even exacerbate them.

THE AMERICAN EXPERIENCE

Americans are not immune from rejection and humiliation. One of the most painful humiliations came with the decisive defeat in 1975 that followed the nation's ten-year war in Vietnam. The images of Americans and South Vietnamese fleeing Saigon, their hands reaching out in desperation for hastily departing aircraft, stayed with the public for years to come, along with the question of how the U.S. military machine could be defeated by such a small, insignificant country. Soldiers who returned to the United States after Vietnam faced societal disapproval, not the hero's welcome they felt they had earned. The Watergate scandal followed hard on the heels of Vietnam, which was then followed in 1976 by the uninspired presidency of Jimmy Carter—who reinforced Americans' feelings of defeat by constantly reminding them of their cultural angst and low morale.

The hostage crisis in Iran added to Americans' collective sense of humiliation; why couldn't the United States, a mighty superpower, free forty-eight hostages held by a small group of "students" who had seized the American embassy? The helicopter mission to free the hostages, Desert One, failed miserably, leading to the public resignation of the secretary of state, Cyrus Vance, who claimed he was not informed of the rescue attempt. The sense of humiliation was reinforced every night on the network news as Walter Cronkite of CBS intoned, "This is the 345th day, the 346th day," of the hostages in captivity. When Dan Rather took over the anchor job, he continued, reminding the viewers of the dishonor that was inflicted on their nation each day the captives were held. The hostages were held for 444 days and weren't freed until President Ronald Reagan took office in

January 1980. An ABC-TV show, *America Held Hostage*, aired every night, becoming *Nightline*, a late-night television show hosted for a quarter of a century by Ted Koppel.

President Reagan, it was said, made Americans "stand tall" again, helping them regain their lost pride by eliminating their sense of defeat. He entered office with an enormous electoral mandate, and in speeches throughout his presidency he relentlessly attacked the Soviet Union as the "Evil Empire." On a more concrete level, Reagan doubled the defense budget, which actually did more to bring about the demise of the Soviet Union than the president's inflammatory rhetoric. In trying to compete with the United States in defense expenditures, the Soviets crippled their economy, and with it, their government.

The crumbling of the Berlin Wall and the West's victory over Communism failed to offset the string of humiliations suffered by the United States during the 1980s and 1990s that left the nation mystified, angry, and frustrated. In Beirut, the U.S. embassy was bombed several times; so were its embassies in Kenya and Tanzania. Attacks on the marine barracks in Saudi Arabia (Khobar Towers) and on the warship USS *Cole* in Yemen yielded no perpetrators, but cost many American lives and frustrated law enforcement officers who were unable to elicit effective cooperation from the Yemeni or Saudi governments. U.S. peacekeeping efforts in Somalia resulted in the humiliating spectacle of insurgents dragging the bodies of two dead U.S. soldiers through the streets of Mogadishu, an event later portrayed in the film *Black Hawk Down*. Then came September 11, 2001, when a small group of Al Qaeda suicide pilots hijacked four airplanes and flew three of them into the Pentagon in Washington and the World Trade Center towers in New York. The fourth crashed in a field in Pennsylvania, thanks to the efforts of the passengers to overcome the hijackers. Over three thousand people lost their lives, most of them in the World Trade Center; the U.S. economy—particularly the airline industry—was impacted for several years; and security became the paramount political issue for Americans in the early twenty-first century. Declaring that he would capture bin Laden—whom he rightly blamed for the catastrophe of 9/11—"dead or alive," President Bush promised Americans that he would avenge this tragedy, which would affect U.S. foreign and domestic policy for years to come.

"Fear and rage are different sides of the same coin," wrote Willard Gaylin, a psychiatrist who specializes in the role of emotion and political behavior.[7] Americans were incredulous that so few people could inflict such heavy damage on a mighty nation; they were equally shocked by television images of people dancing in the streets of Middle Eastern cities in celebration of their nation's worst civilian disaster in history.

The overwhelming fear, rage, and collective humiliation led the nation's top leaders to respond with policies that reflected the national traumas of Vietnam, the first Gulf War, and 9/11. In the last two decades, the United States took significant steps away from the international community: the Senate could not muster the votes to sign or adhere to international treaties, including the Kyoto Protocol (on the environment) and the Law of the Seas (on the oceans). The successful efforts of former senator Jesse Helms (R–NC) to hold back U.S. dues from the United Nations reflected his—and his allies'—disappointment with efforts by the world body to implement its goals for a peaceful world. The second war in Iraq represented another move by the United States to break away from the global community, this time separating from traditional allies, like France and Germany. The Star Wars program, a missile defense system strongly supported by President Reagan and opposed by the international arms control community, also showed that the nation was willing to act independently when it believed its own interests conflicted with those of its allies and trade partners. It looked as if America's leaders had taken to heart British foreign secretary Viscount Palmerston's advice, issued in 1848: Nations have no friends, only interests.[8]

Critics of American policy like psychohistorian Robert J. Lifton have charged that the U.S. response to 9/11 acted as a stimulus to further terrorism, and that the United States should have dealt with terrorist zealots and Al Qaeda with a "more focused, restrained, internationalized response."[9] The emotion of "unadulterated humiliation," he added, characterizes "much of the 'Islamic stance toward the West.'"[10] This now leaves the daunting question of how the rest of the world should deal with a population whose anger derives from such deep-seated feelings of resentment and humiliation.

COLONIALISM, DEPRIVATION, AND "WRENCHING MODERNIZATION"

The experience of colonialism exacerbated national humiliation and collective anger. East Indians painfully recall a practice known as "ritual humiliations," which included edicts from their British colonial masters, such as "crawling orders" that forced them to squirm on their stomachs down special lanes created on local roadways for such purposes. Designed to compel "natives" to "grovel" before Europeans, these cruel "ritual humiliations" were all too common among colonial powers. Even worse than public spectacles designed to degrade and humiliate subject populations were more brutal acts of suppression, such as the incident in India when a British military leader, General Dyar, ordered his troops to fire into a crowd of protesters, causing the deaths of over one thousand people and the wounding of hundreds more. "Humiliation is always an act of disempowerment," wrote Myra Mendible, a professor of English at Florida Gulf Coast University, "a compelling motivator of collective behavior, a profoundly damaging experience."[11] Mendible links this to modern episodes of "reality TV . . . designed to humiliate and degrade people," which have already led to two retaliatory murders among other less disastrous, but still violent consequences.

Anger, fear, resentment, and humiliation have all risen concurrently with the communications revolution. Anger comes from feeling cheated—cheated out of a higher standard of living, out of being able to participate in political life, and out of being able to protest injustice. People from countries where poverty is the rule not the exception, and where democracy as Westerners know it is virtually unknown, can now see more easily how others in the industrialized world live. Some of these countries have elections, but all too often they are sham elections, especially when only one candidate is running for office and voters have no real choice. In other nations calling themselves democracies, the rule of law remains sadly lacking: India has free elections, for example, but what about all those incidents when Hindus and Muslims engage in mob violence against each other without the instigators being apprehended? In some of the Middle Eastern nations, there might be show elections, but mullahs, dictators, and kings rule with an iron hand, treating protesters with harsh punishments—torture, long incarcerations, and occasionally death. Acceptable protests, like those against America or Israel, fall into a different category and are either tolerated or encouraged; some observers have viewed them as safety valves for people who would otherwise protest against their own system of government but are fearful of the consequences.

Deprivation is a cousin of humiliation; seeing what is missing quickly turns into the "smoldering anger of political resentment . . . an explosive rage that can destroy any society."[12] The extent of the anger depends in large measure on what people expect, what society promises, and what society can deliver: the wider the gap, the greater the anger. Often rage is not directed toward the proper object—such as those Middle Eastern tyrannies where people can protest almost anything as long as it doesn't challenge their rulers—and is leveled at the weaker groups, those who cannot retaliate. (An old joke from Cold War days recalls an American boasting to a Soviet citizen that in the United States he could "march up the steps of the White House and criticize the president." The Russian replied that free speech was just as strong in his country, where he could "climb the steps of the Kremlin and also criticize the [U.S.] president.") Political anger in the nineteenth century was not leveled at the colonizers who were too powerful to vanquish, but often at other tribes or groups. Even today, the two major tribes of Rwanda, the Hutus and the Tutsis, still battle each other and not the colonial power, Belgium, that encouraged and then abandoned them to this fratricidal state.

Rage comes from resentment at one's lot in life; it need not be actual deprivation but "psychological feelings of deprivation [that] generate a powerful rage that seeks a justifiable outlet."[13] That is why anger spawned by feelings of deprivation is so highly dependent on culture and why this kind of anger is called a "relative" emotion. Culture also helps determine why a Pacific Islander without a video game, e-mail, or Manolo Blahnik shoes might be perfectly content to live on the equivalent of three hundred dollars a year, while angry French farmers will clog the main arteries of Paris with their trucks to protest the impending removal of protective tariffs on their tomatoes. The Pacific Islander won't know what he is missing and therefore won't feel deprived; the farmers, on the other hand, are Internet savvy, they have the information at their fingertips that predicts their losses to the euro, and they are secure in their ability to influence government policies in their favor.

In other words, extreme poverty might not cause as much anger as "relative deprivation," or fears of impending marginality. In the case of the Aum Shinrikyo cult in Japan—whose adherents spread nerve gas in the subways—"most of the followers were middle class and many of them professionals . . . frustrated in their careers."[14] The rioters in France in the fall of 2005 were all second- and third-generation Muslims.

Even in cultures without much freedom, there are citizens willing to sacrifice Western-style political rights for a more comfortable lifestyle. "Women in Saudi Arabia are very satisfied," said Taqwa Omer, a Saudi woman in a traditional dress of beige and gold silk. "American women are so stressed, but *they* feel sorry for *me*. I didn't feel deprived not driving. I have a chauffeur. We have the choice to study and to work. I never heard the word 'suppressed' until I got here in the U.S. I never felt oppressed at home." Women's issues get "people to ignore other issues," added Samar Al-Rayyis, a Saudi student in Western dress. "We are pampered. We like to be pampered."

"My father had three wives," continued Mrs. Omer, describing the advantages of the polygamous household in which she grew up: "My mother and my two 'aunties.' There was always someone around to talk to." When asked how she would feel if her husband took another wife, she laughed and said, "Just let him try!"

The vast improvement in communications adds to elevated levels of anger, particularly in places that had been relatively starved for information, not to mention the new affordability of telecommunications that has put cell phones in the hands of many citizens whose countries still don't have land lines. Increased media opportunities have simultaneously led to rising expectations of what government can provide. "We can endure the fact that we do not have something, unless we feel that something has been taken away from us," wrote Gaylin. "We will then experience a sense of violation. . . . The smoldering rage which comes from being cheated [will be extended] to the society which allowed us to be so cheated."[15] In Saudi Arabia, for example, citizens expected jobs, houses, and funding from the government because that is what the government had provided for the last fifty years. When the kingdom's oil riches began to diminish, some of these privileges were withdrawn or reduced. "It all happened in a very short time," said Adel Bashatah, a graduate student of nursing administration at George Mason University. "We have 25 percent unemployment among college graduates. We import everything. People feel anger as they see expatriates from India and Pakistan taking their jobs." There is a lot of resentment from businessmen, added Mrs. Omer. "Foreign nationals are cheaper. They've been working for Saudi businesses for years. Now there's a campaign to hire Saudis and solve the unemployment problem. Businesspeople don't want to get rid of experienced foreign workers to replace them with inexperienced Saudis. Also, Saudi nationals need [more] benefits and expect high salaries."

Similarly, in Western Europe, where budget-busting social welfare benefits are more generous than they are in any other part of the world, leaders face an uncertain economic future—and fear the political anger that they know is certain to follow if they dare to reduce these benefits in the interest of fiscal sanity.

Leaders know instinctively that collective humiliation is the most important first step to goad people into "aggressive behavior." World War

I left the economy of Germany in tatters, ripe for Nazi picking. Returning German soldiers were "beaten men, many of them wounded," who faced "national misery and threatened revolution."[16] Osama bin Laden keeps referring to eighty years of "Muslim humiliation and disgrace" as the major source of his litany of grievances. Bin Laden's first fatwa (edict), which was issued in 1996, attacked the "Zionist-Crusader alliance," linking the Jewish state with the Christian crusades, though Jews had nothing to do with the Crusades, and Israel didn't even exist until seven hundred years later. With both Al Qaeda and the Nazis, "humiliation, through manipulation but also powerful self-conviction, was transformed into exaggerated expressions of violence. Such psychological transformation from weakness and shame to collective pride and a sense of life-power, as well as power over others, can release enormous amounts of aggressive energy—a dangerous potential that has been present from the beginning of the American 'war' on terrorism."[17]

"The psychic utility of rage," said Dr. Kenneth Kessler, a psychiatrist, "is that it transforms helplessness, powerlessness, and low self-esteem into a sense of power and high self-esteem. The problem is, of course, that it leads to doing violence. The rage needs to be expressed repeatedly, or it becomes a reinforcement of the original problem of powerlessness."

Modernization can also lead to societal humiliation, primarily because there are winners and losers in the world's inexorable march toward global-ization. The wrenching consequences of international competition produce all the components of anger for what seem like obvious reasons. Why "deny any meaningful connection between Germany, Russia or Japan and the modern Arab world?" asked Michael Mazarr, an expert in Islamic terrorism. "Modernization is a homogeneous and homogenizing force. The social tremors look roughly the same the world over"[18]—as do the roadblocks: poverty, alienation, and memories of a "glorious past."

Wrenching modernization produces winners and losers in the industri-alized as well as the less developed world, since resentment affects all strata of society, such as the middle-class Saudi nationals responsible for 9/11. The rise of Nazism following World War I included many middle-class Germans facing economic collapse during the Weimar Republic. Stalin's acts of genocide targeted the entire officer class, as well as rich farmers, middle-class professionals, and merchants. Neither deprivation, economic hardship, nor the numerous humiliations of history excuse these horrors, but they nevertheless contribute to the explosive anxiety that erupts into patterns of unspeakable violence. What causes victimization to be such a profound part of Islam's self-identity, and why have some Muslims succumbed to paranoia, while most have recovered?

Unlike the Nazis or the Bolsheviks, however, modern Muslims have no universal ideology; a secularized Turkish Muslim, for example, has little in common with a Saudi who practices the strict Wahhabi interpretation of Islam. Nor do Muslims look to a leader whose influence stretches across the borders of the more than seventy nations with Islamic majorities. The failure of Muslims in the Middle East to come to the aid of Muslims slaughtered in Srebrenica, as well as other Muslim victims of ethnic cleansing in the former Yugoslavia, underscores the atomized culture of the Islamic world.

LEADERS AND THE MANIPULATION OF ANGER

Whether it is the stoning of a prostitute in Taliban-controlled Kabul or the mercurial crowd in ancient Rome that switched its allegiance so swiftly from Julius Caesar to Brutus, the mobilization of anger for evil purposes redounds to those leaders who are most effectively able to dip into the spring of existing emotions. Islamic populations were prepped psychologically to hate the West—with much of that emotion cresting in the last 150 years. In the aftermath of the bombing of a commuter train in Madrid on March 11, 2004, the leaders of Al Qaeda issued a statement taking full "credit" for the attack, couching their rhetoric in broad, historic terms aimed at countering the widespread disaffection among their followers. The success of the attack, read the statement, will lead to a collapse of "the international system built-up by the West since the Treaty of Westphalia . . . ; and a new international system will rise under the leadership of a mighty Islamic state."[19] Al Qaeda also took "credit" for the suicide bombings of three hotels in Amman, Jordan, in 2005.

Humiliation is directly related to a feeling of victimization: the idea that one group has held sway for a long period of time and has taken advantage of the other group. There is often a certain amount of historical legitimacy to that claim: the Sunnis, clearly in the minority in Iraq, held power over the majority group, the Shiites, who chafed under their heavy-handed rule for centuries. Knowing they would be outvoted, Iraq's Sunnis boycotted the elections in January 2005 and led the violent insurgency that followed. Rabbi Meir Kahane, a Jewish extremist, viewed the struggle of the

Jews as a series of humiliations, and all their efforts since as an "effort at ennoblement, empowerment and dehumiliation."[20]

One of the reasons the Israeli-Palestinian conflict has defied resolution for so long can also be traced to defeat. Each side brings to the negotiating table its own legacy of defeat and humiliation, baggage that has often proven too heavy for each side to lift toward a peaceful settlement. Etched on the Israeli mind is the devastating genocide of the Holocaust; many families remember close relatives who were killed; others feel threatened, and worry that it could happen again, "tomorrow," as the actress Lotte Lenya said. Israelis bury past images of Jews walking meekly to the gas chambers with vows of "never again," bolstered by strong support of their government's policies to create and maintain a strong military presence to guard their small piece of land. The defeat of the Holocaust still resonates with many Israeli citizens, compounded by the state of siege they now feel, living in a sea of hostile Arab nations. For their part, the Palestinians also feel defeated, victimized by Israel since 1948, when many were summarily evicted from their homes to make way for a Jewish state. Palestinians long for their own country; they, too, regard themselves as living in a state of siege. The problem has continued for so long that refugee camps now house the third generation of Palestinian families. Although they are armed and financed by neighboring Arab states, none of these nations have offered them refuge, land, or territory they can call their own. From an international perspective, the problem defies solution; indeed, some of the "solutions" only aggravate the crisis. When the Israeli government built a 480-mile fence between Israel and the Palestinian territories, the number of casualties caused by suicide bombers was reduced; at the same time, however, the fence reinforced Palestinians' feeling of being the Other and living in a state of siege. From their perspective, "religion and violence [have become] antidotes to humiliation."[21]

Feelings of victimization often go beyond reality into a state of paranoia, which can also have devastating effects. Hitler and Stalin were labeled paranoid personalities who were able to channel the frustrations of their followers into political power for themselves. Populations are not paranoid; they need leaders to organize their emotions into unhealthy directions. "Chronic anger becomes a way of life with paranoids," wrote Gaylin. "The anger is not always expressed but can remain dormant, awaiting an opportunity for excessive and often explosive emotion. . . . When rage is sustained over time, and when it is attached to an enemy who has been designated as the cause of their misery, paranoids enter the realm of hatred."[22]

A leader who has drunk heavily from the well of victimization, anger, and paranoia is Jean-Marie Le Pen, a French politician and founder of the nationalist party Front National. Le Pen blames a plethora of groups for France's current troubles—Arabs, Jews, AIDS victims, and immigrants. Some of his xenophobic remarks include the following:

- accusing President Jacques Chirac of France of being in the pay of Jewish organizations, specifically B'nai B'rith;
- advocating the isolation of those infected with AIDS from society and putting them in special institutions;
- referring to the Holocaust as a "detail of history";
- arguing that "massive immigration is the biggest problem facing France, Europe, and probably the world"; and
- supporting a ban on immigration to France from countries outside Europe.

Unfortunately Le Pen's political support has climbed steadily in recent years, particularly from regions in the south of France. Winning almost 17 percent of the national vote in 2002, he faced Jacques Chirac in a runoff election and was fortunately resoundingly defeated. His anti-immigrant rhetoric, particularly against those from Muslim countries, has infected other European countries as well as France. The Italian representative to the Organization of Security and Cooperation in Europe (OSCE) conference in Brussels in 2004 charged, "There is an irrational xenophobia against Islamic countries under the pretext of fighting terrorism."

Le Pen and his allies blamed "outsiders" for France's troubles, an excuse that was readily adopted by some of his compatriots who still smarted from the defeats at Dien Bien Phu in 1954, Suez in 1956, and Algeria in the late 1950s. Le Pen, a decorated paratrooper who fought in all three wars, emerged from those campaigns determined to right the "wrongs" against his country. Representing the extreme right wing of the French political spectrum, he proved totally incapable of accepting the demise of colonialism and the emergence of independence movements. These "external" defeats loom large in the minds of Le Pen's adherents, because they resonate with internal defeats that they have experienced—and imagine that they have experienced.

Attacking Muslims, immigrants, Jews, and other "outsiders," Le Pen used the classic political ploy of scapegoating: assigning blame to particular groups to hide the paranoia, fear, and hatred that lurk beneath the surface in many cultures, including and especially his own. In addition to extremist politicians like Le Pen, this pattern also extends to terrorists. "Scapegoating is an essential element of the fanatic's toolbox," said Mazarr. "Generating hatred against an enemy held responsible for the debasement of the present and the destruction of the glorious past focuses energy. . . . All the old existential themes are here—alienated individuals in search of authentic identity amid a debased mass society that has forgotten or destroyed its virtues. . . . In a desperate search for identity, the terrorist becomes doubly alienated."[23]

Leaders rarely scapegoat groups that can effectively fight back. Franz Neumann relates anti-Semitism in Germany in the 1920s and 1930s to mass anxiety manipulated by leaders who needed a handy scapegoat for their political difficulties. Only the Jews, he wrote, were sufficiently weak politically; the Nazis knew that the Bolsheviks, big business, and the Catholic Church were too strong to attack. And although many Nazi leaders realized that *The Protocols of the Elders of Zion* was a forgery, they used the publication to stir up anti-Semitism because they needed "an enemy worse than other countries . . . [and because of] their inability to understand the problems causing real anxiety: inflation, depression, [a] non-functional political system . . . [and] moral, social and political homelessness." The only way to integrate people was through "hatred of an enemy."[24]

MARTYRDOM

At the heart of political anger are the acts of martyrdom, with all the attendant tragedies that result from those deeds. The term *martyr* originally comes from the Greek term for "witness," as in the martyr bears "witness to evil with his own life."[25] A martyr is someone who protests what he (or she) sees as evil by taking his own life, such as the Buddhist monks who set themselves on fire in South Vietnam to declare their opposition to the government in power. In the past, martyrdom has assumed a close identification with Christianity and sacrifice, as in martyrs willing to suffer the penalty of death rather than renounce their religion. For Catholics, the difficult path to beatification and sainthood considers martyrdom the most important criterion, and is known as the "highest degree of sainthood." In view of the church's resistance to conversion indicated by its view of martyrdom, it seems paradoxical that Christianity at many times in its own history tried to force its faith on others: convert or die was the choice given to non-Christians—particularly Jews—during the Spanish Inquisition from 1350 to

1400. Many Portuguese and Spanish Jews, called Marranos, chose life over martyrdom, and practiced their religion secretly for many years afterward.

Although Christian history is replete with tales of martyrdom, today acts of martyrdom are more closely associated with the Palestinian territories as well as with neighboring Arab countries where most of the suicide bombers operating in Israel and Iraq had lived. The intifada campaign against Israel led many Palestinian activists to strap bombs on themselves and explode them in buses, restaurants, markets, and other highly populated destinations, causing their own death in addition to the deaths of hundreds of innocent civilians. Palestinian leaders who recruited these youngsters brainwashed them, trained them, and assigned them their deadly tasks. They forbade them from seeing their families for two weeks prior to their missions, fearful that they would change their minds. Suicide bombers were promised that as "martyrs" they would go straight to heaven, where seventy virgins awaited them. The political head of the Hamas movement encouraged suicide bombings as a better way to die than "to die daily in frustration and humiliation."[26]

Other reasons for religion-based terrorism fall in the areas of culture and economics, but they all lead back to defeat, humiliation, and the persuasive power of the leadership in linking these feelings to current problems. Some observers also attribute religious terrorism to sexual frustration. One example: the unemployment rate among young men in their late teens and early twenties in the Palestinian territories has "hovered around 50 percent," leading to all kinds of problems, not the least of which is sexual frustration: "Without jobs, which is usually a prerequisite to searching for a wife in traditional societies, they cannot marry. Without marriage, in strict religious cultures . . . they cannot have sex."[27]

All of the Abrahamic religions are ambivalent about suicide. In Christianity and Judaism, the rules against suicides are loosened in cases when their adherents are prevented from practicing their faith. The Koran enjoins its believers to refrain from suicide, yet leaves the door open if conditions warrant expelling infidels from their land. Countering Jewish prohibitions against suicide is the Masada legend, when about one thousand Jews committed mass suicide—a collective martyrs' death—in 73 CE rather than submit to Roman rule, which they feared meant instant death. When Israeli prime minister Golda Meir was asked whether her besieged country had a "Masada complex," she retorted, "You say we have a Masada complex. . . . It is true. We do have a Masada complex. We have a pogrom complex. We have a Hitler complex."[28]

THE PSYCHODYNAMICS OF ANGER

The widespread anger in response to political events has its roots in childhood. Children's anger bears a significant relationship to adult global anger. Many children grow up and never outgrow their hatreds; indeed, many are given guns and ordered to fight at very young ages, such as the children pressed into service in Africa and Latin America to fight tribal wars, drug wars, and other conflicts. The sense of hopelessness that today affects tens of millions of people involves many groups that have from childhood only seen a bleak future of poverty, joblessness, political corruption, and continued oppression by brutal rulers who govern with an iron hold on power.

Anger in children, even anger caused by external forces, is a complex emotion. In their study of anger in children, Fritz Redl and David Wineman uncovered its three basic components: ego development, contagion, and revenge. When egos cannot perform normally, children are unable to develop a realistic vision of the future. Instead, they substitute fantasy lives—borrowed from "radio, movies, or comic books"—in place of their own desolate reality, often the result of parental neglect or "traumatization" from war, terror, and historical or natural disasters.[29]

Redl and Wineman also found "contagion," a potent element of anger. From mob psychology in ancient Rome to modern groups of Shiite and Sunni religionists, contagion becomes a powerful force when anger is the impetus for unity. The emotion of contagion—like Moshan stoning the prostitute in Kabul—operates destructively even among people with strong egos; in the weak-minded, it knows no bounds. Contagion leaves the "ego more than usually helpless, . . . [with] the melting point of ego control under the impact of excitement and group psychological intoxication . . . *extremely low.*"[30] With an unstable population, "the law seems to be that exposure to almost any type of excitement . . . is 'catching,' and that even extreme behavior forces imitation."[31]

The last important element of anger, the desire for revenge—or the question of how one human being can stick a bayonet into another's stomach—becomes even more relevant here. How intense do the powerful emotions that are evoked have to be to get people to reach that state? Soldiers who have experienced the heat of battle can more easily comprehend the kind of demonization necessary to kill an enemy; others find it more difficult. While killing is sinful in any religion or culture, guilt feelings are minimized if a "specific act can be proved to be 'revenge' for an unjustified hurt."[32] Actually, an individual's perception of the degree of hostility leveled on his community from the outside world cuts down considerably on his guilt at killing his fellow human beings and his obligation to obey society's moral codes.

Translated into hostile behavior, or anger toward other cultures, nations, and leaders, this means that there are fewer brakes on global anger than there were before.[33] When cultures and their leaders feel that the outside world is hostile, they acquire a siege mentality that manifests itself in "negative attitudes" that become "barriers" to the "resolution of conflict." Negotiation in this context becomes almost impossible, as witnessed by conflicts involving the "Albanians, Tokugawa Japanese, Iranians, the Afrikaners of apartheid South Africa, and post–World War II North Koreans."[34]

THE OTHER

The attitude that the "world owes me this" demotes long-held values to a secondary role. In the United States, it goes far to explain the rise of homophobic, anti-immigrant, and miserly local referenda that are otherwise uncharacteristic of American political culture. To get to this point of anger, citizens must develop a concept of the "Other," a term that can lead to xenophobia as well as wars in the name of religion, tribe, or nationality. The Other is anyone different—a necessary prop for leaders like Jean-Marie Le Pen, who blame the Other for a host of societal problems. In the short term, newly arrived immigrants cost money—particularly in the European countries whose high level of social welfare benefits attracts millions to their shores. Add to that the death of colonialism, the rise of independent states, reduced financial resources, and many Europeans' ongoing commitment to some of their former colonies—Algerians were considered French citizens—and the mix presents a host of social problems that in many cases fall well beyond easy solutions. In Germany, for example, workers are guaranteed six weeks of paid vacation by law. Child care, health care, education through university, and maternity and paternity leave are all financed by governments in the European Community. Even with these generous benefits, immigrants face the vicious cycle of discrimination in hiring, which leads to growing unemployment, poverty, rising crime, and in the case of France, widespread rioting. Higher government expenditures are required to meet these new conditions, leaving more fertile ground for Le Pen and others like him to resort to scapegoating, hate language, and paranoia.

Leaders who manipulate their followers into feelings of hatred toward the Other find that at first their task seems relatively easy. Perhaps this is because children are taught for their own safety from early childhood to distrust the Other. They are warned not to talk to people they do not know, not to answer the door if they are home alone, and never to go anywhere with strangers. Most people agree that it is good to teach children the difference between the familiar and the alien for self-protection, so that they can develop a healthy sense of distrust toward anyone who could do them harm. But at the same time, their primary agents of socialization—schools, parents, peer groups, mass media, and religion—may also create negative feelings toward the Other that make them more vulnerable as adults to xenophobia, racism, and related emotions. Few religions emphasize multiculturalism, for example; on the contrary, most faiths emphasize a sense of distinctiveness, the feeling that they are special or superior to other belief systems. The three major sects of Judaism, for example, talk about Jews as the "chosen people," selected by God for a special place in history. Where does that leave other cultures? The schisms in Christianity all confer a position of superiority on Lutherans, Protestants, Methodists, or any of the faiths that broke off from the Catholic Church.

"Identity politics," a term denoting an individual's connection with a particular group or culture, can also lead in its more malevolent forms to racism and xenophobia; in its healthier form, it explains how children can also identify positively with their parents and their community. To identify with one group exclusively means that everyone else has to be categorized as the Other. Identification is the most "powerful of the behavior-determining forces . . . [and] explains the hereditary nature of personality."[35] This trait can also extend to cultures that encourage hatred, such as the "Yanomano Indians in Southern Venezuela, the Albanians under the Communists, and . . . North Korea."[36] In these cultures, a "channel of hatred between parent and child" perpetuates malevolent influences in generation after generation.

Identity politics can also lead to racism, which has led to a myriad of emotions under the expanding rubric of hatred and anger. Hatred comes first, then anger; indeed, anger implies acting on hatred. Many psychological studies talk about innate racism, which gives the false impression that racism is hardwired into human beings. Rather, racism is culturally induced; like anti-Semitism, racism occurs even when there aren't even any racial groups to scapegoat, or even when they seem almost identical—such as the genocide by Muslims in power in the Sudan against darker-skinned Muslim groups in Darfur. In the United States, seven out of ten Caucasians were found to have negative feelings about blacks, most of them unconscious. Contrast this to what is really hardwired into the human psyche, such as the "fight or flight" syndrome, of which few can figure out the relevance to modern times.

Real problems arise when prejudice against the Other, or negative identity politics, leads to public policies that create built-in disadvantages for groups just because of who they are, or where they were born. To get there, leaders have to tap carefully into ongoing feelings of resentment and then manipulate them into full-fledged political anger. Only then do you get full-fledged battles over political and economic resources, such as affirmative action, referenda prohibiting gay marriage (passed in eleven states in the 2004 election), and limits on public spending for the disadvantaged. Feelings of hostility toward African Americans on welfare during the 1996 election, for example, bore no relation to reality, which was that over 63 percent of the welfare recipients were white.

Anger, then, is the natural by-product of fear and humiliation. For centuries it has been stoked by rulers who manipulate ancient ethnic, religious, and national hatreds to sustain their own power. Their efforts have left a legacy of millions of corpses and vast populations that still live in terror, all too aware of the depths of brutality that their rulers are capable of inflicting. Demonization of the Other should be recognized for what it is: an attempt to distract people from the pressing problems of hunger, corruption, and hopelessness, and to discourage them from ousting their rulers. The antidote is respect, dignity, and the transparent resolution of conflict.

NOTES

1. Michael J. Mazarr, "The Psychological Sources of Islamic Terrorism," *Policy Review* 125 (June–July 2004).

2. Yasmina Khadra, *The Swallows of Kabul* (New York: Doubleday, 2004).

3. Alex Alvarez, "Ideology and Genocide," in *Preventing Genocide: Threats and Responsibilities*. Paper presented at the Stockholm International Forum, January 26–28, 2004.

4. Charles Hutzler, "Yuppies in China Protest Via the Web—and Get Away with It: Nationalistic Dissidents Press for Hard-Hitting Policies on Japan, Taiwan, U.S.," *Wall Street Journal*, March 19, 2004.

5. Winston Churchill supposedly created Iraq in a hotel room following World War

I. British rule of Saudi Arabia before World War II was described by pundits as "Made in England." See also Gilles Kepel, *The War for Muslim Minds: Islam and the West* (Cambridge, MA: Belknap Press of Harvard University Press, 2004).

6. Robert J. Lifton, *America's Apocalyptic Confrontation with the World* (New York: Nation Books, 2003), 101.

7. Willard Gaylin, *Hatred: The Psychological Descent into Violence* (New York: Public Affairs, 2003), 46.

8. What he actually said was, "We have no eternal allies and we have no perpetual enemies," in Martin Tolchin and Susan J. Tolchin, *Selling Our Security: The Erosion of America's Assets* (New York: Knopf, 1992), 138.

9. Lifton, *America's Apocalyptic Confrontation with the World*, 88–91.

10. Ibid., 102.

11. Myra Mendible, "A Woman's Place: Gender, Honor, and the Culture of Humiliation". Unpublished paper, Florida Gulf Coast University. The paper will be part of a new book, tentatively titled: *Mediated Humiliations: Culture, Politics, and the New Mass Media.*

12. Max Scheler, Lewis B. Coser, and William W. Holdheim, *Ressentiment* (New York: Marquette University Press, 1994). Quoted in Susan J. Tolchin, *The Angry American: How Voter Rage Is Changing the Nation*, 2nd ed. (Boulder, CO: Westview Press, 1999), 27. See also Willard Gaylin, *The Rage Within: Anger in Modern Life* (New York: Simon & Schuster, 1984), 143.

13. Gaylin, *Hatred: The Psychological Descent into Violence*, 48–62.

14. Mark Jergensmeyer, *Terror in the Mind of God: The Global Rise of Religious Violence* (Berkeley: University of California Press, 2000).

15. Gaylin, *Hatred: The Psychological Descent into Violence*, 143.

16. Lifton, *America's Apocalyptic Confrontation with the World*, 108–9.

17. Ibid.

18. Mazarr, "The Psychological Sources of Islamic Terrorism," 51.

19. The Treaty of Westphalia was signed in 1648.

20. Jergensmeyer, *Terror in the Mind of God*, 184.

21. Ibid., 187.

22. Gaylin, *Hatred: The Psychological Descent into Violence*, 114.

23. Mazarr, "The Psychological Sources of Islamic Terrorism," 44.

24. Franz Neumann, "Anxiety and Politics," in *Identity and Anxiety: Survival of the Person in Mass Society*, ed. Maurice R. Stein, Arthur J. Vidich, and David Manning White (Glencoe, IL: Free Press, 1960), 284. Quoted in Tolchin, *The Angry American*, 29.

25. Lifton, *America's Apocalyptic Confrontation with the World*, 29.

26. Jergensmeyer, *Terror in the Mind of God*, 187.

27. Ibid., 191.

28. The question was posed by columnist Stewart Alsop in Robert S. Robins and Jerrold M. Post, *Political Paranoia: The Psychopolitics of Hatred* (New Haven, CT: Yale University Press, 1997).

29. Fritz Redl and David Wineman, *Children Who Hate: The Disorganization and Breakdown of Behavior Controls* (New York: Free Press, 1965), 66, 96, 142, 258.

30. Ibid., 104, 107.

31. Ibid., 108.

32. Ibid.

33. Ibid., 171.

34. Robins and Post, *Political Paranoia: The Psychopolitics of Hatred*, 59.

35. Gaylin, *Hatred: The Psychological Descent into Violence*, 164.

36. Ibid., 153.

5

BLOOD DIAMONDS: ECONOMIC RIGHTS AND WORLD ANGER

Many of the worst genocidal and human rights excesses of the last century were perpetrated under the guise of creating a more perfect society.

—Professor Alex Alvarez[1]

SIERRA LEONE

When God created the world, he endowed Sierra Leone with such a wealth of natural resources that the angels protested. "Oh, that's nothing," God told them. "Just wait and see the people I have put there." A joke that is often repeated in Sierra Leone, it takes the edge off the brutal, ten-year civil war that has torn apart the nation for much of its recent past.[2]

The war in Sierra Leone was known as the "diamond-powered conflict," for the illegal diamond trade that financed rebel groups and prolonged the country's devastation. The tribal and ethnic struggles that have focused the world's attention as the true culprits of the war were secondary to the real reasons: power and profits. Many of the world's conflicts look like Sierra Leone: on the surface, tribes and ethnic groups battle each other over nuances in their culture or religion—how many people really know the difference between Sunni and Shiite Islam?—while beneath the surface lurk the real reasons.

"It was a conflict over diamonds, a war for diamonds," said Dr. Barba Koroma, a biochemist from Sierra Leone. "Arms and ammunition were sent in exchange for diamonds. Wherever there were diamonds, there was this [illegal] traffic. They were branded 'conflict diamonds.' Others called them 'blood diamonds.' Journalists quipped that 'diamonds are a war's best friend.'³ Diamonds were also easy to smuggle: they are small, and unlike drugs, they have no smell and no taste. By the time they ended up in the diamond capital of the world—Antwerp, Belgium—it was impossible to tell blood diamonds from legal ones, especially if the buyers and sellers did not care about the difference.

Rebel forces in Sierra Leone were financed by a scheme in which diamonds were exchanged for illegal shipments of missiles, grenade launchers, and AK-47 assault rifles—which cost about $100 each on the black market. The cash from diamond sales was transferred through Liberia, the Ukraine, Libya, and Burkina Faso, countries notorious for their complicity in the international arms trade. Their leaders' linkage with the rebels prolonged the war and devastated the country: in one three-week period in January 1999, more than four thousand people were killed in the siege of the capital city of Freetown. (In light of the scandal involving the UN Food for Peace program, it is not surprising that the arms trade flourished in spite of arms embargoes and sanctions imposed by the United Nations.)

Even in peacetime, profits from the world's most perfect diamonds did not benefit the citizens of Sierra Leone. Despite its rich natural resources, Sierra Leone ranks today as one of the world's poorest countries, with a high infant mortality rate, the highest maternal death rate in the world, a life expectancy of 38.9 years, and a literacy rate that hovers slightly above one-third of the population. Very little manufacturing exists, and two-thirds of the population is forced to live off subsistence agriculture—less than 7 percent of the land is arable.⁴ One million miners desperately pan for gold and diamonds in the nation's mineral-rich provinces for about a dollar a day, but only a thousand of them have licenses. No matter: the government does not enforce the licensing regulations, or many of the other laws.

Sierra Leone was founded in 1462 by Portuguese explorers who called the country "Lion Mountains." For the next three centuries, Europeans used Sierra Leone as a source of slaves, but in 1787, Freetown, the current capital, was established as a city that would serve as a refuge for former slaves then living in London. In 1808, Sierra Leone became a British colony until it declared independence in 1961. Since that year, Sierra Leone found itself prone to the same problems of governance plaguing many of the other newly independent states in Africa: economic mismanagement, corruption, and the growing stagnation of its social and political life. The resulting chaos made the country ripe for a series of coups and wars, whose wounds continue to plague it today.

In Sierra Leone, tribal, ethnic, and religious conflict took second place to the fight for diamonds. "In our time," wrote John Gray, one of the world's leading scholars of international trade, "international conflict does not come from 'clashes of civilization.' As it has done in every age, it arises from the conflicting interests and policies of states."[5] The longest-serving prime minister in the postcolonial era, Siaka Stevens, smoothed over tribal conflicts by creating his own version of a Tammany ticket: although he came from a very minor tribe, the Limba, he embraced every one of the nation's ethnicities; spoke its two major languages, in spite of the fact that he was illiterate; and was, admittedly, a very good politician. Others recalled him as corrupt, since he quietly encouraged illegal mining and became involved with other economic activities that were also regarded as illegal. Unfortunately, his political instincts leaned toward cronyism, charged Dr. Koruma, who described how Stevens handed the nation over to his protégé, a brigadier general, who "manipulated individuals, didn't respect education, played one group against the other, plundered the country, and isolated groups from each other." Needless to say, promised elections were never held. In opposition to the turnover of power, "a disgruntled corporal from the Sierra Leone army (Foday Sankoh) went into the bush and led a 10-year war. He also stayed in Liberia and Chad, from where he and his followers waged mayhem from 1991 to 2001. His following cut across ethnic boundaries. It started in Nigeria, with the worst atrocities occurring between 1997 and 1999. The rebels entered the capital city, Freetown, in 1997 and ended up in Liberia. Sankoh's party, the RUF (Revolutionary United Front) had no ideology, only a desire to seize the country's diamond and mineral resources."

The ten-year civil war led to the nation's horrific devastation and loss of life, with civilians—as usual—the main victims. The war claimed over 75,000 lives and displaced over 2.5 million people, many of whom fled to the neighboring countries of Liberia and Guinea. Thousands of children were kidnapped and conscripted into military service by rebel forces, who released very few of them after the war. Many people were maimed—their hands and legs cut off—as punishment for voting, and the number of rape victims was incalculable.

Neither religion nor ethnic conflict played a large role in the nation's horrific civil war. The majority of the population of Sierra Leone is Muslim, 10 to 15 percent are Christian, and the remainder worship indigenous gods. Since the people of Sierra Leone are relatively tolerant of religious differences, there has always been very little religious conflict. Conflicts among tribes are marginally worse, but nowhere as bad as they are in many other

African countries, where hundreds of tribes try to coexist in nations without viable mediating bodies. The largest tribes in Sierra Leone are the Mende (in the southern and central parts of the country) and the Temne (in the north); these two tribes have always had skirmishes, but never full-scale wars. The Mendes are more politically savvy, more educated, and—most important—the owners of the diamond fields, the nation's "cash crop." The Temnes are better at running businesses. Together with the Mendes and the Temnes are eighteen other tribes, making up about 90 percent of the population. Although English is the nation's official language, most of the people speak Krio—a form of the Creole language derived from English—in addition to their tribal language.

Most of the blame for the atrocities was attributed to the rebel leader, Foday Sankoh, who was eventually captured in 2000. But the responsibility more accurately falls to the international diamond trade, which prolonged the war by ignoring the conflict, specifically the companies that tried to corner the market and turned a blind eye to the origin of the diamonds; the countries, like Belgium, that knew what was going on but neglected to police the trading system; and the greedy political leaders of Sierra Leone, who exploited fellow citizens just the way their colonial predecessors did. Critics of the tragedy in Sierra Leone also cite Charles Taylor, the former president of Liberia, for engineering many of the diamonds-for-weapons deals that perpetuated the war. According to *Washington Post* reporter Douglas Farah, Taylor also "hosted diamond buyers from al Qaeda and Hezbollah . . . [which allowed them] to earn and hide their wealth in an asset that is untraceable and easily convertible to cash."[6]

The civil war mercifully ended in 2002, when the United Nations—with the help of Great Britain—stepped in to quell the rebellion. A massive UN force of 17,400 foreign troops disarmed the remaining rebels and militia fighters, whose numbers ran into the tens of thousands (official counts ran as high as 70,000). Ordinarily, peacekeeping is a thankless task, but so far the UN has resettled hundreds of thousands of refugees in Sierra Leone, and is now attempting to rebuild their towns and dwellings. The UN effort was the largest peacekeeping effort in Africa, and the most successful. President Ahmad Tejan Kabbah, who was toppled from office by disgruntled soldiers in 1997, returned after winning a five-year term in 2002. Since 2002, elections have been held every year, and legal diamond exports have risen dramatically—although estimates of illegally smuggled diamonds today still range from 20 to 60 percent. The British came back and stayed to run the police and the army. They were there to "help," their representatives said, not to occupy the country.

Today, Sierra Leone still struggles with many of the same problems that caused the civil war in the first place: poverty, tribal rivalry, the spotty enforcement of the rule of law, and official corruption. All of those factors can only flourish in an environment of a weak government that is inadequate to the task of rebuilding a ravaged infrastructure and a distressed economy. But perhaps the widespread awareness among the people of Sierra Leone of the role that diamonds played in their country's devastation will help them build a future that will avoid the mistakes of the past.

THE WITHERING AWAY OF GOVERNMENT

Would Sierra Leone have been better off with no government? A weak government? Colonial masters? Theocracy? Dictatorship? None of the above? What Sierra Leone needed so desperately during the years following independence was a fair and strong government, to mediate conflict, avoid violence, and guarantee that a fair percentage of the nation's resources helped the people they were intended to benefit.

Yet many of the major theorists of both the left and the right have recommended the reverse: that government is unimportant in a universe of market forces. Karl Marx wrote about the withering away of the state more than 150 years ago. Once the workers owned the means of production, he predicted, the state would be unnecessary; in a worker's paradise, goods would be meted out according to "means" and "needs," and for the benefit of many, not just a few. Instead, the reverse occurred: nations that followed the Marxist model became parodies of big government, where everything from votes to grain production was controlled by the state.

With exquisite irony, the very theories touting the withering away of the state have been espoused today by libertarian and conservative thinkers, most of whom would view with horror any identification with Karl Marx or with the legions of Marxists who have adopted his name. Yet the ideas that have made the most impact on public policy around the world in the last half century have all viewed government from the same perspective as Marx, and in different ways call for such an extensive reduction in government that whatever is left looks very much like the rudimentary state that Marx viewed as ideal. Deregulation, privatization, and globalization all seek to reduce the role of government, each for very different reasons from those the "withering away" theorists talked about.

Taken one at a time, these theories don't seem very threatening to government; they even profess to improve government—to make it leaner, more efficient, and less open to abuse. The United States has even taken the lead in promoting these ideas around the globe, despite its uneven record at home. America's influence was most profoundly felt at international lending institutions, such as the World Bank and the International Monetary Fund (IMF), recalling H. L. Mencken's famous warning: for every problem, there is a solution—neat, plausible, and wrong.[7]

What the world really needed was a more nuanced approach to problems, one more sensitive to the needs of countries, cultures, and available resources. One size did not fit all, despite the best intentions of those convinced that privatization, deregulation, and globalization would work in practice. The overriding theory that government should be minimal may work in certain situations, but whenever there is a crisis—and there are many—people cry out for a governmental presence. At the scenes of airplane crashes, wars, train wrecks, hurricanes, tsunamis, and all the massacres set in motion by leaders inclined to practice genocide, victims and their loved ones seek help from government, which they still view as the best and most neutral source of relief. But by the time crises strike, governmental bodies and the resources that sustain them have been reduced to the point that renders them virtually incapable of addressing the public's needs. This was certainly America's experience in the wake of Hurricane Katrina in 2005, when state, local, and federal government found themselves unable to communicate with each other, resulting in a tragedy of enormous proportions.

PRIVATIZATION

Privatization in the United States has had a spotty record, but this did not stop the nation from attempting to convince the rest of the world of its merits, or from inflicting its views on international financial institutions, which often made privatization a basic condition of their loans. Today, there are more private police—security guards and Wackenhuts, for example—in the United States than police employed by the public sector. Many of the private police officers lack the training required for their counterparts in city, county, or state police departments, although they often provide similar services. Public hospitals throughout the country continue to close, to be replaced by privately owned health maintenance organizations that can pick and choose ("cherry-picking" is the popular term) their subscribers according to how healthy or how sick they are. And in an increasing number of states, prison systems rely on private companies to contract out management functions, personnel, and food and laundry services. Many municipalities today use private garbage collection, and others have gone back to privatized fire protection—reminiscent of colonial times when firefighters watched houses burn down if their owners had failed to pay their annual fees.

The advantages of privatization include the avoidance of onerous pensions, lowered administrative costs, and the diffusion of blame. A prison riot was no longer the governor's fault; the problem fell instead into the lap of the Corrections Corporation of America, a private company that does not have to depend on the next election for its survival. In some cases, it is true that privatized services were cheaper—at least at the beginning—but after a few years, prices tended to ratchet up faster than police pensions. And the niceties of civil liberties for prisoners could be avoided by many of the privatized corrections companies, whose executives eschewed the reach of meaningful oversight. ("Axe-handle Charlie" was the nom de guerre of one such prison guard working for the Corrections Corporation of America.) The privatization of health care probably had the most disastrous effect on the largest number of people: many municipalities, for example, lacked burn units in their hospitals after they were eliminated by private companies that found them unprofitable. And those accustomed to getting their health care from clinics in large municipal hospitals either went without medical attention or patronized overtaxed emergency rooms with problems that could more efficiently have been treated elsewhere.[8] By 2005, over 44 million Americans lacked health insurance, a problem that seemed to be no one's responsibility: not the HMOs, the public sector, or the privatized and virtually unregulated health care system. Over one-half of all federal government activities now operate under the aegis of the private sector, with scant oversight and little data on long-term results.

With the fading of accountability, everything is fair game, including foreign policy. Iran-Contra revealed the privatization of the war power, expressly granted to Congress by the U.S. Constitution. One of the most popular presidents in history, Ronald Reagan, allowed his aides to sell arms to Iran in exchange for money to fund the Nicaraguan Contras—a group attempting to overturn the legitimately elected, decidedly leftist Sandinista government. Once the president's policies were exposed, they were stopped, but this privatized war was waged for several years in direct contravention of specific congressional orders. The last time the war power was so blatantly privatized occurred over two hundred years ago, when Senator William Blount, Independent of Tennessee, incited two Indian tribes and the British to wage war against the Spanish, who owned a great deal of land in the Louisiana Territory that Blount had illegally purchased. Blount was impeached by the House of Representatives, but the Senate declined to convict him.[9]

On a global level, privatization met heavy resistance. In the poorer countries, even the threat of privatization often led to uprisings by groups that feared privatization would only lead them to more indebtedness and poverty. The policy of privatizing water in drought-stricken African countries as a condition of granting IMF or World Bank loans met with very heavy opposition. The idea behind the privatization of water was that people would appreciate those services more if they had to pay for them. That is certainly not true of a farmer earning one hundred dollars a year who cannot grow his crops, feed his children, or bathe without clean water. "Water is life, and because we have no water, life is miserable," said a Kenyan citizen.[10]

In El Alto, Bolivia, the privatization of water costs each family $450 a year to pay for the hookup to the nation's water system, which is run by a company called Aguas del Illimani, a subsidiary of Suez, a French multinational corporation. Unable to pay such a large fee, Remedios Cuyana was forced to bathe her three children in "frigid well water beside a fetid creek." After many people like her rose up in protest, the government cancelled the contract of the company, and President Carlos Mesa—seeking to avoid the fate of his predecessor who was thrown out of office in 2003—assured citizens that the state would henceforth assume the responsibility for providing clean water.[11]

Charging citizens for utilities as basic as water instills a rage that is particularly acute in Latin America, where one out of every ten children who dies before the age of five is the victim of diseases related to the ingestion of impure water. "You see . . . the battle lines are being drawn," said Michael Shifter, a senior fellow with the Inter-American Dialogue. "It builds great resentment and rage that things so essential to people, like water, like electricity, are not being delivered in a fair and equitable way. That's a formula for rage that leads to mobilization and . . . a convulsed region."[12]

Even though some of the mandarins of international finance seem to turn a blind eye to poverty, genuine solutions continue to elude the planners. On the one hand, privatization leads to social unrest and political volatility from citizens who resent the profits big companies are making from their misery. Yet when companies leave, there is a vacuum that cannot readily be filled by governments, many of which remain notoriously inefficient at providing even such basic services as electricity and water, and are left to face an angry populace when they can't deliver. Foreign companies, fearing that they will be closed down by the same angry populace that previously confronted them, refuse to return. Foreign investment, particularly in utility services, has fallen off drastically in Peru, Ecuador, and Argentina, as well as in Bolivia. It is now a classic catch-22 situation: resistance to privatization as a remnant of colonialism is intense, but no viable alternatives exist to take its place.

On the other side of the world, privatization offered a ray of hope to former Communist countries attempting to throw off the shackles of state control. But the problems were remarkably similar: privatization occurred without meaningful oversight, and without a government able to enforce the rule of law in commercial transactions and in the prevention of violence. In Kosovo, for example, the defunct Plastika Company factory stood ready to reopen—a good sign in a country ravaged by unemployment. In its former life, Plastika made body panels for Yugoslavia's state-run auto industry; in its present life, Plastika looked forward to becoming a full-fledged, profit-maximizing manufacturer eager to compete in a capitalist world.

What stopped it from succeeding was the same thing that has stopped Bolivia, and so many other countries, from benefiting from the fruits of globalism: privatization without governance. The United Nations had moved into Kosovo under the banner of a peacekeeping bureaucracy, embracing privatization as a solution to chronic joblessness. UN officials took control of "both large state-owned companies . . . and around 400 small, worker-run firms." Under UN auspices, auctions were held, and foreign investors provided start-up capital to revitalize the "remnants of a defunct socialist order." Amid much fanfare, the head of the UN property office (an Albanian) traveled to Washington and posed with President Bill Clinton under a banner that read, "Privatization Has Started."[13] Alas, by 2004 it was clear that Plastika was a failing enterprise, largely because of the frequent fights between the company's Albanian and Serb workers. Their fights reflected ongoing conflicts between the Serbs and Albanians that not only plagued other industries in Kosovo but prevented peace as well. Unlike the other countries in the former Yugoslavia that were considered independent states (Bosnia-Herzegovina, Croatia, and Macedonia), Kosovo found itself in political limbo, with Serbia steadfastly clinging to its claim that Kosovo and its assets were part of Greater Serbia.

Given the experiences of the rest of the world, it was hardly a surprise that privatization of the "third rail" of U.S. politics, Social Security, never got the political traction its supporters expected. Even the Enron debacle should have given pause to the devotees of pension privatization, especially since the very word *privatization* lost 20 percent of the public immediately— one reason the Bush administration chose to call them "personal savings accounts"—and the nation's pension regulatory agency (the Pension Benefit Guarantee Corporation) was swimming in red ink.[14]

As in Sierra Leone, no governmental presence in Kosovo mediated the perennial conflicts between groups bent on each other's destruction. The UN turned out to be too weak to meet the challenges of the ongoing ethnic conflict, and it lacked the legitimacy either to bring peace to the war-ravaged region or to oversee the transformation of the nation's economy. Privatization may work under certain conditions, but lawlessness, war, and ethnic conflict—conditions that affect a good part of the world—are not among them.

THE RUSH TO DEREGULATE

The United States has also taken the lead on implementing another questionable theory: deregulation. From the time President Reagan won a massive victory in 1980 on a platform of "getting the government off the backs of the people," the idea of overregulation has remained a popular theme with Republicans as well as Democrats. Reagan was able to continue President Jimmy Carter's deregulatory initiatives with even greater enthusiasm, since he wasn't bothered by doubters in his own ranks as Carter was. Reagan solidified the role of the Office of Management and Budget (OMB) in the rule-making process, and successive presidents happily joined in— after all, more power for the White House was always a popular move with presidents. At this point, the OMB is now involved in the regulatory process even in the pre-rule-making stages, which means that the president has a hand in stopping all rules, regardless of what the laws provide.

Economic deregulation continued apace, affecting the banking, airline, telecommunications, and transportation industries. The net effect was the undoing of government's role in vital areas in which the public still expected protection. Banking deregulation, for example, encompassed the worst attributes of socialism and communism, encouraging high-risk behavior from savings and loan industry executives at the same time the federal treasury insured deposits up to $100,000 against risk. In the good old days (specifically, the early 1980s), customers could buy certificates of deposit that paid an interest rate of 16 percent for accounts that were insured up to $100,000. That meant that the banks had to earn more than 16 percent to make a profit, and even in a good economy, investments that pay that much are hard to find.

A crisis finally forced Congress to confront the problems inherent in banking deregulation, which opened the door for criminal behavior and increased the taxpayers' burden. The case of Charles Keating, a California savings and loan entrepreneur, caused a great deal of grief to the five senators known as "the Keating Five," who suffered a two-year ethics probe into their activities. Through generous campaign contributions, Keating had "convinced" some of his friends in the U.S. Senate into pressuring federal and state regulators to ignore glaring accounting discrepancies in his savings and loan business. Keating eventually went to jail for cheating depositors of millions of dollars, but the real criminals, according to former senator Warren Rudman (R-NH) who headed the ethics investigation, were the 535 members of Congress who allowed the passage of banking deregulation. The final tab for the taxpayer? At last count, it was $400 billion, but no one to this day has ever owned up to the real amount.

Banking, airlines, telecommunications, energy, and transportation have long been regarded as quasi-public utilities. That means that unrelated businesses depend on these industries. Goods can't get transported without reliable transportation; since the Depression, businesses and private citizens count on banks not failing; and people can't communicate with their physicians in a medical emergency without a telephone. Soon after the airlines were deregulated, many rural areas found themselves without service, affecting their businesses, property values, and economic development. The former governor of California, Gray Davis, blamed electricity deregulation for the energy crises that crippled his state in the harsh winter of 2001—and probably led to the recall vote in 2003 that cost him his governorship. The notorious energy company Enron was also blamed for California's problems; the company, many recalled, was able to expand rapidly—too rapidly, in fact—because of the state's deregulatory policies.

Clean air? Pure water? Worker safety? Social regulation? Under the White House OMB meat ax, safety and environmental regulations have suffered, although no one will ever know the full extent, thanks to the secrecy ingrained in the process. Add to that a political environment hostile to the costly demands of cleaning up the rivers and the air and of making the mines and factories safer, and the future looks somewhat bleak. Does America really want to inflict these problems on the rest of the world?

GLOBALIZATION AND ITS DISCONTENTS

In an ideal world, globalization also makes perfect sense. You make shoes, and I grow grain. You have oceans, so you can keep the fishing industry; I'm landlocked, so I'll stick to cattle raising. Free trade and open markets are cousins of deregulation and privatization, and on paper they all look good: resources are optimized, work expands, and jobs grow exponentially. Yet even Adam Smith, the father of free trade, believed in government protection of gunpowder at the end of the eighteenth century; and, pressed by 535 legislators with Chrysler franchises in their districts, the subsidy-resistant U.S. government bailed out the auto company from bankruptcy nearly two hundred years later. At this point, it is safe to conclude that with all the exemptions to the rule, globalization remains an ideal—honored by those who have something to gain, and dismissed by the losers as a false promise.

In fact, "free trade" made even more sense than deregulation and privatization. Confused by the fast-paced global economy, Republicans as well as Democrats espoused a "virtual" trade policy since World War II, marking a sharp reversal from their more interventionist approach in the past. Inward investment policy, for example, followed a model reminiscent of the Articles of Confederation, in which the states dominated a weak federal government. States have long taken the lead in deciding which industries to locate in the United States, with virtually no federal presence around, even when conflicts occurred. Often these states competed with each other, while foreign multinationals simply sat back and waited for the best incentive package. Toyota, for example, got the best deal from Kentucky, which spent $325 million to lure the company to the town of Georgetown. State officials argued that they would rather spend money on incentives to attract business than on welfare.

Even the most zealous globalists fail to see that this theory does not always work in practice. At a PhD dissertation defense on voluntary restraint accords, a lone political science professor suggested to a room full of economics professors touting the glories of free trade that they all submit their jobs to the university administration to test out whether they could compete with professors earning a fraction of their wages in the United Kingdom or Uzbekistan. The negative reaction was predictable. "We can compete with them any time," was the typical response. "Don't bet on it, particularly if your global competitors speak English," retorted the naysayer. Tenure among college professors—even those who vociferously support free trade—remains the last bastion of protectionism, indicating once again that most people support protectionism for their own industries, while they favor free trade for everyone else.

Americans' ambivalence toward free trade often evokes angry responses from their trading partners around the world, and even among its own citizens who find themselves in the awkward position of talking free trade while carrying out protectionist measures. "The U.S. preaches free trade, but we have subsidies," complained Dinah H. McDougall, the Brazilian desk officer with the International Trade Administration at the Department of Commerce. "In Brazil they must buy American feed for farm-raised shrimp after U.S. shrimpers raised an action. The Department of Commerce raised the issue. The big guys. The effect was that whole areas were wiped out in Northeast Brazil by U.S. anti-dumping laws. Like steel, U.S. companies depended on cheap imports. We need to change American law."

Political factors often trump trade. When the Cold War was in full swing, the United States refused to ask Japan to remove its trade barriers, fearing a breach in relations with such a staunch political ally. Now, with China holding over $600 billion of U.S. debt—as of 2005—America is similarly loath to offend a nation on whom it has become so dependent. The battle over whether to accord China most-favored-nation status was over before it began.

NAFTA, the North American Free Trade Agreement, was lobbied hard by the Clinton White House, which continued the policies of its Republican predecessors in adopting a wholesale ratification of free trade. Environmental and labor guarantees were shunted off to side agreements on the premise that there was no room for them in the two-thousand-page document. NAFTA was followed by CAFTA (the Central American Free Trade Agreement) in 2005, which critics called a boon to corporate America, because it provided yet another incentive for manufacturers to export jobs offshore.

In its zeal to shrink the global marketplace, the United States continued an "anything-goes" stance on workplace conditions, child labor, prison labor, and a host of other practices that would not be tolerated in the industrialized world. Six-year-old children tethered to looms in Pakistan? This will give them the money to go to school, argued apologists. Prison labor in China? At least we're keeping the lines of communication open to the world's largest market, explained the defenders of renewing China's most-favored-nation status.

In trade policy, American leaders and their Western counterparts contributed to irresponsible economic behavior by encouraging foreign investment in such instruments as U.S. Treasury notes, and by ignoring rampant breaches in reciprocity between themselves and the Arab nations. Kuwaiti nationals, for example, were allowed to invest in U.S. oil fields, but American investors were prohibited by Kuwaiti law from investing in that nation's oil industry. They also ignored the hollowing out of the middle classes in these countries, as small investors in Latin America, the Middle East, Africa, and Asia sent their money abroad for safekeeping.[15]

Perception is key, and ever since communications technology has greatly improved, people know far better than they did before how other nations live. And although the benefits of globalization are clear, the poorer nations tend to regard the promises of a better future as yet another form of economic exploitation inflicted on them by the industrialized world. After all, when they finally threw off the shackles of colonialism, many of these countries embraced the free market: they sold off companies that were owned by the state, reduced government regulation, and wooed foreign investors. Yet, after decades of independence, most of these nations have little to show for their efforts. Europe stands out as the only region without a growing inequality of wages. According to the United Nations, the richest 5 percent of the world's people receive 114 times the income of the poorest five percent.[16] In America, the 25 million richest Americans have as much income as almost two billion of the world's poorest people.[17]

Increasing poverty exacerbates anger, especially among elites who link their country's fortunes to their declining future. "In Ecuador 40 percent of the people live under the poverty line," said Henry Vega, a doctoral student in public policy at George Mason University. "Immigration is not the issue; corruption is." His views were echoed by Gonzalo S. Paz, a Fulbright fellow from Argentina: "In Argentina, the middle-class has disappeared. They are the new poor. Children are a source of the anger; they are not getting enough for their basic needs, particularly food and medicine."

"In Bolivia, 60 percent of the people live in poverty; 40 percent of them in extreme poverty," added Roxana Loaiza, from Bolivia. "One of the reasons was the Bolivian/Paraguayan War in the 1930s. In Bolivia, there is no 'trickle down' effect from the oil companies. Particularly with the indigenous populations. You get a real capitalism versus labor division. The jobs go to the high classes, like the engineers."

The only countries that are "catching up with the industrialized world" are China and India, although they, too, are experiencing a widening income gap due to "slow growth in rural incomes . . . relative to rich OECD countries," as well as "shrinkage in the world's middle income group."[18] In other words, the same patterns that hold back poorer nations seem also to hold true for nations on the move: the perpetuation of rural poverty, and the absence of an emerging middle class to bolster economic gains with a stable and enduring political base.

At times, the facts contradict perceptions. As countries become richer, the incidence of income poverty falls, and other indicators of progress, such as education and health, also tend to improve.[19] Poverty may be somewhat alleviated, but communications and other technologies have made it easier for people to see how richer countries allocate their resources, how others live so much better than they do, and how their lot in life could be improved. "Poverty is . . . low salaries and lack of jobs," said a member of a Brazilian discussion group. "And it's also [about] not having medicine, food and clothes."[20] In addition, it takes some degree of prosperity to mount a decent and effective resistance to the status quo. Witness the French, American, and Russian revolutions: people didn't revolt when they were truly oppressed; they revolted when they had a measure of resources, and when an embryonic middle class emerged, such as the French bourgeoisie, American planters, and well-fed Russian peasants and urban dwellers. Revolutions also occurred during times of weak leadership, such as the short-lived reigns of Kings Louis XVI and George III, and Czar Nicholas II.

Virtually every United Nations report attacks inequality, but very little is done to address it. At her address at Notre Dame two days after the tragedy of 9/11, Baroness Shirley Williams, a member of the House of Lords in Great Britain and an international social activist, attacked the "excessive inequalities around the world." She linked terrorism to inequality—not to justify terrorism, she emphasized, but to deal with the sources of terrorism by treating one of its basic causes: social and economic inequities. The income of the poorest 20 percent is one-sixtieth of the wealthiest 10 percent, said Baroness Williams, who added that the average income in the richest twenty countries is thirty-seven times the average in the poorest twenty—a "gap that has doubled in the past 40 years," according to the World Bank.[21]

Widening income gaps inevitably go hand in hand with economic and social injustice. In fact, statistics show a definite linkage between a more equitable distribution of income and the reduction of poverty. For example, in Uganda, rising equality led to "strong poverty reduction," while in Bangladesh, rising inequality in income redistribution "tempered [its] poverty reduction."[22] Still one of the poorest countries in the world, Sierra Leone looks toward a bleak future, since it persists in maintaining a pattern of gross inequality in income distribution.

Income inequality invariably correlates to dysfunctional government: political leaders who spirit their ill-gotten fortunes to Swiss banks, oppressive regimes that quell public discontent, volatile politics, the absence of stable foreign investors, inefficient and corrupt political leaders, corporate executives that siphon off resources, and the complicity of governments that allow the illegal arms trade to continue unabated.

It is hardly an understatement to say that wars also exacerbate poverty. Wars occur "disproportionately in poor countries" and fall "disproportionately on the world's poor people." Not surprisingly, 90 percent of war deaths are civilian, not military, and are attributed more to disease than to guns. "During 1987–1997 more than 85 percent of conflicts were fought within national borders (14 in Africa, 14 in Asia, 1 in Europe). . . . In Cambodia, 1.7 million people died in 20 years of fighting and mass murder. . . . Civilian victims are also singled out because of their ethnic identity; as many as 800,000 Tutsis and moderate Hutus were killed by extremist Hutus in Rwanda in 1994."[23] Many national governments and international institutions claim to be helpless in the face of such ethnic violence.

A cause of very deep resentment involves the huge debt incurred by the world's poorest nations, a debt that most countries cannot hope to pay off in this millennium. The issue of debt relief has sparked demonstrations against the World Bank, the International Monetary Fund, the United Nations, and the World Trade Organization at meetings as far apart as Seattle; Prague; Montreal; Genoa; Washington, D.C.; London; and Johannesburg. It was no accident that the planners of the WTO meeting in 2001 selected as the site for their conference the city of Doha, Qatar—an island in the Persian Gulf that was largely inaccessible to demonstrators.

Crushing debts mean the loss of jobs, medical care, food, water, and the most basic life services:

- Haiti pays twice as much on debt service as it does on health care, even considering its virulent HIV/AIDS epidemic;
- debt service constitutes more than half the annual budget of the Philippines, or more than double what the government pays for social services;
- Africa pays more than $15 billion annually to the IMF, the World Bank, and richer countries just for debt service; and
- the privatization of water and other basic services, as well as the elimination of subsidies, are often attached to loans.[24]

Led by Great Britain, the industrialized countries—known as the G-8—have agreed to cancel the debt owed to them by the HIPC (Heavily Indebted Poor Countries) nations. Pleading poverty, the World Bank and the IMF declared they could not follow suit, refusing to accept the suggestion offered by a number of NGOs that they sell their gold reserves and force the International Bank for Reconstruction and Development to use its retained earnings and future income allocations to bankroll these crippling debts. What the World Bank and IMF offered instead was "debt relief," which was better than nothing and helped in concrete ways to alleviate some of the worst problems, particularly in education. Tanzania was able to eliminate user fees for elementary school, which put 1.5 million children back in school. Uganda doubled its elementary school enrollment, and Honduras saved enough money to ensure universal access to junior high school. In Mozambique, half a million people were vaccinated.[25]

Economic inequality is a powerful source of anger, particularly now that people can see how "the other half" lives. "To the more educated . . . globalism has become a new word for imperialism," wrote authors Ian Buruma and Avishai Margalit, who described what they termed a "destructive loathing of the West" by the rest of the world.[26]

Signs of a sporadic resistance to globalization have recently appeared in votes against the new constitution of the European Union in both France and the Netherlands. Europeans fear that Brussels will be making decisions that may not be either in their national interest or in the interest of a particular economic sector, such as farming. The new entrants from Eastern Europe find that after years of Communist oppression, their newfound experience with democracy will be too short-lived if they have no control over decisions that are made far away from the Czech Republic, Latvia, or Hungary. And perhaps most important of all, the fear of cheap labor has become a potent fear driving voters away from the EC. During the French vote in the spring of 2005 on the EC constitution, the "Polish plumber" became a key issue, so much so that the enterprising Polish travel bureau took out advertisements featuring a handsome "Polish plumber" as a way of attracting French tourists to Poland.

Resistance to many of globalism's unsavory features has exacerbated anger and will continue to do so unless some of these problems are seriously addressed.[27] Fear of globalization was also seen in the riots in France in the fall of 2005, perpetrated mainly by second- and third-generation Arabs from North Africa who had already experienced decades of joblessness and discrimination in France, and face decades more. Official silence on these issues from the French government only aggravated the deep-seated alienation and anger that were already there.

THE POLITICS OF INSECURITY: OUTSOURCING, OFFSHORING, AND OTHER EUPHEMISMS FOR JOB LOSS

"In many countries," wrote John Gray, "opening up to global markets has evoked a new politics of insecurity."[28] Even in the United States, job losses have created a sense of insecurity in a wide array of occupations, from manufacturing in the Midwest to the high-tech companies in Silicon Valley. Each week, workers at companies all over the country wonder if pink slips will appear in their mailboxes, and if they do, how will they pay the mortgage?

Outsourcing and offshoring have recently become code words for job loss—job loss incurred by globalization, or a combination of privatization, deregulation, and free trade. By the end of 2005, the issue had become a political minefield, as well as the frequent butt of jokes. When President George W. Bush went on an eight-day pre-Thanksgiving trip to Asia, late-night television comic David Letterman quipped that he was just "visiting U.S. jobs."

The real question raises the issue of winners and losers. Sending jobs abroad is unquestionably better for the beneficiaries overseas, but a hard sell for politicians at home. U.S. technology companies are sending jobs out of the country, where English speakers in India, the Philippines, and Russia claim to do just as good a job answering telephone queries as their counterparts in the United States. Computer programmers in China and India earn about $9,000 a year; in the Russian Federation, they earn $5,000; and in the

United States, they bring home from $60,000 to $80,000. With quarterly returns full of red ink and so many companies no longer affiliated with one country, it makes all kinds of sense for companies to send jobs abroad: it improves their bottom line, impresses their stockholders, and there are no laws preventing them from exporting jobs.[29] A recent problem with a Hewlett-Packard printer led one customer to hold a two-hour telephone conference with an expert in Mumbai, where it was cheaper for the company to outsource its customer-service functions and pay for the long-distance telephone call than it was to keep that job in the United States. Outsourcing has also affected service professions that always regarded themselves as immune, such as accounting and tax professionals, medical transcriptions and billing specialists, insurance claims processors, technical writers, architects and drafters, and legal and investment researchers.[30]

What exactly does a jobless recovery mean? It started out with the loss of manufacturing jobs. Now the United States is losing service jobs, and in the next few years it is predicted that 3.3 million jobs will move abroad, primarily to India and China. The argument that this development is good for the U.S. economy was articulated by Treasury Secretary John Snow, who said that "it was part of trade, and there couldn't be any doubt about the fact that trade makes the economy stronger, one could outsource a lot of activities and get them done just as well, or better, at a lower cost."[31]

But abstract trade theory should not be confused with losing jobs, as those too cavalier about this development have learned. Gregory Mankiw, chairman of President George W. Bush's Council of Economic Advisers, was forced to apologize after making remarks in Ohio about how outsourcing jobs was good for the economy. In Ohio, one out of every six factory jobs has gone overseas.

Politically, the ayes have it: outsourcing never became a full-fledged issue either in the U.S. presidential campaigns of 2000 and 2004, or in any other elections in the industrialized world. The influential conservative columnist George Will claimed that 40 percent of the job losses that occurred during the first Bush administration occurred in the aftermath of 9/11. The United States, he argued, would trigger "retaliation that would cost more jobs in export industries that [were] lost to imports if the nation took any measures to retain jobs that could be interpreted as protectionist."[32] Noted trade expert Jagdish Bhagwati added that jobs disappeared because "technical change has destroyed them, not because they [have] gone anywhere."[33] He argued that globalism moved progressive causes like "gender equality" and the "reduction of poverty" forward, and he fears that antiglobalism appeals to an element of the right wing's "fortress mentality against immigration."[34] Bhagwati blamed the antiglobalization movement on young people who "arrive[d] at their social awakening" in "fields other than economics," such as sociology, comparative literature, and English, which were heavily influenced by postcolonialists—called "nihilists" by Bhagwati—like Jacques Derrida and Michel Foucault. Opposing globalization and its inevitable job losses adds up to a form of protectionism that is bad for the economy because it inhibits trade, the country's major engine of growth. And when "stupid" policies impede that growth, he added, poverty is bound to increase.[35]

The most influential opponent of outsourcing is Lou Dobbs, the anchor and managing editor of CNN's *Lou Dobbs Tonight*, former anchor of *Lou Dobbs' Moneyline*, and columnist for *Money* magazine and *U.S. News & World Report*. Dobbs has inveighed against a loss of three million jobs that have been outsourced, totaling fifteen million unemployed Americans, and has published a list of hundreds of companies that have exported jobs overseas. Attacked by editorials in the *Wall Street Journal*, the *Economist*, the *Financial Times*, and the *Washington Post*, Dobbs has held steadfastly to his view that no evidence exists that supports the thesis that outsourcing has created jobs in the private sector, and that there are millions more jobs at risk of being outsourced to "cheap overseas labor markets."[36]

The root of the problem, argues Dobbs, is that outsourcing is not good for the economy. He vigorously opposes U.S. fiscal policies that put the nation in the position of "borrowing foreign capital to buy foreign goods that support European and Asian economies while driving us deeper into debt."[37] At this writing, the current account deficit of the United States stands at $3 trillion, with most of the money owed to China, Japan, and Great Britain, in that order.[38]

There is more hyperbole defending outsourcing than objective data, and more ad hominem assaults than rational discussion. "Our principal trading partners, Canada, China, Japan and the EU all . . . maintain annual trade surpluses and pursue balanced trade. Why don't my critics call *them* protectionists?" queried Lou Dobbs in response to all the attacks against him. "Why not call them economic isolationists?"[39]

Given the paucity of objective data that can be used to solve the "problems created by offshore outsourcing," it is not useful to label anyone challenging the practice "protectionist."[40] Still, name-calling and rigid responses have replaced any semblance of rational dialogue on this important issue. Not so in many other countries, especially industrialized countries, where the issue of job retention assumes more political importance than it does in the United States. Japan, for example, was willing to risk a trade war with the United States over a joint venture involving the development and construction of the FSX fighter plane in order to save five thousand jobs at Mitsubishi's Nagoya plant.[41]

Job loss never became a political issue in the United States primarily because Americans feel so optimistic about the future; they believe America is a big, rich country that will always have a rosy economic outlook, create jobs, and remain a wellspring of new ideas. This has created another source of anger abroad, as many people also look to America as the source of plenty; and when America doesn't come through, the resentment heightens. At a United Nations Social Summit in Copenhagen in 1996, First Lady Hillary Clinton arrived in her husband's stead to offer $10 million in U.S. aid to address the problems discussed at the conference. The reaction was swift: why was the United States so cheap? Nine years later, when the devastating tsunami hit Indonesia, President Bush's initial offer of $35 million was greeted with similar incredulity, after which he quickly raised the sum to several hundred million dollars. The reaction of the world is ironic in view of the fact that the United States, perceived as the richest nation on earth, is also the world's largest debtor nation.

BLOOD DIAMONDS REDUX

The saga of Sierra Leone shows what happens when angry clashes take the place of good governance, when the daily struggle for the basics of life confronts theories imposed by the outside world that are largely irrelevant to time, culture, and place. Privatization may work for garbage collection in Newark, but privatizing water in Bolivia is a different story. Banking deregulation's spotty history around the world held back similar experiments in Germany and sent Charles Keating to prison in the United States; why, then, does the United States expect other nations to follow suit? In theory, since globalization benefits everyone, why hasn't it also helped countries that have not yet industrialized?

The vacuum between theory and reality generates a great deal of anger: anger at the World Bank for imposing unrealistic conditions on nations that have no hope of meeting them, anger at governments that can't govern, and anger at the continued exploitation that many thought had evaporated with the demise of colonialism and the birth of independence. Sierra Leone's experience represents a microcosm of theory gone wrong, wasted resources, unbounded anger, and weak government. Since independence, the national government of Sierra Leone has been virtually incapable of providing social services, protecting its people, and allocating the nation's rich natural resources in the public's interest. There were no institutions to impose the rule of law, guarantee transparency in business dealings, or mediate conflicts. Manipulative leaders played upon tribal conflicts, and disputes were settled according to who had the most guns. Numerous conflicts arose without any of the mediating institutions—courts, police, military, legislature, legitimate rulers, or free elections—that sustain daily life elsewhere.

The fragile peace that has come to Sierra Leone depends on how successfully the current government can run the country. So far, some glimmers of hope have emerged. Several elections have been held without incident; one town established a mining cooperative of NGOs and business interests to educate miners and lend them money. And most important, a course of action known as the Kimberly process has finally been put in motion by the diamond–producing countries (including Sierra Leone) and the diamond-trading countries (particularly Belgium and the United States) to certify the legality of their diamond transactions, although a large percentage of illegal diamond transactions still occur.

The devastation of Sierra Leone would not have been possible without the complicity of the international community. What delayed the implementation of the Kimberly process for so many years? And where were the laws and mechanisms of enforcement that should have halted all the drug dealing, arms smuggling, and illegal diamond sales that financed and prolonged the war that terrorized the country? If the fragile peace is to be maintained, that means the governments of industrialized countries must take more responsibility for the woefully underregulated diamond industry if they are serious about avoiding further inroads into the diamond trade by organized crime, and stop the money flow that has been fueling African civil wars. International multinational corporations should stop buying diamonds, particularly those originating in Liberia and the Ivory Coast, until their legality has been certified. Similarly, the United Nations also needs to impose a full embargo on diamonds—at least until their legality is established—and then develop internationally accepted standards for the diamond trade.

Unfortunately, all these reforms are proceeding slowly, if at all. Until then, it is still a world in which "beleaguered . . . governments find little formal international protection against internal predators, and are forced into Faustian bargains in order to survive."[42] No wonder their anger grows.

NOTES

1. Professor of Criminal Justice Alex Alvarez, Northern Arizona University, "Ideology and Genocide" (paper delivered at the 2004 Conference on Preventing Genocide: Threats and Responsibilities, Stockholm, Sweden).

2. Radio Netherlands, *A Brief History*, January 28, 2000, www2.rnw.nl/rnw/en/features/humanrights/historysl.html (accessed February 13, 2006). See also John L. Hirsch, *Sierra Leone: Diamonds and the Struggle for Democracy* (Boulder, CO: Lynne Reiner Publishers and the International Peace Academy, 2001).

3. Amy Goodman and Juan Gonzalez, *Diamonds Are a War's Best Friend: The Trade of Arms for Diamonds in Africa*, April 19, 2000, www.democracynow.org/index/pl?issue = 20000419 (accessed February 13, 2006).

4. Central Intelligence Agency, *Sierra Leone*, www.cia.gov/cia/publications/fact book/geos/sl.html. See also Douglas Farah, "Salving Deep Wounds, Sierra Leoneans Vote," *The Washington Post*, May 15, 2002.

5. John Gray, "Global Utopias and Clashing Civilizations: Misunderstanding the Present," *International Affairs* 74, no. 1 (1998): 150–52. See also Jared Diamond, *Guns, Germs, and Steel: The Fate of Human Societies* (New York: W. W. Norton, 1997).

6. Douglas Farah, "A Protected Friend of Terrorism," *Washington Post*, April 25, 2005.

7. H. L. Mencken, "The Divine Afflatus," in *A Mencken Chrestomathy* (New York: Vintage Books, 1982), 443.

8. Some of the material on privatization came from a series on the subject by Martin Tolchin, published in the *New York Times* from 1985 to 1994. Specific articles on prisons ran on February 11, 1985; March 2, 1985; February 2, 1985; December 15, 1985; and September 17, 1985; on hospitals on January 25, 1985; on airports on March 7, 1985; July 26, 1985; and February 6, 1986; and on the outsourcing of foreign policy on January 20, 1987; February 20, 1986; and November 11, 1985.

9. Susan J. Tolchin and Martin Tolchin, *Glass Houses: Congressional Ethics and the Politics of Venom* (Boulder, CO: Westview Press, 2001), 22–26.

10. World Bank, "World Development Report: Attacking Poverty," ed. Oxford University Press (New York: World Bank, 2000–2001), 52.

11. Juan Forero, "Latin America Fails to Deliver on Basic Needs," *New York Times*, February 22, 2005.

12. Ibid.

13. Andrew Higgins, "Could U.N. Fix Iraq? Word from Kosovo Isn't Encouraging," *Wall Street Journal*, August 2, 2004.

14. Paul Krugman, "Stopping the Bum's Rush," *New York Times*, January 4, 2005.

15. Martin Tolchin and Susan J. Tolchin, *Buying into America: How Foreign Money Is Changing the Face of Our Nation* (New York: Times Books, 1988), chaps. 14–17.

16. United Nations Development Programme, "Human Development Report" (New York, 2002).

17. Ibid.

18. United Nations Development Programme, "Human Development Report" (New York, 2003), 39.

19. World Bank, "World Development Report," 45.

20. Ibid., 46.

21. Fred Dallmyr, "Lessons of September 11," *Theory, Culture and Society* 19, no. 4 (2002): 139. See also Shirley Williams, *God and Caesar: Personal Reflections on Politics and Religion*, Erasmus Institute Books (Notre Dame, IN: University of Notre Dame Press, 2003).

22. World Bank, "World Development Report," 51.

23. Ibid., 50.

24. Jubilee USA Network, "Drop the Debt," Spring 2004, www.jubileeusa.org/dropthedebtspring04.pdf (accessed February 13, 2006).

25. Soren Ambrose and Mara Vanderslice, *G7 Debt Relief Plan: More Grief Than Relief* (Jubilee USA Network, June 2002), www.jubileeusa.org/jubilee.cgi?page=briefings.html (accessed February 13, 2006).

26. Ian Buruma and Avishai Margalit, *Occidentalism: The West in the Eyes of Its Enemies* (New York: The Penguin Press, 2004).

27. Ibid.

28. Gray, "Global Utopias and Clashing Civilizations," 154.

29. Bill W. Hornaday, "Outsourcing Didn't Pay Off for Conseco," *Indiana Star*, April 22, 2004, www.indystar.com/articles/5/140262-9565-092.html.

30. Kris Mahr, "Next on the Outsourcing List," *Wall Street Journal*, February 2, 2004.

31. John Snow Interview on CNBC, March 23, 2004.

32. George Will, "The Perils of Protectionism," *Newsweek*, March 20, 2004, 84.

33. Jagdish N. Bhagwati, "Why Your Job Isn't Moving to Bangalore," *New York Times*, February 15, 2004.

34. Jagdish N. Bhagwati, *In Defense of Globalization* (New York: Oxford University Press, 2004), 4, 25.

35. Ibid.

36. Lou Dobbs, *The Dobbs Report* (CNN, 2004). See also Lou Dobbs, *Exporting America: Why Corporate Greed Is Shipping American Jobs Overseas* (New York: Warner Books, 2004).

37. Dobbs, *The Dobbs Report*.

38. See also Martin Tolchin and Susan J. Tolchin, *Buying into America: How Foreign Money Is Changing the Face of Our Nation* (New York: Times Books, 1988).

39. Dobbs, *The Dobbs Report*.

40. Ron Hira, "Implications of Offshore Outsourcing" (George Mason University, 2004). Dr. Hira's work on outsourcing became an excellent book. See Ron Hira and Anil Hira, *Outsourcing America: What's Behind Our National Crisis and How We Can Reclaim American Jobs* (New York: AMACOM, 2005).

41. See Martin Tolchin and Susan J. Tolchin, *Selling Our Security: The Erosion of America's Assets* (New York: Alfred A. Knopf, 1992).

42. Ian Smillie, Lansana Gberie, and Ralph Hazleton, *The Heart of the Matter: Sierra Leone, Diamonds and Human Security*, Africa Action, 2000, www.africaaction.org/docs00/sl0001.htm (accessed February 13, 2006).

6

SADAT AND THE
"OCTOBER 6 VICTORY":
FROM ANGER TO PEACE

> It was regarded as a stalemate, yet it shocked the Israelis. . . . The
> Egyptian people were jubilant. Sadat moved quickly after the war
> to make peace with Israel. We were tired of war.
>
> —Amr Abdalla

The Egyptians called it the Ramadan War, or the October 6 Victory
War. To the Israelis, it was known as the Yom Kippur War. The Egyptians and their allies, the Syrians, referred to it as Operation Badr, after the first victory of the Prophet Muhammad, when he entered the holy city of Mecca in 630 AD.

Regardless of its name, Egyptian leaders hailed the war as a victory and convinced their followers that after centuries of defeats, they could finally claim a military triumph. Like others in the Arab world, Egyptians still smarted from the Crusades, from three years of colonization by the French and seventy-four by the British, and from a string of military defeats by Israel in 1948, 1956, and 1967. The war in 1967 was especially painful to Egyptians, who lost the Sinai as well as control over the Suez Canal; Israel also wrested strategic territory, including historic Jerusalem and the Golan Heights, from Jordan and Syria. To the rest of the world, the 1973 war was a stalemate, but President Anwar Sadat was able to convince his people otherwise as part of a "grand strategy" that led to his peace initiative with Israel. Instinctively, Sadat grasped an important element of political anger: that the worst of it stems from a profound sense of defeat and humiliation, and that before people can move toward peaceful coexistence with their enemies, they have to conquer those feelings of defeat. For the Egyptians, the only way to erase defeat from their collective memory was through military victory.

Planned in secret, the Egyptians and the Syrians launched a two-pronged surprise attack on Israel. Egyptian forces crossed the Suez Canal and moved into the Sinai Peninsula, while simultaneously the Syrians struck the Golan Heights. Israel was left to defend itself on two fronts at the same time, in what military strategists termed a "pincer movement." Blindsided by their own complacency, as well as by the fact that they were observing Yom Kippur, the holiest day of the Jewish year, Israelis found that they were unable to mobilize quickly and were totally unprepared for the attack.

"What Egyptian Air Force?" an Israeli general was widely quoted as saying, typifying the contempt with which Israeli military officers had mistakenly viewed their adversaries. The Israelis finally fended off their attackers after suffering heavy losses in the first few days of fighting. They were also saved by the United States, which airlifted $2.2 billion in arms and ammunition into Israel. This included "22,000 tons of tanks, artillery, helicopters and ammunition . . . and involved more than 560 sorties . . . the biggest such operation since the airlift to Berlin after the end of World War II."[1] Many Arabs who never forgave the United States for its role in the creation of the state of Israel were doubly incensed by America's intervention.

After the war, the Israelis referred to the Golan Heights "as the only place in the world where you can ski and get shot at—at the same time," leaving cannonballs in the fields below the Golan to remind citizens of the ongoing threat from Syria. As the United States came to Israel's rescue, Syria was "saved from crushing defeat by the intervention of Iraq. Key elements of Syria's physical infrastructure were smashed, and the country would suffer blackouts from the lack of electricity for months after the war."[2]

Finally, a cease-fire was negotiated between the warring parties, but before that, Sadat announced, "No matter what happens in the desert, there has been a victory which cannot be erased. According to any military standard, the Egyptian armed forces have realized a miracle. The wounded nation has restored its honor, and the political map of the Middle East has changed."[3] Sadat originally planned the strike for 1971, but the war between India and Pakistan intervened and upset his plans for world attention. He had hoped for international intervention in the Middle East stalemate—ideally from the United Nations—but his hopes were constantly being dashed by a world divided by the political realities of the Cold War.

As it turned out, the wait was worth it; Sadat preserved his hold on power, declared victory, and revived his economy from the constant drain on it from escalating military expenditures. Most importantly, he counteracted the profound sense of defeat that had gripped Egyptians since Israel's military victory in 1967.

The superiority of the Israeli military machine was regarded as a threat throughout the Arab world. "The depth of bitterness among Muslims," wrote French scholar Gilles Kepel, "was matched only by their sense of powerlessness. . . . Israel's crushing military superiority was so obvious that protests in Cairo and Damascus . . . were immediately dismissed as . . . hot air."[4]

The loss of the Suez Canal and the Sinai were devastating to Egypt, all the more so in view of the importance that land and water have always assumed in the desert cultures of the Middle East. (And, indeed, in other nations as well: the expression "water is life" is often heard from members of the U.S. Congress pleading for dams in arid states like Arizona, New Mexico, and California.)

Military historians have often observed that defeat in one war usually leads to another war, as anger from people who are conquered festers and grows from one year to the next until it explodes. Egypt had been plotting revenge since 1967 and based its military victory on the principle of "tactical surprise." To ward off such a "surprise," Israel constructed a "110-mile fortification known as the Bar-Lev line along the [Suez] Canal . . . to prevent an Egyptian crossing . . . [consisting of] 26 forts and an enormous continuous sand rampart that rose to a height of 75 feet."[5] The "surprise" was that the fortification was permeable: Egyptian forces were able to cut sixty openings in the Bar-Lev line, enabling them to drive five hundred tanks into the Sinai. Although Israel's construction of another fence separating it from the Palestinian territories in 2003 has dramatically reduced suicide bombings, the structure would most likely be as vulnerable to military invasion as the Bar-Lev fortification was in 1973.

Sadat was able to sell the war as a victory, specifically, the "October 6 Victory," naming the war after the day he ordered the air force to attack Israeli air bases. This example of "spin control" underscored Sadat's conviction that it was necessary to convince the citizens of Egypt that they had achieved a military victory before he could move them to consider peace with their ancient enemy. The "victory" has also been taught since 1973 in Egyptian military academies to illustrate the successful technological and military tactics that enabled Egyptian forces to cross the canal in only four hours, and dispel once and for all the myth of Arab backwardness in military campaigns. The sense of intoxication that gripped the country was attributed to a war that "demonstrated that we are a nation with vitality, a nation that did not die," wrote Baha' al-Din, the editor of *Al-Ahram*, the leading Egyptian newspaper. Bookstalls in Cairo carried many books on the war, with titles like *The War of Ramadan*, *The Myth Was Shattered at Noon*, *The Six-Hour War*, *The Crossing*, and *The Air Force Heroes in the War of Ramadan*.

October 6 was also the tenth day of Ramadan, the holiest month in the Muslim year. Muslims fast from dawn to dusk for a whole month to commemorate this holiday; they can eat only after sunset. From 1973 on, Egyptians commemorated the war with symbols of victory. The October Sixth Bridge, for example, crosses the Nile from the Ramses Hilton Hotel to the Ghezira Sporting Club. On June 17, 2002, President Mubarak unveiled a new site dedicated to preserving the memory of the October 6 War through architectural, literary, and artistic exhibits. On the site is a model of the point on the Bar-Lev line that was stormed by the Egyptian armed forces during the war, regarded ever since as a "shining period of Egypt's modern history." A sound and light show dramatizes the collapse of the Bar-Lev line, the capture of the Suez Canal, and how the "Egyptian political leadership could [then] wisely . . . lead the peace march . . . [by] fully regaining the Egyptian national soil and proceeding toward peace, development and prosperity. . . . One of the greatest outcomes of the October War was that it opened by force the way to peace since war was the approach to political settlement."[6]

Many other artistic renderings of the war are also on display. Sculptures include *Statue for the Crossing*, by Gamal as-Seguini, seen in front of Beni Swaif; a large mural painted by the artist Farouq Ibrahim; and *The Boat*, created by a group of young sculptors. Films also commemorate the war, including *Song at the Passage*, *The Road to Eilat*, *The Bullet Is Still in my Pocket*, and many documentaries and other short films with titles like *Men and Ditches*, dealing with dreams of soldiers on the front, and *Tank Hunter*, about an Egyptian soldier who could "single-handedly destroy 20 Israeli tanks."[7]

Sadat also considered it a "victory" that the Egyptian military only lost three hundred soldiers in the first strike, instead of the expected fifty thousand, recalled Amr K. Abdalla, a former prosecutor from Cairo, who is now the dean for academic programs at the University for Peace, in San José, Costa Rica. "I was only eleven years old at the time, and I knew all the planes flying overhead—the MIGs, the U.S. planes. I knew the difference between a MIG 17 or a MIG 21. All of a sudden the military was very important to us. The 1967 war was a punch in the face to Egypt. We had to get the Sinai back. It was a very important issue for us. In 1968 Nasser was criticized by students demonstrating because they thought the government was too lenient toward those who lost the 1967 war. . . . Crossing the canal was a big achievement. (Actually, recent figures report that the Egyptians lost 8,000 soldiers; the Israelis, 2,523.)

"It was regarded as a stalemate, yet it shocked the Israelis," Abdalla continued. "Golda Meir was seen crying on TV. The Americans rescued Israel. The Egyptian people were jubilant. Sadat moved quickly after the war to make peace with Israel. We were tired of war." Sadat's campaign probably should not have shocked the Israelis, since the Egyptians had been conducting air strikes against their country since the end of the Six-Day War.

In retrospect, there was no question that Israel also paid a heavy price financially. "The war had a devastating effect on [the] economy and was followed by savage austerity measures and drastically reduced living standards. For the first time, Israelis witnessed the humiliating spectacle of Israeli prisoners, heads bowed, paraded on Arab television . . . [and] for the first time captured Israeli hardware was exhibited in Cairo."[8] Israel also lost "half of her armored force and nearly one-third of her air force."[9] To put Israel's human losses in perspective, the nation "lost almost three times as many men per capita in nineteen days as did the United States in Vietnam in close to a decade."[10] Israel suffered political turmoil over questions of who was responsible for this debacle for many years after.

Without this "victory," however, Sadat would never have been able to wage peace with Israel four years later. Who can forget his dramatic flight into the heart of Jerusalem on November 19, 1977, his address to the Knesset, and the historic peace settlement with Prime Minister Menachem Begin? It all began with an address by Sadat to the Egyptian parliament on November 9, 1977, announcing that he was ready to go to the "Knesset itself" to argue for peace with Israel. Two weeks later, at Prime Minister Menachem Begin's invitation, Sadat flew to Ben-Gurion Airport and pursued his diplomatic effort. Millions around the world sat riveted to their television screens as they watched the two former enemies clasping hands, the celebrations around the world that followed, and the glimmer of peace that had blossomed into reality only four years after the 1973 war. Although he feared—correctly as it turned out—that he'd be isolated from the rest of the Arab world for his efforts on behalf of peace with Israel, Sadat initially believed that he would change the minds of his fellow Arab leaders by his own example, as well as break the patterns that had for so long prevented all of them from making peace with Israel. And, perhaps most important,

Sadat was forced to rely more on daring and imagination, since Egypt lacked the oil resources that other Middle East countries had long relied upon as a useful bargaining chip with the Soviet Union and the West.

There is no question that Sadat took political risks, but that is what leaders have to do. His grand design worked because he understood that he had to fight for Egypt's national interests, and that the old patterns just didn't work. "The Yom Kippur War was about dignity, about honor," wrote one military analyst at the National Defense University. "It was not against Zionism." Victory was his "ultimate instrument of statecraft."[11]

THE ROLE OF ISLAM

As extra insurance, Sadat peppered his "victory" effort with Islamic symbols. He called the October 6 war a "Holy War," to remind his coreligionists of its divine purpose, and to contrast it with the 1967 war fought by his predecessor, Egyptian president Gamal Abdel Nasser, "in the name of Arab nationalism/socialism."[12] Sadat was also conscious of the widespread feeling by many of his fellow Islamists that the reason for their previous defeats was rooted somewhere in the religion; something "basic must have been wrong, . . . since their [early] history had been conquest and success, never such total defeat." With the demise of Nasserism, the "Arab world groped for an alternative."[13]

In an effort to further distance himself from the Soviet Union and from Nasser, Sadat expelled fifteen thousand Soviet advisers from Egypt in 1972, two years after he took office, explaining that this freed him to pursue the war with Israel. In hindsight, some observers felt that the expulsion of these advisers was a sign of impending war, as well as proof of Sadat's eagerness to show the United States that in contrast with the Nasser years, Egypt was no longer a "client" state of the Soviets. A majority of Egyptians, particularly those who practiced the Muslim faith, opposed the nation's dependence on the Soviet Union, whose leaders they regarded as "godless Communists." Some observers claimed that Nasser was forced to accept Soviet aid for the Aswan Dam after being promised the funds by the World Bank, which had reneged on its commitment under pressure from the United States.

The culture and symbols of Islam infused Sadat's foreign policy at each stage of his "grand design." Before his historic voyage to Israel, Sadat was careful to consult the president of Al-Azhar University, the leading Muslim university in the Middle East, obtaining from a group of Islamic scholars a statement to the effect that "peace with Israel [was] compatible with

An unidentified member of the Jewish community looks at Nazi signs painted on headstones at a Jewish cemetery in Herrlisheim, eastern France.
(AP Photo/Gil Michel)

Supporters of a Pakistani religious party burn a Danish flag altered with a dog cartoon to condemn the publication of cartoons depicting Islamic Prophet Muhammad in a Danish newspaper during a protest rally. Pakistan's ruling party and hardline Islamic groups issued a joint call to hold a nationwide strike to condemn the publication of the cartoons in Western media.
(AP Photo/Shakil Adil)

Miners pan for diamonds near Koidu in the northeast of Sierra Leone near the Guinean border. (AP Photo/Ben Curtis)

President George W. Bush declared the end of major combat in Iraq while aboard the aircraft carrier USS Abraham Lincoln off the California coast May 1, 2003.
(AP Photo/J. Scott Applewhite)

Iraqi women console an elderly lady, whose only son, an Iraqi policeman, was injured during a car bomb explosion, in Baghdad, Iraq, in March 2006.
(AP Photo/Mohammed Hato)

U.S. General Douglas MacArthur, left, watches as the foreign minister Manoru Shigemitsu of Japan signs the surrender document aboard the USS Missouri on Tokyo Bay, Sept. 2, 1945. (AP Photo/C.P. Gorry)

Sen. John McCain, R-Ariz., tells his son Jack about his time as a Vietnam war P.O.W. as they look into a prison cell at the Hoa Lo prison, nick-named "The Hanoi Hilton" by American prisoners, during a visit in April 2000. McCain was a P.O.W. from October 1967 to March 1973 and spent 3 years locked in the Hoa Lo.
(AP Photo/David Guttenfelder, File)

Egyptian President Anwar Sadat, left, U.S. President Jimmy Carter, center, and Israeli Prime Minister Menachem Begin clasp hands on the north lawn of the White House after signing the peace treaty between Egypt and Israel on March 26, 1979. Sadat and Begin were awarded the Nobel Peace Prize for accomplishing peace negotiations in 1978. The rest of the Arab world shunned Sadat, condemning his initiative for peace.
(AP Photo/ Bob Daugherty

Julia Belafonte, left, and her husband Harry Belafonte, second from right, looks on as United Nations Secretary General Kofi Annan, second from left, greets South African Archbishop Desmond Tutu, right, at the United Nations in New York.
(AP Photo/Osamu Honda)

Islam."[14] He called himself the "Believer President" and encouraged the mass media to cover him praying at local mosques. The famous bump on his forehead was known (in a rough translation from the Arabic) as a "raisin," which the devout develop from repeatedly touching their forehead to the floor in prayer.

To further curry favor with the mullahs, Sadat increased Islamic programming in the media and Islamic courses in schools, he built more mosques, and he regularly "employed Islamic rhetoric in his public statements."[15] He also sought the imprimatur of Islam to add legitimacy to the Camp David peace accords as well as to counter his wife's successful incursions into reforming Muslim family law in the interest of women's rights. (These laws were called "Jehan's laws," after Jihan Sadat—also spelled "Jehan"—who promoted these changes.) To the fury of Muslim leaders, Jihan Sadat was instrumental in the passage of two reforms that vastly improved the lives of Egyptian women: one law involved prohibiting men from ejecting their wives (and usually children) from the family home when they divorced them, and the second mandated a complicated electoral change that compelled citizens to vote for at least one woman per each multicandidate district, thus ensuring that one-third of the Egyptian parliament was made up of female representatives.[16]

Considering the outcome, perhaps Sadat made a personal mistake by allowing the Sufi branch of Islam and the Muslim Brotherhood to operate more freely than they had under Nasser, who had suppressed them. Eventually, Sadat—a ruthless dictator despite his benign appearance—began to restrict the activities of these fundamentalist groups, which led their leaders to accuse him of imitating the SAVAK, the hated secret police of Iran. When Sadat offered sanctuary to the Shah of Iran in 1979 after he left the United States, this only reinforced the accusations of his local enemies about the personal friendship of these two leaders, as well as the similarity of their secular and dictatorial methods. It was no coincidence that Sadat was assassinated right after he had begun to clamp down on the fundamentalists. Today, as Egypt attempts some measure of democratization in its elections, the Muslim Brotherhood (although officially banned) remains the only political organization that continues to increase its power.

GEOPOLITICS: THE COLD WAR AND PEACE IN THE MIDDLE EAST

To his people, Sadat was a hero. As morale improved, Sadat's prestige grew. He was no longer referred to in Cairo salons as Nasser's "pet poodle." On the contrary, he was very much his own man, in control of the government, ruling by fiat, and capable of implementing those programs he accorded top priority. The message was that at least two Arab countries, Egypt and Syria, had demonstrated that Israel was not militarily invincible and that the defeats of 1948, 1956, and 1967 were finally "avenged."[17]

But the Middle East doesn't operate in a vacuum. The victims of colonialism, overtaken by Western technology before that, and partitioned without regard for tribe or culture, Arab countries seized on this "victory" with a vengeance, albeit short lived. None of them, however, reckoned with the Cold War and its politics. In late October 1973, the United States stepped in, negotiated a peace settlement, and called the war a "stalemate."

At that point, Sadat swallowed his pride and asked the Soviet Union for help. The Soviet leaders stalled, thinking that the cease-fire negotiated through the United Nations by the U.S. secretary of state, Henry Kissinger, was in effect: on October 22, the UN passed Resolution 338 calling for a temporary cease-fire by all parties within twelve hours. Egypt accepted, but Israel, "alleging Egyptian violations of the cease-fire, completed the encirclement of [Egypt's] . . . Third Army and its supply lines . . . cutting off two divisions and 45,000 men."[18] The Soviets were furious, accusing Kissinger of double-crossing them, and threatening to act alone if the United States didn't cooperate in imposing a cease-fire. The United States took this threat so seriously that the government ordered the country on nuclear alert for the first time since the Cuban missile crisis in 1962. To further complicate matters, the Syrians accused Sadat of disloyalty for failing to inform them that he had accepted the cease-fire.

Two months later, negotiations were resumed that led to a permanent cease-fire, and on January 18, 1974, the first agreement was signed by Golda Meir and Anwar Sadat. A product of Kissinger's famous "shuttle diplomacy," the cease-fire agreement resulted in awarding Israel and Egypt permanent status as the top recipients of U.S. foreign aid—a status that continued for many years afterward. Egypt also gained back the Rudays oil field in western Sinai, and the Israelis secured secret promises from Kissinger to maintain Israel's arms superiority and to continue to refuse to recognize or to negotiate with the PLO, the Palestine Liberation Organization.[19]

The rest of the world—and especially the Western powers—didn't reckon with the politics of oil in the aftermath of the Yom Kippur War. Following the lead of King Faisal of Saudi Arabia, Arab oil producers announced a 5 percent cutback in output to punish Israel's Western allies, to be followed by unspecified reductions every month until Israel withdrew from the occupied territories and restored rights to the Palestinians. After causing huge gas lines and economic turmoil in the West, OPEC (the Organization of the Petroleum Exporting Countries) finally backed down, perhaps because their members needed the revenue as badly as the West needed oil.

A SAD FINALE

Hopes for a permanent peace in the Middle East faded with the demise of those leaders who risked their lives and careers to promote peace. After being returned to office in a close election in 1981, Begin retired two years later. The war had another, more important effect on Israeli politics, and one that affected the policies of all the leaders who followed: it demonstrated that "the state of Israel [was no longer] a safe haven for Jews. Its security [was] precarious, its survival dependent upon the support of a great power."[20]

Sadly, in a serious setback for the Middle East peace process, Anwar Sadat was assassinated on October 6, 1981, at the eighth annual pageant celebrating the very victory that was the cornerstone of his political career. As Sadat proudly saluted his military officers in a live broadcast to the entire nation and in full view of two thousand dignitaries, shocked Egyptians watched their leader gunned down by "at least five bullets and pieces of shrapnel in his chest, thigh, forearm and neck."[21]

The assassins were identified as members of a fundamentalist group called the Organization for Holy War, led by an officer, Lt. Khalid Islambuli. As the shots rang out, Islambuli shouted, "I have killed Pharaoh and I do not fear death."[22] The group was linked to a broader coalition of intelligence officers, civil servants, university professors, students, religious leaders, and radio and television workers who were particularly resentful of Sadat's recent crackdowns on their activities. They also objected to widespread economic inequalities that they charged were exacerbated during his administration, official corruption, his failure to liberate Jerusalem, and the sanctuary he had given to the Shah of Iran. The linkage of Sadat with Pharaoh was particularly significant, since the religious, fundamentalist group responsible for his assassination regarded the Egyptian pharaohs as symbols of the secular power they hated so much.[23]

Many Egyptians also opposed Sadat's "eagerness to bring Western business into Egypt, sometimes at the expense of local entrepreneurs," and resented his closeness to the United States. "In the eyes of the militants, the defiantly proud Egyptians, who once ruled the Mediterranean, were becoming another satellite of the United States."[24]

Also ironic was the role played during the October 6 War by current leaders Egyptian President Hosni Mubarak and Israeli Prime Minister Ariel Sharon. Mubarak was the air force general who led the attack on the Suez and paralyzed Israeli troops in the early hours of the war; Sharon was the major general who led the counterattack and crossed the canal into Egypt, cutting off the Egyptian Third Army. Upholding the tradition of the victory theme, Mubarak in later interviews termed the war "the glorious Ramadan war."[25]

Sadat's assassination was later deemed the result of a massive intelligence failure. It also doomed future overtures to peace with Israel by discouraging other leaders from following his strategy. And it gave more strength to anti-Western forces promoting violence and terrorism as a substitute for peace and security.

NOTES

1. Abraham Rabinovich, *The Yom Kippur War—The Epic Encounter That Transformed the Middle East* (New York: Schocken Books, 2004), 2.

2. Ibid., 457.

3. J. C. Moulton, "The 1973 War: The Egyptian Perspective" (GlobalSecurity.org, 1997).

4. Gilles Kepel, *The War for Muslim Minds: Islam and the West* (Cambridge, MA: Belknap Press, 2004), 20–21.

5. Ahmad Faruqui, "Splitting Egypt from the Arab World—Lessons of the October War," *CounterPunch*, 2003.

6. "Let October 1973 War Be the Last in the Middle East," *Egypt Magazine*, Fall 2002, 5.

7. Ibid., 8.

8. Federal Research Division, U.S. Library of Congress, "The October 1973 War," in *Egypt: A Country Study*, ed. Helen Chapin Metz (Washington, DC: U.S. Library of Congress, 1991), http://countrystudies.us/egypt/41.htm (accessed February 13, 2006).

9. Marcia L. McDermott and Alan W. Wallace, "Anwar Sadat and the 1973 Yom Kippur War Force: Sadat's Ultimate Instrument of Statecraft" (National Defense University, 2000).

10. Rabinovich, *The Yom Kippur War*, 498.

11. McDermott and Wallace, "Anwar Sadat and the 1973 Yom Kippur War Force."

12. John L. Esposito, *The Islamic Threat: Myth or Reality?* (New York: Oxford University Press, 1992), 17.

13. Robin B. Wright, *Sacred Rage: The Wrath of Militant Islam*, updated with new chapters (New York: Simon & Schuster, 2001).

14. Mark Tessler and Jodi Nachtwey, "Islam and Attitudes toward International Con-

flict: Evidence from Survey Research in the Arab World," *Journal of Conflict Resolution* 42, no. 5 (1998): 624.

15. Esposito, "The Islamic Threat," 94.

16. Susan Tolchin and Martin Tolchin, "The Feminist Revolution of Jihan Sadat," *New York Times Magazine*, March 16, 1980.

17. Federal Research Division, U.S. Library of Congress, *The October 1973 War*.

18. Ibid.

19. Ibid.

20. Charles Liebman, "The Myth of Defeat: The Memory of the Yom Kippur War in Israeli Society," *Middle East Studies* 29, no. July (1993): 412.

21. Wright, *Sacred Rage*, 173–77.

22. Esposito, "The Islamic Threat," 95.

23. Milton Viorst, *In the Shadow of the Prophet: The Struggle for the Soul of Islam* (New York: Doubleday/Anchor Books, 1998), 56.

24. Wright, *Sacred Rage*, 173–77.

25. Hamdi Lifti, "Air Force Commander Explains October War Victories," interview with Commander of the Air Force Husni Mubarak, August 23, 1974, in *Al-Mussawar*, in JPRS tables of contents, translations on Near East in Arabic. See also George W. Gawrych, "The Egyptian High Command in the 1973 War," *Armed Forces and Society* 13, no. 4 (1987): 535–59; Haggai Ashad, "War Hailed as Great Military, Political Victory: Suez Crossing was Trump Card in Negotiations," February 1, 1974, in *Davar*, in JPRS tables of contents, translations on Near East in Hebrew; Musa Sabri, "Al-Sadat Reveals New Information on October War," August 3, 1974, in *Akhbar al-Yawm*, in JPRS tables of contents, translations on Near East in Arabic; Muhammad Basha, "Egyptian Forces Claim Smashing Victory in October War," November 17, 1973, in *Al-Ahram*, p. 3, from JPRS tables of contents, translations on Near East in Arabic; Dr. Marwan Asmar, "The Valiant October 6, 1973," Gulf News Research Centre, June 10, 2003, www.aljazeerah.info/Opinion%20editorials/2003%20Editorials/October/6%20 0/The%20Valiant%20October%206%20197320By%20Dr%20Marwan%20Asmar.htm; and "Egypt Marks 27th Anniversary of Ramadan War," www.arabicnews.com/ansub/ Daily/Day/001207/2000720744.html.

7

HEARTS AND MINDS: FOREIGN POLICY AND WORLD ANGER

We make war that we may live in peace.

—Aristotle[1]

PREEMPTIVE WAR: IRAQ

The world has long had a love-hate relationship with the United States. Lately there has been a lot more hate than love, but it wasn't always so. The United States has a singular history of feeding the world's poor, battling tyrants, and rebuilding war-torn nations. No country in the history of the world has been more generous in dealing with defeated enemies. But much of the goodwill engendered by its generosity has been squandered. Simmering hostility has become much more overt with the nation's ill-considered invasion of Iraq, and the occupation that followed. The Iraq invasion brought to a head anti-American feelings that had long festered, largely because of the United States' history of supporting despots, its unstinting support of Israel, and the perception of an American lifestyle that was considered both materialistic and libertine. As the world watched in horror, the United States discovered in Iraq that it was difficult for an occupying power to be both humane and effective, and in many instances, the United States was neither. At the same time, many Americans justifiably felt hurt at not being fully appreciated for their nation's many humanitarian efforts, including aid to earthquake victims in Pakistan in the fall of 2005, and to the tsunami-ravaged towns in Southeast Asia the year before.

The problems stemmed from a difference in perception. While the United States viewed its role in Iraq as fostering democracy, Iraqis and many others in the Middle East viewed the United States as the latest in a long

135

line of Western powers that coveted its oil. Aggravating the problem was the changing nature of war. Difficult to identify, impossible to predict, and without leaders with whom to negotiate, today's enemy is a faceless network of adversaries, instead of nations pitted against each other. Some of these adversaries, operating under the banner of fundamentalist Islam, poured into Iraq from neighboring countries to support insurgent groups that attract their followers with a long list of grievances. There was never a shortage of recruits.

After the tragedy of 9/11, which took the lives of more than three thousand people, mostly Americans, the United States conducted two military operations intended to destroy the major terrorist group that claimed responsibility for demolishing the World Trade Center and a corner of the Pentagon: Al Qaeda. Virtually unknown to most Americans before the attack, Al Qaeda emerged as a highly efficient international organization with units strategically placed around the globe. The group was led by Osama bin Laden, who was believed to be hiding in the impenetrable warren of caves that bordered Pakistan and Afghanistan. A gaunt giant of a man from Saudi Arabia, bin Laden and his billion-dollar fortune were instrumental in financing Al Qaeda and its deadly activities.

The first U.S. action, a land and air assault on Afghanistan, uprooted the governing Taliban—an Islamic fundamentalist group with ties to Al Qaeda—and brought democratic elections to that nation within three years. Ironically, the United States had supported Islamic fundamentalists in their decade-long effort to overthrow Soviet rule, and had during that period funneled money and weapons to bin Laden and his allies.

The second action, the invasion of Iraq, was not as successful and continued far longer than its planners intended. (Although sporadic fighting continued in Afghanistan right up to and following the elections, the Iraqi insurgency was much more violent.) The goals of both invasions were virtually the same: to bring about "regime change" in nations that had long served as launching pads for world terrorism. Following the 9/11 catastrophe, President George W. Bush emphasized that America considered its enemies to be not only the terrorists themselves, but also the nations that harbored them. "Rogue nations" was the original term until the State Department, fearful of offending these nations, changed the name to "nations of concern."

Afghanistan had been notorious for harboring terrorists: evidence of Al Qaeda training camps, for example, was found throughout the mountains of Afghanistan. And even though Pakistan sided with the United States in its war in Afghanistan, its military and intelligence services were known for their divided loyalties; they were, in fact, suspected of protecting bin Laden—a major reason he has eluded capture for so long.

Initially the rationale for invading Iraq was different from the reasons for "regime change" in Afghanistan. President Bush claimed that Iraq had developed weapons of mass destruction (WMD) that threatened to obliterate America and the rest of the world. When subsequent investigations led by the United Nations revealed that no such weapons existed, and the U.S. invasion of Iraq bore this out, the president's reasons changed. The invasion was justified by the president in order to eliminate a brutal dictator, Saddam Hussein; to bring order and democratic government to a nation that had experienced only chaos and widespread violations of human rights; and to show that Western-style democracy could thrive in the Middle East. Regime change was seen as the only way to allow the Iraqi people to flourish in a democratic society, especially since diplomatic sanctions had failed to work. Unspoken was another compelling reason: oil. Iraq was home to the world's second largest reserve of oil fields, which served as the source of much of the world's energy. The oil wells also explained the country's wealth—Saddam Hussein built himself a spate of palaces with his profits from oil revenues—as well as its relative independence from (as it later turned out) weakly monitored United Nations sanctions. These sanctions were mitigated by a program called "Oil for Food," which was designed to control Iraq through diplomatic means and avoid going to war. Stronger than UN sanctions, however, was the ease with which individuals and nations could bypass the rules through the use of complex, multilayered, multinational corporations designed specifically to evade scrutiny.

The war turned out to be enormously unpopular around the world, unleashing a torrent of anger against the United States. At the beginning of the war, the Bush administration failed to enlist the support of many of its traditional allies, including France and Germany, with Great Britain the only major country to join its "Coalition of the Willing"—perhaps better named "Coalition of the Bribed" for the economic strings that bound them to the United States. The coalition included fifty-four countries that supported America's efforts in Iraq, most of them in very limited ways, such as sending only a few dozen soldiers to Iraq. (Of the fifty-seven members of the Organization of Islamic States, only five joined the American effort.) The reluctance of its major allies should have been a warning to the United States, but their concerns were ignored. Secretary of Defense Donald Rumsfeld jeered publicly that France and Germany represented the "Old Europe," an insult that only served to offend and stiffen the spines of those two nations.

If France, Germany, and much of the world refused to join the "Coalition of the Willing," America would go it alone with or without its allies, so certain was the Bush leadership of the rightness of its cause. The war also had the effect of further destabilizing other countries in the Middle East, many of which were already suffering political unrest, such as Jordan and Saudi Arabia. The bombings in Jordan in early November 2005 were yet another sign that the "instability stirred up in Iraq [was affecting] its strategically crucial next-door neighbor."[2] All told, sixty people were killed, including members of a wedding party in the Radisson Hotel. Reasons for increasing instability in Jordan linked to the Iraq war involved the following: (1) the fact that Jordan remained a steadfast ally of the United States, and one of the two Middle Eastern nations to recognize Israel; (2) Iraqi and Palestinian refugees were superheating the economy, as well as taking jobs away from Jordanians; and (3) for security reasons, many U.S. companies and NGOs had relocated their headquarters to Jordan, which they now considered their home base.

The loss of lives, the rise of terrorism in Iraq—many of the insurgent fighters came from other countries in the "neighborhood"—the failure to revive the economy and restore order, and the intractable insurgency that arose after the invasion, all led to worldwide condemnation of the American-led intervention in Iraq.

As the twenty-first century dawned, Americans kept asking themselves the question, Why do "they" hate us so much? By then, "they" meant most of the rest of the world, which had a hard time grappling with Americans' almost messianic view of their own "exceptionalism," which meant not only their right but their obligation to deliver democratic governance to the rest of the world,[3] preferably through persuasion, diplomacy, and economic sanctions, but if all else fails, "preemptive war." A historic change in U.S. policy, "preemptive war" justified the invasion of another country that threatened the United States—in the same way that America had always defended its borders from foreign invaders. Iraq and its "weapons of mass destruction" qualified in the minds of the nation's leaders as legitimate external threats, since biological, chemical, and nuclear weapons could cross borders with far deadlier efficiency than troops.[4] Americans also felt strongly about encouraging the federal government to protect them by being more aggressive and "proactive" in preventing terrorism before it happened. The polls showed that the major reason George W. Bush was reelected in 2004 was his strong leadership in the post-9/11 period, support that quickly declined in the years that followed.

The rest of the world did not share America's ambivalence; quite the contrary. On the eve of the Iraq war, public opinion surveys in countries that were considered traditional U.S. allies—Morocco, Saudi Arabia, and Jordan—showed that less than ten percent of those surveyed expressed a positive view of the United States. A postwar survey by the Pew Research Center for the People and the Press indicated that the "bottom had fallen out of support for America in most of the Muslim world," according to Pakistani journalist Husain Haqqani.[5] In January 2005, the foreign editor at the *New York Times* asked some of the newspaper's far-flung overseas reporters to identify specifically their region's major problems with the United States. In Europe, it was the war in Iraq; China feared economic dependence; Latin Americans wanted more (economic) attention, in other words, more foreign aid; Africa, relief from its foreign debts and fairer trade; Russia, an end to what President Vladimir V. Putin called "meddling" (as in elections in the Ukraine); and the Arab world, some proof that American policies would bring peace and stability to the region.[6] Only in Europe was the war in Iraq a source of animosity toward the United States.

With the end of the Cold War and the emergence of the United States as the world's only superpower, America's every action is intensely scrutinized, its "hegemonic" power is feared, and its standard of living is resented the world over. It is as if all the neighbors are constantly watching one house: the occupants of the house might feel safer, but they resent the lack of privacy all the same.

The world spotlight also beamed its harsh rays on political life, with the 2004 election watched more carefully abroad than any recent presidential election. The day after the election, the London *Daily Mirror*'s page-one headline under a picture of George W. Bush asked, "How Can 59,054,087 people be so *dumb*?"[7] Normally neutral world leaders and erstwhile allies went on record with sharp critiques. "The Americans have voted for a militarised Rambo rather than someone who appeals to their reason," exclaimed Bolaji Akinyemi, a former foreign minister from Nigeria. "Sweden and Europe will continue to criticise Bush the same way as earlier," said the Swedish prime minister, Göran Persson, and a former French foreign minister noted that "almost all nations . . . wanted a change."[8]

Since WMD and foreign terrorists continued to cross borders with impunity, simple logic determined that "preemptive war" would be justified on the grounds of U.S. national security. But America's propensity to thumb its nose at the United Nations—by refusing to pay its dues in a timely way, for example—and to continue to make decisions without its allies, explains to some extent why the nation continues to confront accelerating hostility around the world. It also helps to answer the question of why the outpouring of sympathy for the United States from the tragedy of 9/11 evaporated so quickly.

Many Americans also found the idea of "preventive war" troubling and disagreed with the change of U.S. foreign policy from responding to attacks to anticipating attacks. Indeed, this is why the approval ratings for President George W. Bush's handling of the war fell below 33 percent by the end of 2005. The public no longer felt in imminent danger from either Iraq or Afghanistan; people were secure in the knowledge that gunboats no longer threatened U.S. shores; vast oceans protected the nation on both coasts; and its neighbors to the north and south were counted as "friendly" and, more important, too weak to constitute a physical threat. Other perils could be dispatched with missiles, the major reason for President Ronald Reagan's unwavering support for the "Star Wars" missile defense system.

But terrorists are different: they don't announce themselves in gunboats, they steal airplanes and use them as weapons, and they cross borders with false IDs. The problem is, who decides whether and when to go to war? More specifically, who decides that the United States will go to war? Who decides where the most serious threats are posed? And who decides how serious those threats are to the security of the nation?

THE AWOL CONGRESS

Since World War II, U.S. presidents have exercised the sole power to make critical decisions about external threats to the nation. Indeed, the only reason that "preemptive" war has succeeded without any serious challenges is that the war power has quietly shifted from Congress to the executive branch. Congress has assumed the role of cheerleader, the exact opposite of what is explicitly guaranteed by the Constitution, which grants Congress the sole power to declare war. Nevertheless, the United States has fought five major wars in the last half century: Korea, Vietnam, Afghanistan, and the two wars in Iraq—all of them without a congressional declaration of war.

How did this happen? And how did it happen relatively unnoticed by the American public? All presidents since World War II have justified their seizure of the war power on the grounds that the Constitution grants them the role of commander in chief, and therefore the authority to deploy troops. But neither the president nor the military can move without money, and Congress remains in charge of the country's purse. The war in Vietnam ground to an unsatisfactory halt after ten years of fighting, only after Congress finally began to reduce funding for the war. The United States was soundly defeated in Vietnam, although the end of the war was officially termed a "stalemate."

(It was ever thus. Congress tried to set the tone as early as 1815, when the Barbary pirates threatened American ships, but ended up giving President James Madison the power to repel them. In the early 1900s, Teddy Roosevelt outfoxed the Congress, which had flatly turned down his request to send the navy around the world in a show of force. With just enough money in the Treasury to ship them out, Roosevelt dispatched the ships in 1907 and challenged the legislators either to leave the sailors in Tokyo Bay indefinitely or bring them home—which, of course, they did.)

Prior to 2006, Congress had spent more than $258 billion on the wars in Afghanistan and Iraq, not to mention the human cost of the loss of American and Iraqi lives. The war in Iraq looks eerily like the war in Vietnam, which raged for ten years before ending in inglorious defeat for the United States. AWOL from their constitutional duties then as now, Congress gave President Lyndon Johnson the go-ahead with the dubious Gulf of Tonkin Resolution in 1964. Were the two U.S. destroyers in the Gulf really fired upon by North Vietnamese gunboats? Were the attacks launched in retaliation for U.S. commando raids on the coast of North Vietnam? Were the sailors shooting at flying fish or whales? No matter. If Congress had been forced to declare war rather than simply ratifying Johnson's fait accompli, perhaps the conduct of the war would have been different: either the United States would have tried to win the war early and decisively, or it would have abandoned the effort much sooner. Instead, Congress didn't even begin to withhold funds until the war began to wind down and the protests grew uglier.

Remember President Richard Nixon's 1968 campaign pledge that he had a "secret plan" to end the war? After 58,000 American and 3 million Vietnamese deaths, Congress at long last protested presidential seizure of the war powers with passage of the War Powers Resolution in 1973. The act, too little and too late, reads more like a joke on late-night television than a serious piece of legislation, especially in view of Congress's constitutional powers. It requires the president to inform Congress after taking an aggressive military action that could be considered an act of war, and to terminate hostilities within sixty days unless by then Congress has declared war. Sixty days? In a thermonuclear age?[9] Perhaps the founding fathers were right all along.

Fast forward to the U.S. invasion of Iraq, also led by the president, who argued that Iraq harbored weapons of mass destruction that posed a serious global threat. Although these weapons were never found, the search for them took place over a two-year period and was finally called off on January 13, 2005. Yet public opinion polls in 2004 revealed that many Americans still saw Iraq as a rogue nation that instigated the horror of 9/11, even though no hard evidence has ever emerged linking Iraq to 9/11.[10]

The question of civilian rule of the military also comes into play—another reason Congress supercedes the president in this most important decision of government: waging war. The president may be the commander in chief, but the Founding Fathers purposely put a civilian president in charge of the military and gave a civilian Congress the power to fund the military and to declare war. The nation's first president, George Washington, who bore the rank of general, warned the nation not to succumb to the dangers of foreign entanglements—particularly those necessitating military action. One hundred and seventy years later, another war-hero president and general, Dwight D. Eisenhower, warned of the dangers of allowing the combined efforts of the military-industrial complex to lure America into war.

The war in Iraq has brought a new dimension to the president's power to wage war without Congress. Simple logic defends this view on the grounds that only the president has the intelligence reports and the leadership capacity to act militarily to protect the nation against threats to its security.

The decision to go to war, therefore, depends solely on the president's judgment, leaving Congress far behind as the rubber stamp it has become, that the nation is threatened, that armed assault is the only method to counter that threat, and that the rules that govern the rest of the world do not apply to the world's only superpower.

NATION BUILDING: MACARTHUR'S EXPERIENCE IN JAPAN

As the war in Iraq progressed, it began to bear an uncanny resemblance to the ten-year "quagmire" in Vietnam. In many ways, the American occupation of Iraq provides a sharp contrast with how General Douglas MacArthur led the U.S. occupation of Japan after World War II, compared with how L. Paul Bremer, the U.S. choice to lead the Coalition Provisional Authority, attempted to rebuild Iraq. True, there are many differences between Iraq and Japan, but when MacArthur left Japan, this "American Caesar" enjoyed widespread popularity among the very people his nation had just conquered. In hindsight, his methods were the mirror opposite of the U.S. liberation of Iraq, raising the question of why the nation learned so little in fifty years about what it takes to build a democratic society from the ravages of war.

When MacArthur arrived in Japan six days after the Japanese surrender in August 1945, he brought with him an extensive knowledge and appreciation of the area. He had lived for many years in the Philippines and was a student of Asian history and culture. By contrast, Bremer had only a passing knowledge, and interest, in the Middle East. To his credit, General George Casey, who succeeded General John Abizaid as commander of U.S. forces in Iraq, brought with him two books to read en route from Washington: the Koran and William Manchester's biography of MacArthur, *American Caesar.*

MacArthur viewed his immediate task as rebuilding the nation's infrastructure and feeding the people. "Give me bread or give me bullets," he implored bureaucrats in the Pentagon and the State Department who were holding up his request for 3.5 million tons of food for Japan. Riding through twenty-two miles of "devastation and charred rubble" to get to the American embassy convinced him—as the United States later found out to its great disadvantage in Iraq—that people without work and without food would soon become formidable adversaries.

At first, MacArthur confronted enormous hostility on the part of the Japanese people, as well as from Americans whose memories of Japanese atrocities during World War II were still fresh in their minds. Why should Americans sacrifice tons of food for Japan when their own citizens were still suffering from the war? Similar questions arose with Iraq: why are U.S. lives and resources being poured into a part of the world that has proven so hostile to the nation and its interests?

And why did democratization work in Japan, when it has proven so elusive in Iraq? Of course there are many reasons why a particular strategy works in one part of the world and in one culture, and not in another. MacArthur's military background influenced his understanding of how quickly defeat and humiliation turned to anger, and how that anger could be channeled toward war. He realized very quickly how important it was to break that connection before it impeded Japan's progress toward healing and renewal, and before it could become a threat to the security of the region—and to the United States.

To prepare for the task of leading the Japanese toward democratic government, MacArthur immersed himself in Japanese culture—folklore, ritual, tradition, politics, and economics—a relatively easy task for him since he had lived for so many years in the Far East. Few Westerners have ever come closer than he did to understanding the Japanese mind, and in particular, how important it was for an Asian culture to "save face." Under heavy pressure from fellow Allies, MacArthur managed to resist calls for prosecuting Emperor Hirohito, fearing that "bringing him [Hirohito] to justice would lead to [his] abdication, which, in turn, would bring anarchy, chaos, and guerrilla warfare" to Japan.[11] Instead, MacArthur treated the emperor with respect, called him "Your Majesty," and permitted him to stay in office. At the same time, however, many of Japan's top generals, admirals, and civilians involved in the war machine were found guilty of war crimes and executed. And although MacArthur allowed the emperor many privileges, the general was still responsive to American sensibilities and refused to enter the emperor's palace.

The general's lenient treatment of him led the emperor to return the favor. Hirohito addressed the nation in a radio message, announcing that he was not a god, and that the belief that the emperor was divine was a "false conception" that fed into the similarly false perception that the Japanese people were "superior to other races and fated to rule the world."[12]

The radio address had a devastating impact on the Japanese people; MacArthur later wrote that their world had "crumbled."

The United States also sought to rebuild Iraq's war-torn infrastructure and feed its people, but these efforts were thwarted by an insurgency that appeared to grow stronger by the hour. Unlike MacArthur, who exercised tight control over Japan, the U.S. military in Iraq allowed widespread looting, including of munitions warehouses that armed the insurgents. And although MacArthur immediately asked for food and jobs, American commanders lacked his clout with the American public and their representatives in Congress. Three years into the war in Iraq, Major General Peter Chiarelli, commander of the army's First Cavalry Division in charge of Baghdad, sounded "more like a social worker than a soldier," noted a reporter. "I want jobs in January, not February," the general said. "Let's put people to work. . . . Money is ammunition. Food is ammunition. Health care, education, new schools, fuel, employment and respect are ammunition."[13] In other words, his heart was in the right place, but he lacked the effectiveness to back up his rhetoric. Also, the lack of troop strength made it impossible for the commanders in Iraq to accomplish the same kinds of advances that MacArthur was able to accomplish.

And in contrast to MacArthur's immersion in Japanese culture, few American commanders knew either the Arabic language or the rituals, traditions, politics, and economics of the Middle East. Since the invasion and aftermath in Iraq, there has been some discussion at the top levels of government about introducing more "culture training" for Foreign Service officers and some military officers.

MacArthur disarmed returning Japanese soldiers by getting the enemy's own commanders to ask for their troops' weapons on a "voluntary" basis. In this case, explained MacArthur, it was also a question of "face," although privately he worried that the millions of highly-decorated samurai swords in the soldiers' closets would constitute a potential threat to the U.S. occupying army.[14] Self-government? Democracy? MacArthur ran Japan "through the Emperor, the cabinet, and the Diet [the Japanese legislature] thus preserving the continuum of government." He also encouraged—some say ordered—Japanese officials to pursue reforms—among them women's suffrage, unionization, liberalization of schools and corporations, and income redistribution, as well as political, civil, and religious freedom. All political prisoners were released, torture chambers were destroyed, and freedom of the press allowed newspapers to publish whatever they wished—as long as they didn't provoke "controversy" or criticize MacArthur.[15]

By the time MacArthur left Japan in the late 1940s for his new post in Korea, he had achieved a semblance of order and democratic government. He gave Japan a new constitution that empowered the Diet to make laws, abolished the feudal aristocracy, guaranteed civil liberties and collective bargaining, and established "equality of the sexes" and the rights of habeas corpus. He also implemented some land reform and encouraged the United States to support Japan's bid to become a member of the United Nations.[16] He displayed his contempt for advocates of racial supremacy, was always available to government officials, and (in contrast to the Halliburton experience in Iraq) "sharply limited the amount of profit foreign traders could take out of the country." He also "suspended banks that had financed Nipponese imperialism, seized their assets, and ordered all war profits returned to the government. Then he set about smashing the great monopolies."[17] In addition, unlike the U.S. military in Iraq, MacArthur also had a huge civilian staff whose advice he frequently took, along with the credit.

The contrast between MacArthur's occupation of Japan and the U.S. occupation of Iraq was stark. When L. Paul Bremer, U.S. administrator of the Coalition Provisional Authority (CPA), left Iraq in 2004, the CPA had become a "symbol of American failure." Bremer's pledge to "mount a massive reconstruction effort and create a competent security force" was never fulfilled, and polls of Iraqis showed 85 percent of them expressing a lack of confidence in the CPA.[18] Other polls gave the CPA an even lower approval rating: only from 2 to 8 percent of the Iraqi public expressed confidence in the CPA. A civilian, Bremer lacked MacArthur's clout, which would have made a difference in two major areas: (1) getting the $18.6 billion allocated for Iraq spent fast enough to make a difference, and (2) recruiting senior diplomats with experience in the Arab world instead of relying on "young, inexperienced staffers with Republican Party connections."[19] Would MacArthur have tolerated party hacks around him? Or the budget cutters back home, whom he easily vanquished with threats of "give me bread or give me bullets"? Of course, there are a lot of differences that reached well beyond the stature of MacArthur versus the obscurity of Bremer. Japan was homogeneous, while the new Iraqi government sought to reconcile Sunnis, Shiites, and Kurds, with hundreds of years of disputes among them. Also, MacArthur never faced the kind of insidious guerrilla warfare, financed and supported by neighboring nations, that kept the insurgents in business.

Of course, MacArthur was no saint, and Japan is not Iraq. He was notorious for his outsized ego and dictatorial personality, and he openly defied President Harry S Truman over the president's policy in the Far East.[20] Ultimately fired by President Truman, whose orders he had ignored, MacArthur nevertheless continued to enjoy the support of many members of Congress whom he had carefully cultivated—often in opposition to the president.

But when MacArthur left Japan, that nation was as close to democracy as any nation in the Far East (even though many question today whether one-party rule is really democracy); in fact, a new word was introduced into the Japanese language: *demokrashi*. Ironically, it took a man of monarchical disposition to bring democratic government to a nation that had never before experienced democratic self-rule.

IRAQ AND THE GENEVA CONVENTIONS

It was a short step from "preemptive war" to the stance that the rules of law governing the treatment of prisoners did not apply to the United States. The

Geneva Conventions, argued members of the Bush administration, applied only to prisoners of war, not to "unlawful combatants" such as members of Al Qaeda and the Taliban, who were captured during the wars in Afghanistan and Iraq and held indefinitely at the naval base military prison in Guantanamo Bay, Cuba.

The president and the secretary of defense were clear about their options, which were diametrically opposed to world opinion as well as to recent court decisions and global treaties. A White House press release read, "The President has determined that neither al Qaeda nor Taliban detainees are entitled to prisoner-of-war status under the Geneva Convention Relative to the Treatment of Prisoners of War."[21] That meant that detainees had no legal rights—no right to a lawyer, a trial, or habeas corpus. Secretary of Defense Rumsfeld echoed the president's view: "Iraq's a nation. The United States is a nation. The Geneva Conventions . . . have applied every single day from the outset. . . . The Geneva Conventions do not apply to terrorist organizations such as al-Qaeda."[22] Rumsfeld repeatedly made public his disdain for the Geneva Conventions, according to journalist Seymour Hersh, calling criticism of America's treatment of prisoners "isolated pockets of international hyperventilation."[23] It is ironic that conservatives, who disdain bureaucrats and cast doubt on the government's ability to deliver basic services, had no qualms about allowing the military to decide who was and was not a terrorist, without benefit of a trial.

President Bush eventually reversed himself and said that only Taliban detainees would be accorded rights under the Geneva Conventions, since Afghanistan was a signatory, while Al Qaeda's terrorist network never signed the treaties. His reversal had little practical effect, however, on the treatment of prisoners. The Pentagon will not even release a list of current Guantanamo detainees, the prisoners who did not file lawsuits protesting what they claimed was their illegal detention.

The Bush administration's opposition to prior human rights agreements might have gone unnoticed as mere legal quibbles had the scandal at the prison Abu Ghraib not erupted. Abu Ghraib quickly became a symbol of human rights abuses inflicted against Arabs by the United States as an occupying power; soon afterward, both issues—POWs at Guantanamo and the detainees at Abu Ghraib—became fused in the public's mind. The Abu Ghraib scandal came to light with the publication of unforgettable pictures of American soldiers abusing naked prisoners: one prisoner was held on a leash by a female soldier; other prisoners faced unmuzzled guard dogs; and still others were forced to assume humiliating sexual positions and commit acts of masturbation, homosexuality, and sodomy. Stories and reports emanating from the prison bore witness to punishments of lengthy isolation, beatings, head blows, and other violence, which sometimes led to death. Photos of these atrocities were taken by U.S. soldiers to show the folks back home—as souvenirs from a holiday abroad. Military commanders defended U.S. management of the prison, saying that those soldiers were not typical and that these infringements of the rules were isolated incidents. Later information that revealed earlier protests from the Red Cross to prison commanders suggested that those arguments were false. Pfc. Lynndie England, the twenty-two-year-old soldier who became a symbol of the abuses at Abu Ghraib—she was the woman jeering over a pile of naked detainees—defended her actions stating that she had been ordered to abuse the prisoners. She was later convicted by the military court in late September 2005. Since the scandal at Abu Ghraib, over 130 low-level soldiers have been punished for abusing detainees, but so far no high-ranking officials have been prosecuted.

The abuses at Abu Ghraib, and later at Guantanamo Bay, Cuba, where the Koran was allegedly desecrated by U.S. soldiers, were broadcast around the world. They were particularly offensive to Muslims, who regard nudity and homosexuality as taboo. These abuses were designed to humiliate, to shame, and to deny prisoners their manhood in order to get them to confess to past crimes and future terrorist plans. As expected, reaction around the world, and particularly the Arab world, was savage. *Al-Ahram*, the semiofficial Egyptian daily newspaper, editorialized, "The torturing of Iraqi prisoners explodes the myth that the Americans are engaged in a war of liberation or that the war in Iraq was part of a struggle against terrorism." Columnist Ahmed Barri asked the United States to pull out of Iraq, since "the era of empire is long passed and will never return!"[24]

From the *Jordan Times*: "They [Americans] should never assume the moral high ground of coming to civilize us and teach us how to behave, how to reform, how to promote human rights. . . . Yes, we need all of that, but not from them."[25] Another newspaper published in London that appeared in several Arab capitals, *al-Hayat*, likened the Abu Ghraib scandal to Nazi concentration camps, reminding readers that "the crimes of Auschwitz were committed under the skin of Western civilization and not in the regressive Islamic Middle East."[26]

But there were exceptions. One notable column by Rajeh Khuri, in *al-Nahar*, a daily newspaper in Beirut, reminded readers that similar abuses existed all over the Arab world: "We are concerned with the detention centers and jails filling the tunnels of regimes in the Arab world . . . without one official batting an eyelash."[27] Some observed that even with the abuses, Abu Ghraib was a far more humane prison than it had been under Saddam Hussein.

A few months after the abuses at Abu Ghraib became public, U.S. federal courts weighed into the debate over human rights with two decisions that took the Bush administration to task. Even though both decisions involved cases of detainees at the Guantanamo prison, the judges were probably affected by the conduct of the war in Iraq, the direction of U.S. foreign policy, the lack of accountability on the part of the federal government, general mismanagement, and, most of all, the official White House denouncement of international human rights law.

The first decision, handed down on November 24, 2004, ruled that President Bush had "overstepped his constitutional bounds and improperly pushed aside the Geneva Conventions" by establishing military commissions that tried detainees at Guantanamo naval base as war criminals—"enemy combatants," in their words. Instead, said the court, the detainees should have been treated as prisoners of war, which would have given them the right to be tried in a court of law. These military commissions held hundreds of trials, although only sixty-three cases were brought on behalf of detainees that forced the government to explain (under writs of habeas corpus) why they were being detained. Judge James Robertson, a Clinton appointee, wrote that the government had "asserted a position starkly different from . . . previous conflicts, one that can only weaken the United States' ability to demand application of the Geneva Conventions to Americans captured during armed conflicts abroad."[28] The decision, *Hamdan v. Rumsfeld*, also held that not only did the U.S. position violate human rights, but it was a strategic mistake as well, one that could seriously affect U.S. citizens' ability to receive humane treatment from foreign powers in current and future wars. One year later, Amnesty International, in uncharacteristically strong language, called Guantanamo Bay a "gulag," after the notorious prison camps run by Joseph Stalin in the former Soviet Union.

The Supreme Court also ruled against the Bush administration's actions. In *Hamdi v. Rumsfeld*, a decision handed down a year before *Hamdan*, the Supreme Court ruled that due process "demands that a citizen held in the United States as an enemy combatant be given a meaningful opportunity to contest the factual basis for that detention before a neutral decision-maker,"[29] and that only U.S. courts (and not military commissions) should have the "jurisdiction to consider challenges to the legality of the detention of foreign nationals captured abroad in connection with hostilities and incarcerated at Guantanamo Bay."[30]

The administration had been swift in opposing the lower court's position, claiming that by conferring legal status on members of Al Qaeda under the Geneva Conventions, the judge had put "terrorism on the same legal footing as legitimate methods of waging war."[31] The basis for the Bush administration's position came from a forty-two-page memo, which concluded that "treaties do not protect members of the al Qaeda organization, which as a non–State actor cannot be a party to the international agreements governing war. We further conclude that these treaties do not apply to the Taliban militia."[32] Their basic argument held that since detainees were "stateless," they were not entitled to the protections of the Geneva Conventions.

Bush administration officials were not in total agreement about the memo, widely credited to Alberto R. Gonzales, then White House counsel, and later appointed attorney general in the second Bush administration. Secretary of State Colin Powell objected vigorously to the memo, arguing that it would "reverse over a century of U.S. policy and practice," as well as accelerate all the negative reactions from abroad.[33]

A week before the Senate Judiciary Committee's confirmation hearings of Gonzales for Attorney General, the Bush administration (through the Justice Department) issued another memo repudiating its former memo's rationale of ignoring the Geneva Convention's prohibitions against torture in the name of national security. The new memo reverses that position, stating that (at least in a de jure sense) "torture is abhorrent both to American law and values and to international norms."[34] However, the administration strongly opposed a ban on torture proposed by Senator John McCain (R–AZ) on October 20, 2005, which won overwhelming majority votes in the Senate and in the House.

The Geneva Conventions state unequivocally that POWs must be treated humanely, with full rights to a court-martial if they are accused of war crimes. No American court would approve of proceedings used routinely by military courts that deprive the accused of the right to confront his accusers, as well as examine the evidence against him prior to a trial. Military commissions, on the other hand, can withhold some evidence from a trial if it is labeled "classified," and if it has to remain "classified."[35] The Geneva Conventions also set minimal standards for the treatment of prisoners that are probably more humane than the standards applied in some U.S. prisons today, namely clean and hygienic quarters, adequate food and drinking water, the right to defense counsel, medical and dental services, the provision of interpreters, the separation of civil and criminal detainees, and the separation of young prisoners from adults.[36]

The rules on torture are also very specific, and had they been applied in Iraq, the horrors at Abu Ghraib might never have occurred. They prohibit "outrages upon personal dignity, in particular humiliating and degrading treatment; murder; torture; corporal punishment; mutilation; physical and moral coercion," and, in reaction to Nazi practices, they prohibit "medical or scientific experiments not necessitated by the medical treatment of a person."[37] Also specified are permission for "ministers of religion to give spiritual assistance" and the acceptance of "consignments of books and articles required for religious needs," as well as the "education of children and young people . . . and contacts with family and the outside world."[38] Finally, the International Red Cross and its affiliates were given the role of monitoring the detention of POWs.[39]

Along with its dismissal of the Geneva Conventions, a policy known as "extraordinary rendition" was secretly carried out by the CIA and approved by the government. "Rendition" involved the use of private planes to transport suspected terrorists to countries notorious for allowing torture in their interrogations. Although the practice had gone on for a number of years—no one knows how long—it did not come to light until early in January 2005, when an Australian national born in Egypt sued the U.S. government, alleging that he had been captured by the United States and sent to Egypt, where he was brutally tortured for six months before being returned to the United States.[40]

Another CIA practice linked to rendition involved the use of "black sites": secret prisons set up by the CIA in Guantanamo Bay, Thailand, Romania, and Poland, where Al Qaeda suspects are allegedly held, interrogated, and tortured. Revealed by Dana Priest, the national security reporter at the *Washington Post*, and known only to a handful of members of Congress and intelligence officials, these detention centers drew protests from the European Commission, Denmark, and Great Britain for widespread human rights abuses of prisoners. Many other countries also protested when they found out that the CIA had used their airports for refueling stops on the way to the "black sites." Both Vice President Richard Cheney and CIA director Porter J. Goss asked Congress "to exempt CIA employees from legislation endorsed by ninety senators that would bar cruel and degrading treatment of any prisoner in US custody."[41]

It was also noted in the week before Gonzales's confirmation as attorney general that even though Gonzales was "credited" with authorship of the infamous forty-two-page memo, he benefited from widespread help and support from the administration. (A draft of the memo had circulated to several executive departments and to the vice president's office.) The Justice Department's Office of Legal Counsel, which issued the memo, was "staffed by advocates of expansive executive powers," telling the president in a "classified" memo that his "authority to wage preemptive war against suspected terrorists was virtually unlimited."[42] In effect, the Constitution was rewritten by participants who failed to recognize the necessity of going through the tedious, but legal, amendment process.

Despite the timing and the substance of the revised policy on torture, Gonzales still faced harsh questioning from Democrats as well as Republicans on the Senate Judiciary Committee. He claimed that he couldn't remember his exact role in the drafting of the memo, but promised that he would honor the Geneva Conventions, stating specifically that torture and abuse would not be tolerated in the future.

ACCOUNTABILITY

Since the United States did not recognize the Geneva Conventions in a de facto sense, it came as no surprise that the role of the Red Cross was considerably diminished in the Iraq war theater as well. In May 2004, the *Wall Street Journal* revealed that officials of the Red Cross had lodged complaints against the abuses at Abu Ghraib as early as March 2003 to senior officials of the U.S. Central Command. The organization's periodic complaints of detainee abuse were ignored; in fact, a criminal investigation was not launched at the Pentagon until January 14, 2004, ten months later. Individual soldiers also protested practices at Abu Ghraib—over two hundred complaints were filed from March to May 2003—with one soldier testifying that the abuses inflicted by his fellow Americans at the prison made him "sick to his stomach."[43] Others spoke of prisoners being held in isolation for twenty-three hours a day, with some forced to remain naked or allowed to dress only in women's underwear. One commander, according to observers, "joked" that he had stopped sending "Victoria's Secret catalogues to detainees."[44] In an understatement, the Red Cross accused the military of being "slow to respond."[45]

President George W. Bush's response to Abu Ghraib failed to satisfy his critics. At a joint press conference in early May 2004 with King Abdullah of Jordan, the president said that the Abu Ghraib abuses did not reflect America and that they were a "stain" on the nation. His critics insisted this did not constitute a formal apology, but his words still conveyed a deep sense of distress. "The American people are just as appalled as Iraqis over images broadcast around the world of naked detainees and gloating U.S. soldiers at the prison," he said in an interview with Arab television networks Al-Hurra and Al-Arabiya.[46]

Bush's regrets were undoubtedly sincere, but he still refused to take any blame for the scandal. The question of who was responsible for the abuses at Abu Ghraib did arise but quickly fell without anyone of stature being held accountable. Instead, lower-level soldiers, the ones who were later court-martialed for "conduct unbecoming," suffered demotions in rank, losses of pay, and incarceration. Neither the president nor the secretary of defense claimed responsibility for the abuses at Abu Ghraib; liability instead devolved to the head of the prison, Brigadier General Janis Karpinski, and to other soldiers far down the chain of command. Eventually, seven soldiers were charged: three pled guilty, and four were court-martialed, including Specialist Charles A. Graner Jr., who was found guilty and sentenced to ten years in prison in mid-January 2005.

The scandal did immeasurable damage to the U.S. position in the Middle East and around the world. Many asked how the United States could continue to cling to a morally superior position in its attempt to democratize Iraq if its own political system failed the rudimentary task of managing a prison. Some expected the secretary of defense, Donald Rumsfeld, to resign after Abu Ghraib erupted; he was also expected to resign after his misjudgments about personnel, materiel, and the conduct of the war in Iraq came to light. But he and the president held firm: Rumsfeld remained the only major cabinet member left in office after Bush was reelected in 2004, while the secretaries of state and treasury and the attorney general were replaced. Afterward, it became apparent that both Rumsfeld and Gonzales were doing the bidding of the president in openly defying the Geneva Conventions and stonewalling the scandal at Abu Ghraib. Similarly, other high-ranking players in the Iraq war not only failed to take responsibility but were rewarded. To name a few, George Tenet, the director of the CIA, received the Presidential Medal of Freedom; Rumsfeld's deputy, Paul Wolfowitz, was appointed head of the World Bank; and Condoleezza Rice, the national security adviser to President Bush, became the secretary of state.

Unfortunately, the military was charged with bringing democracy to Iraq despite all advice to the contrary. In hindsight, it appears that the campaign in Iraq should have been mounted as two distinct operations: (1) removing Saddam Hussein and his Ba'ath party from power, and (2) restoring order and introducing democratic government to a nation lacking the political infrastructure to sustain it. U.S. forces succeeded at the first task: invading Iraq and closing down Saddam's government (symbolized by the toppling of his larger-than-life statue); months later, Saddam himself was finally captured and brought to trial—ironically with more rights than the detainees at Guantanamo.

The second task of bringing democracy to Iraq was much more daunting, but was also handed over to the military, with disastrous results, primarily because the task far exceeded the military's training, culture, and mission. There was no question that some military officers could be remarkably effective in teaching democracy; the problem was whether that was the most efficient use of them.

A prime example involving the confusion of missions occurred in the city of Najaf, where intense fighting was precipitated by the closing of a radical Shiite newspaper in Baghdad, *al-Hawza*, whose circulation of ten thousand readers hardly constituted a real threat to anyone. This sparked a revolt led by a Shiite leader, Muqtada al-Sadr, with riots that spread throughout the city of Najaf, as well as in Baghdad and across Shiite areas in central and southern Iraq. The irony was striking: why didn't the U.S. Constitution's First Amendment guarantee of freedom of the press apply to Iraq?

The order to close *al-Hawza* was signed by L. Paul Bremer, the civilian administrator of Iraq, but the U.S military forces were blamed nonetheless, since they were the most visible symbols of the occupation. And although Bremer was a civilian, he controlled a vast military bureaucracy that was in charge of running prisons, supplying electricity, insuring security—in short, all the things ordinarily expected of the public sector. "Armies have always been viewed with suspicion in democratic societies because they are the least democratic of all social institutions," wrote military historian Bryon Farwell.[47] The assault on Fallujah later conducted by the Marines turned out to be the very "opposite of what [they] had come to Iraq to do. Instead of nation-building . . . they were about to lead a theater-level attack on a large urban area." And if they failed to get the message, Lieutenant Brennan Byrne clarified it: "Gents, let me tell you what this is all about. . . . The CG [commanding general] has changed the order from 'capture or kill' the enemy to 'kill or capture.' He wants the emphasis on 'kill.'"[48]

The notion of using the military for the "construction of a democratic society is preposterous," said Eugene Fidell, a well-known attorney special-izing in military law. "The military is not democratic. It is hierarchical. The right to free speech is reduced. They protect our society by undemocratic means."

The military do not expect to be loved; they do not go into a country to win the hearts and minds of its people: their task is to make it more secure and then to turn the task of nation-building over to government agencies trained for that mission. As it turned out, the armed forces faced more enor-mous obstacles than they expected in Iraq, and since Iraqis saw few civilians, they soon began to associate all Americans with the military. "Most of the Americans have a military mindset," said the mayor of Fallujah. "When somebody kicks down a door to search a house, does he expect to be loved?"[49]

Some outspoken members of the military establishment protested the lack of preparation for the war. Army chief of staff Eric K. Shinseki was harshly criticized by Defense Secretary Rumsfeld and his deputy Paul Wolfowitz—then as some say forced into early retirement—for testifying before Congress that several hundred thousand troops would be required for the Iraq war. Retired marine commandant Anthony C. Zinni initially opposed the war on the grounds that U.S. leaders didn't understand the culture of the region, the intelligence was faulty with regard to the immedi-acy of the threat, the task was underestimated, and the United States failed to internationalize the effort. President Bush appointed General Zinni as his envoy in the Middle East peace process, raising the question of why a mili-tary official was in charge of the peace process in the first place. What kind of a signal did this send both to our allies and our enemies?

Closing down a newspaper with opinions unfavorable to the regime in power is common in dictatorships, but the world expects more of the United States. With the military in charge, however, media "control" was a way of life that would never be tolerated at home. The practice of "embedding journalists" was initiated during the first war in Iraq and was justified by the military leadership as a way to give reporters a firsthand look at the action, as well as to protect them. Many journalists wait to be embed-ded, although relatively few are chosen; others cover the war from press releases and official handouts. Many reporters holed up in hotels, while oth-ers worked the streets and tried to get their stories published despite the grave physical dangers confronting them. Today, the practice of embedding is largely accepted by the journalistic community, although it was protested vigorously when it was first initiated as more restrictive than the freedom enjoyed by the press during World War II and the Korea and Vietnam wars.

In a documentary about Al-Jazeera, a television network that claims 40 million viewers and is based in Qatar, editors and reporters at the network accused the United States of bombing the headquarters of Al-Jazeera and Abu Dhabi TV as an attempt to "control the media." Three of their reporters were killed in three separate bombing strikes, alleged the network's leaders; in addition, a five-hundred-pound bomb obliterated Al-Jazeera headquarters in Kabul. Criticized as a mouthpiece for terrorists and banned in several Arab countries (by governments that censor the network's criticism of regime despotism), Al-Jazeera frequently shows graphic pictures of war, including beheadings, bombings, and other horrific images that other networks deem unsuitable for their viewers. Al-Jazeera is also the network of choice for terrorist leaders like bin Laden, who send their warnings in the form of taped messages, all but certain that they will be broadcast. "The message of Al-Jazeera is to wake up society . . . to show that war has a human cost," said Samir Khader, a senior producer. "Supposedly the U.S. is there to democratize . . . but the policy is to shoot anything that is moving." "To tell you the truth," he added sadly, "if I am offered a job with Fox" (a U.S. cable news network), "I'll do it. I'd send my children to America and they would stay there."[50]

Has media coverage been unfair to the military? The administration of George W. Bush believes that the media focuses on the negative in Iraq—the bombings, the lack of infrastructure, the problems of creating a constitution. Media manipulation in wartime has a long history, from the Crimea to Vietnam, and probably back to the Peloponnesian wars as well. Vietnam brought the horrors of war into living rooms around the world as the first war covered by television. The truth helped professionalize journalism; "truth" is no longer necessarily the "first casualty," and since Vietnam, war correspondents are no longer the heroes, propagandists, and mythmakers that journalist Phillip Knightley wrote about. They now question the necessity for war, the reasons that justify it, and, as Khader pointed out, its human costs.[51]

The media also no longer portray wars simply in terms of good and evil. The flip side is that communications technology has exacerbated anger and has made the idea of a lasting peace that much more elusive. The anger in Najaf sparked a nationwide revolt in Iraq against the U.S. occupation that provoked countervailing anger from Americans, many of whom still believed their efforts in Iraq deserved gratitude, not the brutal and violent opposition they encountered. To Americans, the massacre of four security workers in Fallujah was all too reminiscent of the 1993 incident in Mogadishu, Somalia, where a cheering, angry mob dragged the body of an American soldier through the streets. Eleven years later and thousands of miles away, the burned bodies of two American contractors were hung suspended from a bridge that spanned the Euphrates River, while mobs of Iraqis chanted anti-American slogans: "Fallujah is the graveyard of Americans," and "Viva mujahedeen . . . long live the resistance."[52]

Iraq is not the fault of the military, or of military rule. It was civilians who made the decision to go to war; and the military agencies of government turned out to be the only ones capable of ousting Saddam from power. And certainly the military did not expect the terrible insurgency that followed its rapid victory, or the stubborn pockets of resistance erupting throughout the country. Widespread support from the Iraqi population as well as from groups based in surrounding countries made the insurgency that much harder to vanquish. But as the American experience in Iraq showed, the Defense Department is not capable of negotiating peace, restoring order, and resolving issues between local warring factions that have gone on for centuries. Nor should it be.

NEOCOLONIALISM: THE NEW COLD WAR

Abu Ghraib highlighted another problem in U.S. foreign policy: the importance of the past. The war in Iraq produced a great deal of anger against the United States for a number of reasons, chief among them the checkered history of U.S. intervention in the region—intrusions propelled almost exclusively by the Cold War. A controversial article by political scientist Jeane J. Kirkpatrick argued that the United States would be better off allying itself with right-wing dictators who were pro-American than with left-wing revolutionaries who tended to sympathize with the Soviet Union. The article, which came out in 1979 in *Commentary* magazine, had a profound influence on the incoming president, Ronald Reagan, who later appointed Dr. Kirkpatrick ambassador to the United Nations. Although a great deal of controversy swirled around the article, there was always a question of whether Dr. Kirkpatrick was arguing *for* the concept or merely analyzing the realities of U.S. foreign policy heavily influenced by the Cold War.[53]

Whatever the case, the United States quickly became identified with the policy of supporting right-wing dictators throughout the Cold War until the fall of the Berlin Wall, the demise of the Soviet Union, and the rise of global terrorism. Was there a correlation? No doubt there was, in the Middle East, Africa, and Latin America, where Cold War thinking laid the groundwork for twenty-first-century hatreds. Wars also led to other wars. "My original belief—that unresolved anger and bitterness over the war [in Vietnam] had played a part in Iran-Contra . . . was borne out," wrote Robert Timberg in a brilliant book about members of the Reagan administration who were implicated in the Iran-Contra affair.[54]

No better example occurred than in Iran, when in 1953 the CIA helped the British depose a popularly elected, leftist prime minister, Dr. Mohammed Mossadegh. The pattern of future U.S. intervention in the politics of foreign governments began there, and so did so much of the hostility. The coup restored the shah to power, and for the next quarter of a century his brutal regime remained firmly entrenched under the protection of the West. The United States had no tangible interests in Iran, which had been colonized since World War I by the British, yet today the Iranian leaders refer to America, not Great Britain, as "the Great Satan."

Before the coup, Iran looked like a typical colony, with the "mother country" leeching out its natural resources. An overwhelming majority of its people lived in poverty despite the riches produced by the Anglo-Iranian Oil Company (AIOC), most of whose profits went straight back to Great Britain. In 1953, the country elected Dr. Mossadegh, a European-educated lawyer then in his early seventies, who immediately proceeded to nationalize the oil company through the Iranian Parliament. Viewed by the general public as an honest social reformer who wanted to free the peasants from forced labor, Mossadegh also "ordered factory owners to pay benefits to sick and injured workers, established a system of workmen's compensation, and [took] 20 percent of the money landlords received in rent and placed it in a fund to pay for development projects like pest control, rural housing, and public baths."[55]

Poor losers, the British imposed a crushing embargo on Iran that "devastated" its economy, barred other countries from trading with Iran, and denied visas to oil technicians who wanted to work there. Unlike their colonization of India, where they left an industrial and political infrastructure, the British did not train Iranians to manage the oil fields, which accelerated the collapse of the industry. The British government refused—despite U.S. efforts to convince it otherwise—to share its profits fifty-fifty with Iran, preferring instead to sabotage the machines, repossess the company, and get rid of Mossadegh.[56]

The British succeeded in eventually getting American help in their plot to overthrow Mossadegh, a task the United States might not have embarked upon on its own. President Truman opposed the plan; so did President Eisenhower before the Dulles brothers (Allen, director of the CIA, and John Foster, secretary of state) convinced him to back Great Britain. Although America did not have the economic interests that Britain did, Allen and John Foster Dulles were very concerned about the flow of oil and about the possibility that this precious resource would fall into the hands of an unfriendly government. In 2000, a secret CIA history of the coup surfaced that revealed the "inner workings of a plot that set the stage for the Islamic revolution of 1979, and for a generation of anti-American hatred in one of the Middle East's most powerful countries." Neither the CIA nor the British intelligence service liked Mossadegh, who the CIA said was "prone to tears and outbursts." The operation was code-named "TP-Ajax."[57]

As usual, the United States took the lion's share of the blame. "Operation Ajax taught tyrants and aspiring tyrants that the world's most powerful governments were willing to tolerate limitless oppression as long as oppressive regimes were friendly to the West and to Western oil interests."[58] The CIA was then held responsible for many of the coups that followed, including those in Guatemala, Chile, the Congo, Vietnam, the Dominican Republic, and Lebanon. Except for the abortive fiasco at the Bay of Pigs in Cuba, all of the CIA interventions were considered "successful" in a military sense, although they turned "whole regions of the world bitterly against the United States."[59] In Egypt, a visiting American professor was told in the winter of 1979–1980 by Egyptian university officials that she would be "killed" if her lectures were supported by the CIA. At that time, the United States Information Agency (USIA), which had partially funded her program, had changed its name to the International Communications Agency (ICA), which became a source of great confusion around the world, and a good reason for changing the name back to the original shortly afterward.[60]

The CIA's role in Iran brought consequences many years later that also affected U.S. policy toward that nation, showing that the trajectory from humiliation to anger travels both ways. When Iranian "students" took over the U.S. embassy in Tehran following the revolution that deposed the shah and put the Ayatollah Khomeini in power, fifty-two American embassy employees were held hostage for 444 days. This elicited "an intense degree of hostility and a deep sense of powerlessness that Americans had not been used to." Later polls indicated that the "politics of Islam were confused with the politics of Iran, with many Americans unable to imagine relations with an Islamic government in which the United States was not cast in the role of the Great Satan."[61] Add that to the defeats in Vietnam, Nicaragua, and Somalia, and the U.S. "hegemon" began to look very much like an injured dinosaur, unable to counter the politics of defeat and anger to form a new narrative in its foreign policy.

The Cold War wasn't always so "cold." Policy throughout the period encouraged alliances with private armed groups, many of whom did not hesitate to engage in hostilities. The Contras in Nicaragua, for example, caused a great deal of trouble for top officials in the Reagan administration, who recruited private funds for their military operations in direct opposition to the Boland amendment, a congressional directive prohibiting the executive branch from taking such action. Cultural anthropologist Mahmood Mamdani argued that U.S. foreign policy in general (and the CIA in particular) was responsible for the current outbreak of terrorism through its longtime practice of "proxy wars"—undeclared low-level wars that engage incipient terrorists and terrorist groups that later became anti-U.S. militants. As proof of his theory, Mahmoudi recalled the history of U.S. involvement in Afghanistan, calling Osama bin Laden the "best-known CIA terrorist," because of alleged U.S. support of him. Bin Laden, he argued, was typical of an international cadre of uprooted individuals who broke ties with family, friends, and country to join clandestine networks that targeted a specific enemy.[62] The Cold War was indiscriminate: the United States aided the Taliban in Afghanistan, for example, simply because they were fighting the Soviet Union. (A famous picture showed President Jimmy Carter's national security adviser Zbigniew Brzezinski stationed at the Khyber Pass proudly pointing a machine gun at an undefined target.) Which was worse: the Taliban or the Soviet Union? A terrible choice, but not to Afghan women, who were denied medical treatment and education under the Taliban regime.

The CIA was implicated in the Abu Ghraib scandal, along with military intelligence officials and civilian contractors. In a Pentagon report released on August 25, 2004, officers at the agency were accused of "flouting military procedures . . . inside the prison . . . [eroding] the necessity in the minds of soldiers and civilians for them to follow army rules."[63]

More than half a century has passed since the coup against Mossadegh, yet the Iranian government still reacts very strongly to Western intervention of any kind. The government is also resentful that the world did not come to its aid during its long war with Iraq, when Iraq's chemical weapons killed and injured thousands of Iranians. Fully aware that nuclear energy development could be used for military purposes, Iran nevertheless launched a stiff protest against the UN's efforts to regulate its nuclear technology, concealing key "aspects of its nuclear program from the IAEA (International Atomic Energy Agency), [and] conducting secret research that involved procedures potentially useful in making weapons."[64] In light of its recent history, Iran's reaction to the IAEA is typical of some former colonies who find it difficult to reconcile the increasing globalization of commerce with the loss of their hard-won independence.

But the United States did not have any colonies, with the possible exception of its incursions into the Philippines and Cuba, or lead any long, bloody conflicts like the Crusades, or invade countries to steal their natural resources—although some of its multinationals could be said to be colonizers. In fact, the reverse was true: In the 1950s and 1960s, America tried to build alliances in Islamic states to counterbalance "Godless communism and secular Arab nationalism,"[65] regarding Egyptian leader Gamal Abdel Nasser's secular Arab nationalism, for example, as a threat to the West.

Another interesting view argues that the fact that the United States was not an imperialistic power with a tradition of colonial exploitation acted *against* its interests, particularly in its fight against global terror. Without colonial experience, America lacked the networks, the "trained manpower, the generations of friendships, the easy economic ties, the institutional knowledge, the police files. . . ."[66]

Colonial experience might also have helped the United States in Iraq, particularly in recognizing the need for the kind of bureaucratic infrastructure that many imperialist powers left in their wake. Insurgents found fertile ground in Iraq after American leaders decided "that Baath Party members could not participate in the rebuilding of Iraq," in effect, dismantling "much of the state without installing a suitable replacement."[67]

Aside from its Cold War stance, the United States practiced a form of corporate colonialism that perhaps drew more hostility than the more classic types of conquest. This pattern involved supporting the efforts of a company like United Fruit, which dominated the economy and politics of Nicaragua—another form of exploitation to be sure, but not as overt as the dreams of empire that sustained the colonialism of the imperial powers.

RESOURCES

MacArthur was adamant about keeping war profiteers out of Japan. Although this policy reinforced Japan's insularity, it also helped rebuild local industries and perhaps staved off some resentment against its occupiers. In Iraq, the reverse occurred, with disastrous results. The U.S. company Halliburton was the biggest contractor in Iraq, winning more than $17 billion worth of contracts from Great Britain as well as from the United States. The contracts went primarily to rebuild Iraq's infrastructure and to supply the soldiers with food and other supplies. Bechtel was Halliburton's closest competitor, winning only half the contracts awarded to Halliburton. Many of the awards given to smaller companies were noncompetitive.

Halliburton later found itself in a great deal of difficulty with Congress and was accused of overcharging the military and of shoddy management. Representative Henry Waxman (D–CA) criticized the company for operating without much oversight or competition: "This is a great deal for Halliburton and Bechtel, but it's an absolutely horrendous arrangement for the taxpayer," he said.[68] A year later, a UN auditing board found that the United States owed Iraqis $208 million for contracting work in 2003 and 2004, completed by Kellogg, Brown & Root, a subsidiary of Halliburton. The company also fought accusations of political favoritism, since Vice President Dick Cheney had served as CEO of Halliburton for five years prior to running for vice president. Cheney responded that he had no connection with Halliburton except for deferred annual payments scheduled for five years after his departure.

Halliburton countered congressional charges against the company with the argument that it was the only company with the requisite experience: it built airfields in Vietnam, cleared jungles, capped oil wells in Kuwait in 1991, and aided U.S. troops in Somalia in 1992. In 1962, Halliburton merged with Brown & Root, another politically connected company, also based in Texas and tied to former President Lyndon B. Johnson; war protesters called the firm "Burn and Loot."[69] Halliburton lost thirty-five employees to attacks by the insurgents. The U.S. occupation was strongly criticized for awarding so much business to an American company while ignoring local businesses. It was rumored that local businessmen, left out of what they thought would be a competitive bidding process, took out their resentment by helping to fund the insurgency.

A great deal of hope accompanied American troops after the Cold War. Under congressional direction, they were tasked with the job of defense conversion—building roads and schools in a turnabout from their traditional military roles. Even military hardware was affected: breaking news over the five-thousand-dollar coffeepot, nine-hundred-dollar monkey wrench, and other acquisition scandals moved the Pentagon to a policy of "buying off the shelf," putting sole-source contractors out of business.[70]

But old habits die hard, and even though the armed forces were handed a civilian role, they were never quite able to change either their image or their policies. In Iraq, they found they were unable to protect the nation's museums and other cultural treasures, or to defend the cities against widespread looting. Later they faced many bloody battles against Sunni insurgents who fanned out throughout the country in protest against forthcoming elections. Decisive victories eluded them, as they did in Vietnam; how could it be otherwise, when their mandate now included civilian as well as military tasks, and they lacked adequate resources, troops, and supplies to complete either job?

The lack of resources continues to plague other countries, who find the task of democratization virtually impossible in the face of such widespread economic insecurity. A United Nations survey of nineteen thousand Latin Americans in eighteen countries came up with the striking finding that a majority would prefer a dictator over a popularly elected government if that dictator provided jobs and benefits. Democracy appeared to be losing its momentum in Latin America, even though the region had never before experienced "so many countries living under [robust] democratic systems." The problem: since democracy did not bring with it either economic justice or a redistribution of income, there was "little faith in its capacity to improve living conditions." In 2003, "poverty affected 43.9 percent of the population, and extreme poverty 19.4 percent. . . . The region has one of the highest levels of inequality in the world."[71]

Another problem stalling the distribution of resources is corruption, identified by former president Clinton as one of the three "Cs" (corruption, capitalism, and cronyism) impeding progress in the less developed world, and the leading cause of dissatisfaction with the government in Saudi Arabia. In Ilave, Peru, for example, angry citizens burst into a town council meeting, grabbed the mayor, and dragged him through the streets before beating and killing him, so convinced were they that he had used their hard-earned tax dollars to enrich himself instead of for paving the local highway and building a market for vendors.[72]

"Where there's no economy you get anger," said Marian Douglas, an American field worker who had served in Croatia. "These people [the Croatians] have no jobs, no pensions, and no security. It all happened with the fall of Communism," when the state was dismantled without anything left in its stead.

In Iraq, the question of resources continues to plague both nations. As the United States learned in Vietnam, it is hard to conquer an internal group that keeps the local population in check either through terror or persuasion. The Sunni minority always ran the country under Saddam Hussein even though Sunnis made up only 20 percent of the population. The Shiites, suppressed by the Sunnis for hundreds of years, and the Kurds—also brutally suppressed by the Hussein regime—looked forward to gaining power. Local leaders, fearful of violence, asked to postpone the election; Americans kept up the pressure to keep the date intact, perhaps so they could pack up and go home earlier. Other world leaders supported the idea of guaranteeing Sunni representation in the hope of stopping the violence.

In the absence of resources, nothing is accomplished, while life becomes a daily struggle for such basics as food and water. The unemployment rate as high as 60 percent in the Sunni triangle drew constant complaints about the chronic blackouts and the lack of clean water. Since a "jobless man can still make $100 a day by agreeing to plant a roadside bomb or shoot at the Americans," the insurgents have a relatively easy job finding recruits, while "hard-line clerics . . . attack the [U.S.] occupation and are more popular than ever."[73]

HINDSIGHT

Another factor not facing MacArthur was the global reach of modern communications technology. Who can forget the picture of Boris Yeltsin astride a tank, the brutality of government troops in Tiananmen Square, and the cheering crowds chipping away blocks of the Berlin Wall? The forty-eight million citizens of Ukraine overturned their dubious election results in late 2004, also thanks to global technology. The "orange revolution"—named for the orange flags and garments worn by the protesters—captured on television networks around the world helped the Ukrainians to oust the first winner, Prime Minister Viktor Yanukovych, and install his opponent, Viktor Yushchenko, whose swollen, pockmarked face revealed just how dubious this election was: according to his doctors, Yushchenko was poisoned with dioxin by "unknown" sources during the first election campaign.

But the advent of global communications also has a flip side: it brought the U.S. standard of living to the rest of the world. An object of envy, the picture was often inaccurate, since "culture" continues to be America's leading export. "Do you all live like Hollywood stars?" asked a PhD student at Al-Azhar for Girls, a Muslim university in Cairo, "in mansions with pools?" "No," answered her American professor. "I live in a simple, split-level house with three bedrooms. We live better than you do in Egypt, but our movies have given you the wrong impression of the rest of us."[74]

Accompanying the resentment over the U.S. standard of living is the expectation that America can bring about change, particularly in the Middle East. "Thanks to satellite dishes, shortwave radios, and the Internet, Muslims have longingly watched societies from South Africa to some of the former Soviet republics shed odious ideologies and repressive regimes."[75] America is buffeted by two opposing forces: on the one hand, there are still great expectations of the United States; on the other, the nation has become the target of terrorism, hatred, resentment, and global anger.

"One of the elements of anti-Americanism," said author and journalist Alan Riding, "is America's perception that people hate us more than they really do. . . . We must be important if people hate or envy us." Riding also believes that America must change its narrative or its mind-set about foreign policy, suggesting a "second Monroe Doctrine," which incorporates the realities and experiences of the twenty-first century, but is not seen as negatively by the international community.

"The average Mohammed on the street believes that the U.S. is capable of bringing about change," said Husain Haqqani, who traces the beginning of anti-Americanism to U.S. support of the Shah of Iran. But he also thinks that the U.S. is not bringing about change for the good of ordinary citizens. "Anti-Americanism is a substitute for anger against what seems like American insensitivity to ordinary people. The U.S. only relates to the apex of the pyramid—to the power structure." The Arabs "discovered TV years after everyone else," added Samir Khader, of Al-Jazeera. "That feeds their anger." "Do Americans really think that Middle Easterners actually like beheadings, cutting off hands, things like that?" continued Haqqani. "The rest of the world doesn't hate your freedoms. They hate your tendency not to allow those freedoms to exist in their societies," he added, referring to the Cold War policy of supporting dictators over democratic governments if the dictators favored the United States and the democratic governments leaned to the left.

The fall of Communism has changed the nature of the debate in ways that are still too new to assess. The debate is no longer Communism versus the West; instead, there are a myriad of cultures, theories, nationalisms, and civilizations all reaching out in different directions. The Cold War simplified the debate and left long-standing conflicts to fester unresolved. Now that America and the Soviet Union are no longer in direct competition with each other, it is no longer unpatriotic for citizens everywhere to express their anger, to organize for change, and to press for political change.

Thanks also to the speed of global communications, Americans also see Arab governance at close hand, and are frightened at the visual images. American hostages pleading for mercy, the public execution in Saudi Arabia of young lovers, Palestinians dancing in the streets the day after 9/11—all these images are burned into the American psyche, making communication between the two cultures very difficult. One of the major problems with Iraq is that it has no tradition of democracy, nor do any of the other Arab nations surrounding it. Trying to bring democracy to Iraq, according to *New York Times* columnist Thomas L. Friedman, is the only "right argument for the war," not WMD, but helping Iraqis build a decent government "in the heart of the Arab-Muslim world . . . because it is the pathologies and humiliations produced by Arab misgovernance that are the root causes of terrorism and Muslim extremism."[76]

In hindsight, the question arises as to whether wars are inevitable. Defeat sows seeds of anger, which later reappear as full-blown plants. That day can come decades or centuries later, depending on the depth of the conflict, the cultures involved, and the contours of the defeat. Shiites suffered for hundreds of years under Sunni domination—or repression, in their minds; it comes as no surprise that they would not willingly relinquish power to the Sunnis in the Iraqi elections. When Yugoslavia split into six countries after the death of Tito, resentments reappeared that had festered for hundreds of years.

Preemptive war does not fit in with modern realities or modern ideologies. What American leaders need to be preemptive about are the locations of potential conflicts, what to do about them, and how to avoid a "Lone Ranger" stance that alienates the nation's major allies. They also need to ask the hard questions about whether U.S. involvement will make a difference in helping nations govern themselves. Is it within America's capability to control ethnic hatreds that may go back one thousand years or more? And if not, what should its options and strategies be to ensure the best outcomes?

Political anger propels foreign policy—from all sides. The objective is to manage that anger, to foresee where it is most likely to arise next, and to lead by example. No longer can the United States continue to bomb countries into submission the way it has tried to do in Vietnam, Bosnia, Kosovo, and now Iraq. Instead, it must focus more on winning the hearts and minds of beleaguered countries. The new narrative for the United States must lie not in how to make war, but in how to handle peace.

NOTES

1. Aristotle, *Nicomachean Ethics* (Oxford: Clarendon Press, 1908).

2. Jay Solomon, "In Jordan, Bombs Highlight Changes Wrought by War," *Wall Street Journal*, November 10, 2005.

3. See Seymour Martin Lipset, *American Exceptionalism: A Double-Edged Sword* (New York: W. W. Norton, 1997). Lipset's analysis of "exceptionalism," however, is very different from the direction taken in the text.

4. For the often insuperable difficulties of imposing one nation's political and cultural values on another, see Robert W. Merry, *Sands of Empire: Missionary Zeal, American Foreign Policy and the Hazards of Global Ambition* (New York: Simon & Schuster, 2005). See also Robert Kagan, *Of Paradise and Power: America and Europe in the New World Order* (New York: Alfred A. Knopf, 2003).

5. Husain Haqqani, "The American Mongols," *Foreign Policy*, May–June 2003.

6. Roger Cohen, "What the World Wants from America," *New York Times*, January 6, 2005.

7. *Daily Mirror*, "God Help America—The People Have Spoken," November 4, 2004.

8. Ibid.

9. Louis Fisher, *Presidential War Power*, 2nd ed. (Lawrence: University Press of Kansas, 2004). See also Robert C. Byrd, *Losing America: Confronting a Reckless and Arrogant Presidency* (New York: W. W. Norton, 2004); Peter Irons, *War Powers: How the Imperial Presidency Hijacked the Constitution* (New York: Metropolitan Books/Henry Holt, 2005); Emily Bazelon, "Original Intent," *New York Times Book Review*, August 21, 2005, 6; and Susan J. Tolchin, "War—What Is It Good For?: Chicken Congress AWOL from Battle," *Los Angeles Times*, October 9, 2005, 6.

10. Thomas H. Kean and Lee H. Hamilton, *The 9/11 Commission Report*, ed. National Commission on Terrorist Attacks Upon the United States (Washington, DC: 2004).

11. William Manchester, *American Caesar: Douglas MacArthur 1880–1964* (Boston: Little, Brown).

12. Ibid., 459.

13. Ibid., 466.

14. Ibid., 467.

15. Ibid., 498, 10.

16. Ibid., 499, 501, 32.

17. Ibid., 494, 506.

18. Rajiv Chandrasekaran, "A Grand Mission Ends Quietly," *Wall Street Journal*, June 29, 2004.

19. Ibid.

20. Manchester, *American Caesar.*, 459.

21. White House, *Status of Detainees at Guantanamo*, 2002, www.whitehouse.gov/news/releases/2002/02/20020207-12.html (accessed February 13, 2006). As a result of a victory in federal court of a lawsuit brought by the Associated Press, the Pentagon was forced on March 3, 2006 to release the names of hundreds of detainees at the military prison at Guantanamo. The identities of the prisoners was buried in 5,000 pages of transcripts of hearings.

22. Donald Rumsfeld, "The Geneva Convention Does Not Apply to Terrorist Organizations Such as Al-Qaeda," disinfopedia.org, 2004.

23. Seymour Hersh, "Chain of Command," *New Yorker*, May 17, 2004, 41.

24. Nora Boustany, "Arab Opinion Hits US and Hits Home," *Washington Post*, May

7, 2004. See also Reed Brody, *The Road to Abu Ghraib* (Human Rights Watch, June 2004), http://hrw.org/reports/2004/usa0604/ (accessed February 13, 2006).

25. Jenny Booth and Michael Theodoulou, "Bush: US Abusers of Iraqis Will Face Justice," *The Times London*, May 5, 2004.

26. Boustany, "Arab Opinion Hits US and Hits Home."

27. Ibid.

28. Neil Lewis, "Justice Memos Explained How to Skip Prisoner Rights," *New York Times*, May 21, 2004.

29. *Hamdi v. Rumsfeld*, 542 U.S. 507 (2004). Decided on June 28, 2004, the case was argued April 28, 2004. The Hamdan case was argued on April 7, 2005, and decided on July 15, 2005. See *Hamdan v. Rumsfeld*, 415 F.3d 33, 367 U.S.App.D.C. 265.

30. *Shafiq Rasul, et al., Petitioners v. George W. Bush, President of the United States, et al.*, no. 03-334 (2003). See also *Rasul v. Bush*, no. 03-334; *al Odah v. United States*, no. 03-343, 542 U.S.___ (2004) (slip. op.). The specific opinion held that foreign nationals (noncitizens) imprisoned without charge at Guantanamo Bay were entitled to sue in U.S. federal court to challenge their detention.

31. Neil Lewis, "US Judge Halts War-Crime Trial at Guantanamo," *New York Times*, November 9, 2004.

32. Robert Delahunty and John Yoo, "Memorandum for William J. Hayes II, General Counsel, Department of Defense" (Office of the Attorney General, 2002), 1.

33. *Newsweek*, "Bush Had Decided That Geneva Conventions Did Not Apply to Taliban, Al Qaeda by Jan. 2002," May 16, 2004.

34. Neil Lewis, "US Spells Out New Definitions Curbing Torture," *New York Times*, January 1, 2005.

35. Ibid.

36. *Standard Minimum Rules for the Treatment of Prisoners*, Resolution 663 C (XXIV) and 2076 (LXII) (July 31, 1957).

37. *Geneva Convention Relative to the Protection of Civilian Persons in Time of War* (August 12, 1949), 10. See www.unhchr.ch/html/menu3/6/92.htm.

38. Ibid., 28, 32–33.

39. Ibid.

40. Dan Eggen and Dana Priest, "Terror Suspect Alleges Torture," *Washington Post*, January 6, 2005.

41. Dana Priest, "CIA Holds Terror Suspects in Secret Prisons," *Washington Post*, November 2, 2005.

42. Jeffrey Smith and Dan Eggen, "Gonzales Helped Set the Course for Detainees," *Washington Post*, January 5, 2005.

43. David Cloud, "Red Cross Cited Detainee Abuse over a Year Ago," *Wall Street Journal*, May 10, 2004.

44. Greg Jaffe and David S. Cloud, "Officials in Iraq Knew Last Fall of Prison Abuse," *Wall Street Journal*, May 19, 2004.

45. Jaffe and Cloud, "Red Cross Cited Detainee Abuse over a Year Ago." See also Hersh, "Chain of Command"; and Seymour Hersh, "The Gray Zone," *New Yorker*, May 5, 2004.

46. Booth and Theodoulou, "Bush: US Abusers of Iraqis Will Face Justice."

47. Byron Farwell, "Five Days in Fallujah," *Atlantic Monthly*, 2004.

48. Ibid., 118.

49. Ibid.

50. Jehane Noujaim, *Control Room* (Doha: Magnolia Pictures, 2004). See also Martin Smith, "Beyond Baghdad," *Frontline*, PBS, 2004; Robert Kaiser, "A Foreign Policy Fall-

ing Apart," *Washington Post*, May 23, 2004; Anthony Shadid and Sewell Chan, "Protests Unleashed by Cleric Mark a New Front in War," *Washington Post*, April 5, 2003; and Hugh Miles, *Al-Jazeera: The Inside Story of the Arab News Channel That Is Challenging the West* (New York: Grove Press, 2005).

51. Phillip Knightley, *The First Casualty: From the Crimea to Vietnam; The War Correspondent as Hero, Propagandist and Myth Maker* (New York: Harcourt Brace Jovanovich, 1975).

52. Jeffrey Gettleman, "4 from U.S. Killed in Ambush in Iraq; Mob Drags Bodies," *New York Times*, April 1, 2004. See also Patrick Graham, "Beyond Fallujah: A Year with the Iraqi Resistance," *Harper's Magazine*, June 2004.

53. Jeane J. Kirkpatrick and American Enterprise Institute for Public Policy Research, *Dictatorships and Double Standards: Rationalism and Reason in Politics* (New York: Simon & Schuster, 1982). The article in *Commentary* appeared in the November 1979 issue, vol. 68, no. 5.

54. Robert Timberg, *The Nightingale's Song* (New York: Simon & Schuster, 1995).

55. Stephen Kinzer, *All the Shah's Men* (New York: John Wiley & Sons, 2003), 140.

56. Ibid., 88.

57. James Risen, "Secrets of History: The CIA in Iran," *New York Times*, April 16, 2000.

58. Kinzer, *All the Shah's Men*, 204.

59. Ibid.

60. The professor in question was the coauthor, Susan J. Tolchin, who taught at the American University of Cairo in 1979–1980.

61. Fawaz A. Gerges, "Islam and Muslims in the Mind of American Influences on the Making of U.S. Policy," *Journal of Palestine Studies* 2 (1997): 71.

62. Mahmood Mamdani, *Good Muslim, Bad Muslim: America, the Cold War and the Roots of Terror* (New York: Pantheon, 2004).

63. Douglas Jehl, "Some Abu Ghraib Abuses Are Traced to Afghanistan," *New York Times*, August 8, 2004.

64. Robin Wright, "Desire for Nuclear Empowerment a Uniting Factor in Iran," *Washington Post*, November 14, 2004.

65. Gerges, "Islam and Muslims in the Mind of American Influences."

66. Jonathan Randal, *Osama: Making of a Terrorist* (New York: Alfred A. Knopf, 2004), 25.

67. Edward Wong, "Iraq Is a Hub for Terrorism, However You Define It," *New York Times*, June 20, 2004.

68. Jyoti Thottam, "The Master Builder," *Time*, June 7, 2004.

69. For a discussion of the role of Brown and Root in Vietnam, see Martin Tolchin and Susan Tolchin, *To the Victor: Political Patronage from the Clubhouse to the White House* (New York: Random House, 1971).

70. Susan J. Tolchin, "Missiles to Plowshares," *Journal of Socio-Economics* 25, no. 4 (1996).

71. United Nations Development Programme, "Democracy in Latin America: Towards a Citizen's Democracy," 2004.

72. Juan Forero, "Latin American Graft and Poverty Trying Patience with Democracy," *New York Times*, June 24, 2004.

73. Edward Wong, "In Anger, Ordinary Iraqis Are Joining the Insurgency," *New York Times*, June 28, 2004.

74. The professor was the coauthor Susan Tolchin.

75. Robin Wright, "Will the Modern Era Come Undone in Iraq?" *Washington Post*, May 16, 2004.

76. Thomas L. Friedman, "Axis of Appeasement," *New York Times*, March 18, 2003.

8

MEGABYTES OF HATE

As far as recruiting, [the Internet has] been the . . . biggest break-through I've seen in the 30 years I've been involved.

—Don Black, former Grand Dragon of the Ku Klux Klan[1]

U.S. district judge Joan Humphrey Lefkow arrived home from work the evening of March 1, 2005, to make a horrifying discovery. In the basement of her home on Chicago's north side were the bodies of her husband and elderly mother, both fatally shot. Lefkow had been named to the bench by President Bill Clinton in 2000, and shortly thereafter presided over a case brought by an Oregon church that accused a white supremacist group of usurping its trademarked name, Church of the Creator. Lefkow ruled against the church, but her decision was reversed on appeal, and the case was remanded to her court. She had no choice but to order Matthew Hale, the hate group's leader, to remove the name from its websites and printed material or face fines of one thousand dollars a day. Lefkow was immediately vilified by several hate groups, which posted her name, address, and family photographs on their websites.

Lefkow received federal protection until Hale was arrested in 2003 for openly soliciting her murder. Unfortunately for Hale, he had solicited the murder from a federal informer, who taped the conversation. Hale was convicted of the crime in 2004 and spent two years in solitary confinement in Chicago's Metropolitan Correctional Facility before being sentenced in April 2005, by another judge, to forty years in prison. The day after the double murders, Bill White, editor of the *Libertarian Socialist News*, posted an essay on his website that read, "Everyone associated with the Matt Hale trial has deserved assassination for a long time. I don't feel bad that Judge Lefkow's family was murdered today. In fact, when I heard the story, I laughed."[2]

Following a citywide search for the murderer, an unemployed electrician named Bart Ross, whose legal crusade against the government was dismissed by Judge Lefkow, confessed to the murders. He had been hiding in the basement waiting for the judge when he was discovered by the judge's husband and mother, whom he then killed. After writing his confession and sending it to a local TV station, the electrician committed suicide.

Hale's hate site is one of five thousand such sites found on the Internet, according to the Simon Wiesenthal Center. Most of them are American, but foreign sites also have sprung up since 1995, when the first hate sites appeared. Unlike Europe, where hate speech is severely punished by law, the United States has become the fount of hate on the Internet. America's Internet users are protected by the Constitution's First Amendment guarantees of freedom of speech and of the press. As a result, hate groups around the world peddle their wares on websites created and registered in the United States. The ease of instant worldwide communication makes the Internet an ideal tool for terrorists, racists, anti-Semites, homophobes, and other world-class haters who are among the roughly 533 million people who use the Internet, including 149 million Americans.

The murder of Judge Lefkow's husband and mother rekindled a long-standing debate over hate speech. Some seek to criminalize such speech, pointing to the success of European models. They note that hate speech is infectious and often leads to a proliferation of hate that has an especially perfidious influence on unformed youthful minds. Hate speech also often leads to hate crimes, including murder, mayhem, and the destruction and desecration of property.

But others believe that America's founding fathers correctly protected all speech, trusting that democratic values would emerge triumphant from the free exchange of ideas, no matter how revolting or insidious. They also preferred to have such speech out in the open, rather than dangerously bubbling underground where it could explode unannounced at any time. Then again, hate speech can be difficult to define. Who's to say what constitutes hate speech? Some Jews found Philip Roth's novel *Portnoy's Complaint* to be anti-Semitic. Dubliners smashed the printing plates of James Joyce's masterpiece, *Ulysses*, believing that Joyce had mocked and belittled his countrymen. The smearing of elephant dung on a canvas depicting the Virgin Mary was considered by some, including New York mayor Rudolph Giuliani, to be anti-Catholic. Finally, opponents of criminalizing hate speech point out that when speech leads to violence, those actions are punishable under U.S. criminal law, albeit after the fact.

Without question, the Internet has given purveyors of hate speech a global megaphone. "The Internet is an especially inviting host for the virus of hate," noted a technical assistance brief submitted by the group Partners Against Hate. "Whereas hate-mongers once had to stand on street corners and hand out their message of bigotry on mimeographed leaflets, now these extremists have seized new technologies to promote their causes at sites on the World Wide Web and in chat rooms. The Internet has allowed extremists expanded access to a potential audience of millions—including impressionable youth. It has also facilitated communication among like-minded bigots across borders and oceans, and enhances their ability to promote and recruit for their causes anonymously and cheaply."[3]

Even before the founding of the Internet, hate groups utilized technology to communicate their vitriolic messages. In the 1980s, Louis Beam, a leader of the Ku Klux Klan, and neo-Nazi publisher George Dietz created a computerized bulletin board accessible to anyone with a computer, phone line, and modem. The bulletin board, called the Aryan Nation Liberty Net, was designed to recruit young people, raise money, and incite race hatred. In the early 1990s, many bigots united in organized online discussion groups called Usenets (also called Usernets) that were similar to the Aryan Nation Liberty Net but were easily accessible to anyone with Internet access. Don Black, a former Ku Klux Klan leader and convicted felon who learned to use computers during his two years in prison, created one of the earliest hate sites, Stormfront, in 1995. Black was convicted of plotting to invade the Caribbean island of Dominica, overthrow its government, and turn it into a white state. Stormfront served as a virtual supermarket of online hate, with materials that promoted racism and anti-Semitism. One of the world's most visited hate sites, with more than five million hits over the last decade, Stormfront provides links to hundreds of other white supremacist sites.[4]

The United States has become the home of the most virulent sites, whose sponsors are prohibited from using such vitriolic language and symbols in their own countries. "Political repression is increasing in Europe," lamented the website www.Nazi-Lauck-NSDAPAO.com. (The name stands for National Socialist Deutschland Arbeiten [Workers] Party Overseas Organization.) "European webmasters can reduce their risk by moving their websites to the USA. . . . American National Socialists enjoy a measure of political freedom far greater than our comrades in any other country. Failure to effectively use that freedom would be negligent. Irresponsible action that could endanger that freedom would be downright criminal." The site also advises that the charge for hosting a website in the United States is $60 a quarter, with no charge for setting up the site and no domain or registration fees.

THE FRUITS OF INTERNET HATE

Hate-inspired websites have played a major role in promoting some of the worst violence in recent years, including the terrorist attacks on September 11, 2001. U.S. officials found that the 9/11 terrorists used the Internet to exchange thousands of instantaneous, encrypted messages. They were not isolated examples. "People organize terrorist attacks on the Internet," said Peter Bergen, author of *Holy War, Inc.*, a book about Al Qaeda and Osama bin Laden. "Bin Laden puts his messages on the Internet, where they are not subject to editing by Al Jazeera, where he previously sent them."[5] Experts estimate that terrorist groups are responsible for two thousand websites. On the website of its TV station Al-Manar, Hezbollah started the false rumor that four thousand Jews failed to go to work at the World Trade Center on September 11 because they had been forewarned about the attack. (Federal officials also have found it difficult to catch Islamist terrorists planning or coordinating an attack if the terrorists are using encryption.)

"Legal considerations aside, it is nearly impossible from a technological standpoint, to prevent Islamist terrorists from using the Internet," concluded a 2002 study by the Anti-Defamation League. "If they are restricted from one avenue of online communication, they will simply use another."[6]

The Web also has encouraged violence by homegrown terrorists in the United States. In addition to reading *The Turner Diaries*, a book which played a key role in setting up private militias across the United States,[7] Timothy McVeigh, who destroyed the federal building in Oklahoma City and murdered more than three hundred people, including women and children, had been a frequent visitor to the Aryan Nations' website. The site www.aryan-nations.org proclaims, "We have been constantly fighting for our race for over a quarter of a century," and urged its followers to "wake up, join the Aryan Nations in our fight against this evil, Jewish menace." Similarly, the NSDAPAO site declares, "Our Purpose: The defense of the white race. Our goal: White Power. Our Method: Non-violent political activism in countries where our movement is legal." The site was founded by Gerhard Lauck, aka Gary Lauck, who once published Nazi newspapers in ten languages—English, German, Danish, Swedish, Hungarian, Dutch, French, Spanish, Portuguese, and Italian. In 1996, he began serving four years in a German prison for publishing his hate site in a German-language newspaper.

The influence of the Web on emotionally disturbed youth is also a matter of national concern. Jeff Weise, a sixteen-year-old boy of Chippewa descent, shot and killed five students, a teacher, and a security officer in a high school on an Indian reservation in Minnesota in 2005. He was later found to have posted notes on www.nazi.org, a website that condemned the shooting but added that such events were to be expected. On the website, Weise called himself Todesengel, which is German for "Angel of Death." One member told him, "We welcome you, brother."[8]

Later that year, Captain Michael Haworth of the Pinellas Park, Florida, police feared there may have been snipers posted during the controversy over removing the feeding tube of Terri Schiavo. Haworth reported that the police had received numerous threats traced back to inflammatory messages on the Internet. "There are people out there who want to do us some harm," Haworth said. "All you've got to do is look at the web sites."[9]

Benjamin Smith, who went on a racially motivated shooting spree in Illinois and Indiana over the July 4, 1999, weekend, told documentary filmmaker Beverly Peterson, "It wasn't really 'till I got on the Internet, read some literature of these groups that . . . it really all came together. . . . It's a slow, gradual process to become racially conscious." Smith committed suicide before law enforcement officers could arrest him, Another killer, Richard Baumhammers of Pittsburgh, murdered members of several minority groups after reading hate websites. He was convicted of killing five people and sentenced to death. His victims were a Jewish woman, an African-American man, two Asian Americans, and two Native American men. Baumhammer repeatedly visited several hate websites, including Stormfront. David Copeland, a British neo-Nazi, planted nail bombs in a black neighborhood, an East Indian area, and a gay pub in London, killing three people and injuring more than one hundred. He learned how to make the bombs by downloading two books, *The Terrorist Handbook* and *How to Make Bombs: Book Two*. Copeland received six life sentences.[10]

THE MESSAGE

What kind of messages do the hate sites peddle? The logo of www.stormfront.org shows a cross and a circle, with the motto "White Pride World Wide." The site went online initially as a dial-up bulletin board in 1990 and has been on the Web since 1995, claiming to be the first National Socialist website. A typical article, "What Is Racism?" by Thomas Jackson, argues that, "If blacks are equal to whites in every way, what accounts for their poverty, criminality and dissipation? Since any theory of racial differences has been outlawed, the only possible explanation for black failure is White racism. And since blacks are markedly poor, crime-prone and dissipated, America must be racked with pervasive racism. Nothing else could be keeping them in such an abject state."

Jews also are a frequent target. An article posted on www.stormfront.-com titled "Who Rules America?"[11] states, "No king or Pope of old, no conquering general or high priest ever disposed of a power even remotely approaching that of the few dozen men who control America's mass media of news and entertainment. . . . And who are these all-powerful masters of the media? . . . To a very large extent, they are Jews."

Jews are the sole target of www.jewwatch.com, which provides headlines reading, "Breaking News! Israeli spies, AIPAC (Jewish Lobby) Cover-ups" as well as "N.J. Governor Resigns over Gay Affair with Possible Jewish Double Agent." Other articles include "Jewish Hate Groups (ADL, ACLU, JDL, Simon Wiesenthal Center)," "Jewish Controlled Press," "Jewish Banking and Financial Manipulations," and "Zionist Occupied Governments (Z.O.G—USSR, US, Vatican City, W. Germany, Austria, France, U.K., Poland, and Australia, among others)." Ironically, some hate sites were established by Jews, such as www.Gendercentral.com, which was set up by a rabbi who believes that homosexuals are responsible for all the world's ills.

Islamic extremists also use the Web as a way to communicate, coordinate, and raise funds. In planning the 9/11 attacks, Al Qaeda members sent each other thousands of messages in a password-protected section of the Al Neda website. Al Qaeda operatives relied heavily on the Internet for help in planning and coordinating the 9/11 attacks. Some of the hijackers accessed the Internet in public libraries. Encryption programs are a key tool, scrambling messages so that they can only be read by those who have a special decoding key. These programs are available free of charge.

The Internet is fast, cheap, and efficient. As an organizing and operational tool, it is unsurpassed. If one site is closed down, another quickly takes its place, defying government and private agencies that seek to monitor them. But monitoring also has its occasional successes. The creator of www-.stopamerica.org, James Ujaama of Seattle, was indicted by a federal grand jury as a possible Al Qaeda agent, the direct result of a government investigation. He was charged with conspiring to create an Al Qaeda boot camp in rural Oregon and with helping Al Qaeda with computer training and Internet propaganda. In April 2003, Ujaama was sentenced to two years in prison after pleading guilty to conspiracy to support the Taliban and promising to cooperate with ongoing investigations of Islamic terrorists.

The Houston-based www.Ansarnet.com, the website of Al Ansar forum, targeted for death Jeremy Reynalds, a Christian journalist. The Islamic extremists first posted Reynalds's home address so that he might be "visited," according to www.Haganah.us, an Israeli watchdog group. Ansarnet then posted a photograph of Reynalds and a wish that his ribs should be broken. Finally, the site offered prayers to Allah that he should deliver to them Reynalds's "fatty neck," a clear reference to the current practice by terrorists of decapitating their prisoners.

Another Islamic extremist site, Rabat-based www.mawsuat.com, headlined an article, "Hey Kids, Want to Learn How to Assassinate Someone? Let Mawsuat show you how."[12] The site www.Al-fateh.net, one of dozens of websites linked to Hamas, presents its material in comic-book-style material designed to encourage children to engage in jihad. An excerpt: "Our expectations will not be fulfilled until we fight and kill the Jews, especially as we are standing east of the river (Jordan) with the Jews still standing west of the river; and until the rock and the tree says, 'woe Muslim, woe subjects of Allah, here is a Jew (hiding) behind me. Come and kill him.'"

The Palestine Information site, the primary website representing Hamas, is hosted on computers in North Carolina, while a second Hamas site representing the Izzedine-al-Qassam Brigades (the armed wing of Hamas) originates on computers in Houston. The Houston site seeks to recruit suicide bombers and persuade viewers to be martyrs; to take the Koran as a way of life; to be committed to Allah; and to be willing to leave one's wife, parents, and children for the cause. Hamas also uses www.Palestine-info.co.uk, www.hamasonline.org, and www.sabiroon.net, among dozens of other websites.[13] Similar sites are maintained by the Al-Aqsa Martyrs Brigade, Hezbollah, Hizb ut-Tahir, Palestinian Islamic Jihad, Kavkaz, Spawn of Finsbury Park Mosque, Salafyist/Jihadist, Caliphist/Jihadist, and the Popular Front for the Liberation of Palestine. Hizhb'Allah.org, a website of Hezbollah, posted a speech of Hezbollah's secretary general Hassan Nasrallah, regretting that the Shi'ite Ashoura holiday fell "on the 50th anniversary of the bitter and distressing historical catastrophe of the establishment of the state of the grandsons of apes and pigs—the Zionist Jews—on the land of Palestine and Jerusalem." The site reaffirmed the organization's struggle against America, calling it the Great Satan and urging "Death to America."

The site www.Shareeah.org is the website of Spawn, an organization that is located at the Finsbury Park Mosque in London. The site was created by Abu Hamza Al Masri, who is under indictment in the United States and Yemen for terrorist-related activity. Its primary purpose appears to be to encourage participation in Islam-inspired violence. The site serves as a portal for Albanian, Swedish, Bosnian, Arabic, and English terrorist cells. The site www.kataebalaqsa.com is the website of the Palestine Liberation Organization, which was listed by the U.S. State Department as a terrorist organization. A communiqué from the group called the "terrorist" designation "an honor."

The openness of the United States to Internet hatred was exemplified by Orkut, a site created and run by Google that permits people, by invitation only, to join any of a long list of online communities. "Communities have been created around a shared interest in photography, Miles Davis' music and travel to offbeat places," the *New York Times* reported. "A small minority, however, advance a hatred for Jews, blacks or gays, including a 'Death to the Jews' site and a site called 'Death to Blacks.'"[14] One of the communities that advocates death to all black people was founded by Kiarash Poursaleh, who described himself in his profile as an eighteen-year-old living in Tehran. He listed *Mein Kampf* as his favorite book and "shooting" as his favorite sport. Dozens of other English-language communities include the "Adolf Hitler SS Army Fan Club" and an "anti-Jewry" community. Mr. Poursaleh is an equal-opportunity hater. He is also a member of Anti-Arab Iranian, a community with the motto, "We hate Arabs!!! Kill them All!"

In January 2005, Christiano Jorge Santos, a state prosecutor in Sao Paulo, Brazil, began a criminal investigation of some of the hate communities hosted by Orkut. The impetus was the web-incited assault of a thirteen-year-old black child who lives in Sao Paulo. Those behind a Portuguese-language community called "Antiheroes" posted a copy of the child's picture at the site without his knowledge and then invited visitors to "unload all your fury on this poor, innocent little black kid. Click on him and get revenge." Such an action is clearly criminal under Brazilian law, Mr. Santos said. "That's racism," he said, "and in Brazil, racism is a crime." Many of the Orkut hate sites are written in Portuguese, including "I hate Argentines," "I hate Transvestites," and "I hate the Universal Church." An

English-language site, "Anti-Jews," based in Schenectady, New York, has members from Korea and Iran.[15]

THE LAW

Cass R. Sunstein, a law professor at the University of Chicago and author of *Republic.com*,[16] concluded that the Internet inadvertently helped foster extremist views: "The U.S. is pretty unusual providing the broad protection we do to hate speech. In South America, Europe—Google could have problems with many other jurisdictions."[17]

Christopher Wolf, a lawyer who specializes in Internet law, speaks of the dark side of the Internet. "The Internet has become the new frontier in spreading hate," Wolf said, noting that "from web sites spewing vitriolic messages of hate and recruiting the young to join in sponsor's organizations, to technology attacks, to the consummation of terrorist conspiracies through e-mail, bulletin boards, extranets and downloadable files with target coordinates and recipes for bombs, the Internet has become a potent tool for the spread of hate and violence."

Although it is offensive, hateful, and sometimes leads to acts of violence, hate speech is protected by the Constitution. However, when that speech contains a direct, credible threat against an identifiable individual, organization, or institution, it crosses the line and becomes a crime. In other words, hate speech containing criminal threats is not protected by the First Amendment. Nevertheless, the U.S. Congress has historically shunned legislation to curb hate on the Internet, focusing instead on sexually explicit materials; even so, the courts have struck down much of that legislation as violating the First Amendment's guarantee of freedom of speech. But pre-Internet laws prohibiting obscene materials, threats of imminent violence to specific individuals, and violations of civil rights have been applied to the Internet and upheld by the courts.[18]

Lamentably, the growth of the Internet has coincided with a marked increase in hate crimes. Don Black, former Grand Dragon of the Ku Klux Klan, noted that, "as far as recruiting, [the Internet has] been the biggest breakthrough I've seen in the 30 years I've been involved."[19] The leading case of Internet-inspired hate crimes involved an antiabortion website called "The Nuremberg Files," created by Neal Horsley and the American Coalition of Life Activists (ACLA). Similar to the websites that posted the names, addresses, and family photos of Judge Lefkow and her relatives, "The

Nuremberg Files" posted detailed personal information about physicians who performed abortions. This included their photographs, addresses, phone numbers, license plate numbers, Social Security numbers, and the names and birth dates of their spouses and children. The ACLA justified the site as gathering information to be used to prosecute those doctors when abortion became illegal, just as Nazi leaders were prosecuted after World War II. Names listed in plain black letters were of doctors still "working," those printed in gray letters were "wounded," and those whose names were crossed out indicated doctors who had been murdered. The name of Dr. Barnett Slepian, who was murdered in his upstate New York home by a sniper in 1998, was crossed out within hours of his death, indicating that he had become a "fatality."

Planned Parenthood and several doctors sued the site in a civil action, and a federal district court held that the site was a threat to plaintiffs and ordered the website owners to pay plaintiffs $100 million in damages. In 2000, the Ninth Circuit Court of Appeals unanimously reversed the decision, holding that the defendants were protected by the First Amendment. The court concluded that "unless [defendants] threatened that its members would themselves assault the doctors," the site was constitutionally protected. The court later decided to rehear the case en banc (the entire court) and in a reversal decided eight to three that the site was not protected by the First Amendment.[20] The appellate court set the standard: when a reasonable person would believe that a person vilified on a website would be subjected to physical violence, that site is not protected by the First Amendment.

In *United States v. Machado*, federal prosecutors brought a successful case against Richard Machado, a twenty-one-year-old expelled college student who sent a threatening e-mail message to sixty Asian students: "I personally will make it my life career to find and kill everyone of you personally. OK????? That's how determined I am." Machado's first trial ended in a hung jury. A second trial, in 1998, resulted in Machado's conviction, and he was sentenced to one year in prison to be followed by one year of supervised parole. In 1999, the Ninth Circuit Court of Appeals declined to reverse the conviction.[21]

In *State v. Belanger*, Casey Belanger, a nineteen-year-old freshman student at the University of Maine at Orono, posted his résumé on the university's computer network, which included a statement that he "dislike[d] fags." Later that day, he posted a message to student groups affiliated with gay and lesbian causes, which stated (expletives deleted), "I hope that you dies screaming in hell. . . . you'd better watch your . . . back you little . . .

I'm gonna shoot you in the back of the head. . . . die screaming [name of student], burn in hell. [*sic*]" The state attorney general obtained an injunction against Belanger under the Maine Civil Hate Crime Act.[22]

A year later, in 1998, Ryan Wilson, a white supremacist, started a website for his racist organization, ALPHA, depicting a bomb destroying the office of a fair-housing specialist who regularly organized antihate activities. Posted next to her picture, the site stated, "Traitors like this should beware, fir [*sic*] in our day, they will be hung from the neck from the nearest tree or lamp post." Pennsylvania's attorney general obtained an injunction under Pennsylvania's Civil Hate Crimes Act, and the site was removed from the Internet. Finally, in *United States v. Kingman Quon*, a college student sent e-mail messages to hundreds of Hispanic persons across the nation and threatened to "come down and kill" them. Quon pleaded guilty to violating the students' civil rights and received a two-year prison sentence.

Unfortunately, combating online extremism still presents enormous legal and technological problems. Experts maintain that the international nature of the medium and its complexity render legal regulation virtually impossible.

THE ANTIDOTE

The Simon Wiesenthal Center, one of the leading watchdog groups, has prepared an Internet code of ethics for providers. But most providers compared themselves to the telephone company and said they were merely common carriers, no more responsible for what appeared on their sites than telephones were responsible for what was spoken into them. The Simon Wiesenthal Center has nevertheless succeeded in persuading some providers to take down websites, akin to TV stations refusing to run offensive ads, including a complaint against www.NukeIsrael.com, which accused the site of promoting violence. "We sent a letter to the provider, www.Theplanet.-com," recalled Rick Eaton, a Wiesenthal web researcher. "They took it off." Friends of the Wiesenthal Center, in Toronto, Canada, persuaded the Rack Force of Kelowna, B.C., to take down six hate sites as possible violations of Canadian law. The sites were www.shareeah.org, www.Islam-online.net, www.JewstoIslam.com, www.WorldofIslam.us, www.newsuncovered.org, and www.al-thabaat.com.

Another tracker of Internet hate sites is INACH, the International Network Against Cyber Hate. The group was founded jointly in 2002 by the Magenta Foundation, the Dutch Complaints Bureau for Discrimination on the Internet, and by www.Jugendschutz.net in Germany. The network seeks to remove hate sites and prosecute their creators. Since 1997, INACH members were responsible for the removal from the Internet of thousands of hate sites, as well as many successful prosecutions. They often worked together with Internet service providers (ISPs) and NGOs.

Anti-Semitism became the largest category of hate sites in the Netherlands in 2002, with Islamophobia in second place. The number of these complaints increased from 114 in 1997 to 1,496 in 2003, according to the Magenta Foundation and the Complaints Bureau for Discrimination on the Internet. In 2002 and 2003, the bulk of anti-Semitism on the Web no longer came from "classic" neo-Nazi groups, but from Muslim extremist and left-wing Web forums. "The good news is that our removal rate is higher than ever, 95.3%," Magenta and CBDI reported. INACH reported that there were at least eighty Russian websites regularly engaged in racist and anti-Semitic propaganda, while Swedish groups reported about 120 sites.

In France, most of these sites used to be in English, but now sites in the French language have begun to appear. In Belgium, the Correctional Court of Brussels convicted a person for violating the antiracism law and sentenced him to one year in jail. In Antwerp, Belgium, a court convicted two brothers, each of whom received a one-year suspended sentence. In Germany, www.Jugendschutz.net has documented eight hundred new Internet hate sites a year since 2000, sites which agitate against Jews, anti-Fascists, foreigners, blacks, and homosexuals. In Denmark, TDC, the Danish telecom company, has removed hate sites, while Sweden is preparing to prosecute Radio Islam, which has nothing to do with Islam but instead uses its Web page to spread conspiracy theories demonizing Jews. In England, the Internet Watch Foundation focuses on pornography rather than hate sites, but the group has also investigated sites referred to it by citizens and other groups. The British became more rigorous after the London bombings of 2005. Another vigorous tracker is the Southern Poverty Law Center of Montgomery, Alabama. Mark Potok, the group's Web expert, notes that "the only thing that can be done is to complain to the service providers. But now they have their own servers, so there's nothing that can be done to stop them."

In addition to constant vigilance, the antidote to hate speech is to use the Internet to promote tolerance, to educate, to spread positive messages and truthful information, and to facilitate the exchange of ideas. After all, in the final analysis, "the content of the Internet is as diverse as human thought," concluded Supreme Court justice John Paul Stevens.[23]

NOTES

1. Andrew Backover, "Hate Sets up Shop on the Internet," *Denver Post*, November 8, 1999, E1.

2. Jodi Wilgoren, "Shadowed by Threats, Judge Finds New Horror," *New York Times*, March 2, 2005, A1.

3. James E. Kaplan and Margaret P. Moss, "Investigating Hate Crimes on the Internet," eds. Michael L. Lieberman and Stephen Wessler (Partners Against Hate/U.S. Department of Justice, 2003).

4. Ibid.

5. Peter L. Bergen, *Holy War, Inc.: Inside the Secret World of Osama bin Laden* (New York: Free Press, 2001).

6. Anti-Defamation League, "Jihad Online: Islamic Terrorists and the Internet," 2002.

7. Andrew MacDonald, *The Turner Diaries* (Washington, DC: National Alliance, 1978). MacDonald is the pseudonym of William L. Pierce.

8. Shankar Vedantam, "Gunman Found Haven on Nazi Web Site," *Washington Post*, March 23, 2003, A1.

9. Rick Lyman, "As Legal Moves Dwindle in Schiavo Case, the Focus Returns to Governor Bush," *New York Times*, March 26, 2005, A16.

10. Christopher Wolf, "Needed: Diagnostic Tools to Gauge the Full Effect of Online Anti-Semitism and Hate" (paper presented at the Conference of Organization of Security and Cooperation in Europe, Paris, France, June 16, 2004).

11. And bylined "the research staff of *National Vanguard Magazine*."

12. All translations provided by www.haganah.us.

13. Registered at 1010 Wisconsin Avenue, NW, Washington, DC.

14. Gary Rivlin, "Hate Messages on Google Site Draw Concern," *New York Times*, February 7, 2005, C1.

15. Ibid.

16. Cuss Sunstein. *Republic.com* (Princeton, NJ: Princeton University Press, 2001).

17. Rivlin, "Hate Messages on Google Site Draw Concern."

18. Ibid.

19. Backover, "Hate Sets up Shop on the Internet."

20. *Planned Parenthood of the Columbia/Willamette Inc. v. American Coalition of Life Activists*, Civil No. 95-1671-JO (2004).

21. *United States v. Richard Machado*, 195 F.3d 454 (1999).

22. *State of Maine v. Thomas Belanger*, 552 A.2d 27 (1988).

23. *Reno v. ACLU*, 96-511 (1997).

9

THE POLITICS OF HOPE

Peace cannot be kept by force. It can only be kept by understanding.

—Albert Einstein[1]

UGANDA

With raw eggs, twigs, and livestock, Ugandan rebels who cut off the hands, noses, ears, and lips of villagers were being forgiven and welcomed back into their communities. These traditional rites of forgiveness came after a civil war that has lasted nearly two decades and has claimed more than 800,000 lives. The rebels were former followers of Joseph Kony, leader of the Acholi tribe of Northern Uganda, who once was quoted as saying, "If you pick up an arrow against us and we ended up cutting off the hand you used, who is to blame? You report us with your mouth and we cut off your lips, who is to blame? It is you! The Bible says that if your hand, eye or mouth is at fault, it should be cut off."[2]

These reconciliation efforts began when Ugandan President Yoweri Museveni invited the International Criminal Court at The Hague to investigate the war. But when the court announced it was close to issuing arrest warrants, some of the victims appeared expressing their fear that they would be the ones to suffer if the rebel leaders felt cornered. Instead of punishment, they said, they wanted to try "forgiveness." In March 2005, a delegation of tribal leaders led by their chief traveled to The Hague to urge the chief prosecutor not to issue arrest warrants, but instead to allow them to try their traditional methods of reconciliation. "When we talk of arrest warrants it seems so simple," said David Onen Acana II, chief of the Acholi. "But an arrest warrant doesn't mean the war will end."[3]

Consequently, rebels who had killed and maimed, raped and pillaged, underwent a forgiveness ceremony. This involved sticking their bare right feet into freshly cracked eggs, then brushing against a branch of a Pobo tree, after which they were considered symbolically cleansed. After stepping over a pole, they were welcomed back into their villages, where they confessed their misdeeds and made amends by paying the victims' relatives compensation in the form of cows, goats, and sheep.

It is a rite that was used for centuries when the members of one tribe killed members of another, and is now being used to defuse other bloody conflicts, including those in Somalia, Kenya, and Rwanda. In the Darfur region of Sudan, the government, which has been accused of brutality and racism, is now urging reconciliation, although without success so far. South Africa conquered apartheid after pressing for confessions from those who had brutalized the nation's blacks, and then promoting reconciliation.[4]

Time alone can be a factor. In February 2006, Vice Admiral Edward Martin (U.S. Navy, ret.) returned to the infamous "Hanoi Hilton," the prison where he had been imprisoned and tortured for nearly six years—2,066 days, to be exact—during the Vietnam War. He toured the prison, now a museum that emphasizes how the French had imprisoned and tortured Vietnamese "patriots." A section of the prison was devoted to the treatment of American soldiers imprisoned during the Vietnam War. There were photographs of smiling captives, well dressed and well nourished, enjoying good meals and recreational sports.

"They've got to be kidding," the admiral said on entering the American exhibit, which featured photographs of celebrity prisoners John McCain (now a U.S. senator) and Pete Peterson, who became the first U.S. ambassador to Vietnam. The admiral was somewhat emotional after viewing his prison cell, number thirteen. "Did the visit cleanse my soul and give me closure?" he asked rhetorically after the visit. "Nonsense."

But the admiral said he was pleased with the changes he had seen in Vietnam, which has abandoned rigid Communist doctrine and now encourages individual entrepreneurs and foreign investors. "I saw an entirely different country than when I left Vietnam thirty-three years ago," the admiral said. "Vietnam recognized it had to change its ways. They've changed to economic pragmatism. Vietnam has come a long, long way." As a result, he added, "I've changed my position on letting bygones be bygones."

Trade also has brought reconciliation. Although Vietnam, Thailand, Singapore, and Hong Kong were brutally occupied by the Japanese during

World War II, and its citizens have not forgotten the brutality of those occupations, Honda motorbikes and Toyota cars predominate throughout the region.

Pham Hong, a high-ranking official who is head of the Hanoi Chamber of Commerce, noted that three decades after the Vietnam War, "Every major U.S. company was negotiating with Vietnam," hoping to build factories as well as tap into the Vietnamese market. Did the government fear the exploitation of Vietnamese workers? she was asked. "That was in the past," she responded. "U.S. companies in Vietnam now include Ford, Nike, GE, and Hilton and Sheraton hotels."

Forsaking revenge, those who urge forgiveness and reconciliation are seeking to break the cycle of violence that has brutalized their countries for decades. It was a model used by the United States after World War II, and especially by General Douglas MacArthur in Japan. A relatively small number of German and Japanese war criminals were brought before the bar of justice, while most of "Hitler's willing executioners,"[5] as well as most of the Japanese soldiers who tortured and murdered civilians and prisoners of war, were allowed to rebuild their lives. America's forgiveness was underscored by its policy of feeding and rebuilding its vanquished foes.

It took U.S. military might to defeat the Nazis and imperial Japan. The forgiveness and reconciliation came afterward. Since World War II, the United States has been in the vanguard in providing financial aid and human resources to combat poverty and disease around the world. Together with the other industrialized nations of the G-8, America pledged in 2005 to double its aid, reduce trade barriers, cancel the debts of many poverty-stricken nations, and fight the AIDS and malaria epidemics. The initiative was promoted by British prime minister Tony Blair, and approved after fifty-six people were killed in terrorist bombings in London on July 7, 2005. Blair called the aid package an antidote to the terror that had gripped the city. "There is no hope in terrorism nor any future in it worth living," Blair said. "And it is hope that is the alternative to this hatred. So we offer today this contrast with the politics of terror."[6]

Unfortunately, a large percentage of the billions of dollars in aid to less developed countries never reached those who needed it. Instead, the money was seized by corrupt leaders, stowed away in Swiss banks, and used for purchasing foreign real estate and for financing opulent lifestyles around the world. The major challenge today lies in changing political leaders, from those who steal resources and manipulate ancient hatreds, to those who foster reconciliation as a way to change their cultures of revenge to ones of forgiveness.

GOVERNANCE

But with the best will in the world, the international community is helpless to address the problems of poverty, disease, and even brutality in the face of corrupt leaders who have sown and reaped the seeds of hatred to gain power. The same week that the G–8 emptied its pockets, the *Economist* magazine published a series of articles about what was happening in some of the world's worst trouble spots. In each case, bad governance was both the cause and the effect.

- Leaders manipulated their followers into religious, ethnic, and racial frenzies to distract them from their real problems, and to enrich themselves.
- Funds intended to alleviate poverty often ended up either deposited in the numbered accounts of unscrupulous dictators, or in untraceable cash payments to international arms merchants.
- And precious resources were frittered away, leaving ever larger numbers of people in desperate need of food, clean water, shelter, and medicine.

The following are just a few examples of flagrant misgovernance:

The Absence of the Rule of Law

THE TENTH ANNIVERSARY OF
THE MASSACRE AT SREBRENICA

In the worst case of genocide since World War II, eight thousand Muslim men, aged thirteen to seventy-seven, were executed by Serbian forces under the leadership of General Ratko Mladic on July 11, 1995. The killings took place under the umbrella of "ethnic cleansing," the name of an official policy presided over by the notorious Serbian prime minister, Slobodan Milosevic—who remained in office for many years before finally being captured, imprisoned, and tried by the International Criminal Court at The Hague. Srebrenica represented a failure of governance at all levels.[7]

On the national level: for a system that tolerated Milosevic, kept him in office, and allowed him to implement his genocidal policies.

International: for the six hundred Dutch "peacekeepers" who were stationed in Srebrenica by the United Nations but not permitted to prevent the violence from escalating, despite the Bosnians' faith in the UN peace efforts (a sad lesson for the UN, but a lesson that peacekeeping needs to be backed by sufficient force to be taken seriously).

Regional: for the intervention of the North Atlantic Treaty Organization (NATO), too little and too late, earning its widespread reputation of "No Action Talk Only," or "Not At The Office."

And Local: Most of all, the massacre bespoke a failure of local leaders, who stirred up the populace with their very different versions of history, always pitting Serb against Muslim in conflicts that went back centuries.

The False Hope of Elections

ELECTIONS IN THE CONGO

Violence took the place of promised elections, looked forward to by most of the nation's almost fifty-four million people after a brutal civil war in 2003 that killed four million citizens. The peace accord provided for elections, but the "provisional" government of dictator Joseph Kabila, as well as Kabila himself, seemed reluctant to carry out even the basic preliminaries of voter registration. Fearing their strength—and the threat of his own loss at the polls—Kabila also refused to allow opposition parties to operate without government interference.[8]

A classic case of misgovernance all around, the Congo has all the ingredients for a "political culture that is corrupt, mendacious and self-perpetuating." As if that were not bad enough, the future seems hopeless with or without elections, since all the people know of government is a "self-perpetuating machine of immiseration that one Congolese leader after another has operated for over a century"—in fact, since King Leopold II, of Belgium, set the system in motion.[9]

But when elections work, they often stave off just these kinds of conflicts. "Democracy is the worst system," said Winston Churchill, "until you've looked at the alternatives."[10]

Democracy is messy, imperfect, and fraught with scoundrels who all too often win public office over more "virtuous" candidates. And the flow of money? While democracy's advocates would recoil at funneling profits from "blood diamonds" to rebels who cut off people's hands if they dared to vote, the flow of money in the form of campaign contributions still speaks louder than anything else in separating the winners from the losers in the democracies of America, Japan, and Western Europe.

Still, democracies work better because they provide so many outlets: elections that can change leaders; grievance procedures that cool things off; laws that prevent violence and (ideally) deter lesser forms of malfeasance; armies and police forces sufficiently professional to enforce those laws; and the freedom to sound off on a street corner, on the Internet, or in the media. In the face of terrorist threats and outright attacks, Americans and Western Europeans have had second thoughts about the benefits of free speech, with Western Europe taking the lead in limiting Internet use, and the United States following suit with its restrictions on civil liberties in the Patriot and Homeland Security Acts of 2001 and 2002. The United States has also refused to allow suspected terrorists incarcerated at Guantanamo Bay and other military prisons the same legal protections enjoyed by its own citizens and prisoners of war.

Elections hold out the promise of participation—that means real elections, with at least two candidates, and political parties that are free to support any candidate and platform they choose, unencumbered by government interference. In May 2005, President Islam Karimov of Uzbekistan put down a revolt involving armed militants and several thousand civilians in the city of Andijon. After weeks of peaceful demonstrations failed to elicit a response from the government involving the arrest, imprisonment, and trial of twenty-three Uzbek citizens accused of supporting an Islamic terrorist group, a frustrated crowd broke into the prison and freed the twenty-three defendants as well as two thousand other prisoners. The rebels had also taken over a government building before Karimov finally ordered his troops to open fire on the rebels.

If Uzbekistan had benefited from a more open political system, if it had been a genuine democracy instead of a dictatorship, reflected Secretary of State Condoleezza Rice, the nation would have benefited from the kind of built-in pressure valves that could have prevented the rebellion that cost the lives of over five hundred citizens.

At great risk to themselves and their families, a group of laborers in the town of Xizhou, in rural China, chose to go on strike for higher wages during the summer of 2005. No grievance procedure existed that could have acted as a channel for their complaints, leaving them no option but to strike.[11] Still, it was quite daring, since their leaders must have recalled the

Chinese government response to the prodemocracy protest at Tiananmen Square in 1989, when tanks and troops from the People's Liberation Army brutally quelled the disturbance. Estimates of those killed ranged from four hundred to eight hundred; another seven to ten thousand people were injured. After the demonstration, the government imprisoned many of the dissidents and their leaders.

In both Uzbekistan and China, brutal dictatorships prohibited the existence of outlets, each failing to appreciate how well outlets worked in democracies. As legitimate channels of citizen discontent, they absorb anger, resolve disputes before they erupt, and ultimately avoid the kind of violent confrontation so common throughout history. Gunning down protests may work for a while, but the anger that emanated from Tiananmen Square and Andijon will fester and reemerge at a future date, perhaps in an even more lethal and virulent form, as protesters wait patiently for another day.

The restlessness indicated by the pockets of rebellion in China and Uzbekistan has met with more success in other regions of the world where democracy appears to be taking hold. The "rose revolution" in Georgia, the "orange revolution" in the Ukraine, and the "cedar revolution" in Lebanon all point to the emergence of some form of electoral democracy. Even in South America, the spirit of reform has taken hold, as it has in Iran, and in Iraq, where over 60 percent of the people came out to vote in the elections of January and December 2005, despite the violent threats from terrorists attached to the Sunni insurgency. Several years before, Afghan citizens also defied local terrorists to vote, so happy were they to jettison the yoke of Taliban governance. President George W. Bush stood at the site of the "rose revolution" in Freedom Square in Tbilisi, Georgia, to laud that nation's achievements in democracy. The first American president to visit the nation of Georgia, Bush said that "standing in front of 150,000 people who love freedom was a fantastic experience."[12] Even more unbelievable was the location: Tbilisi, a town where former Soviet dictator Joseph Stalin had studied, near his birthplace in Gori, Georgia.

Why now? Why is democracy breaking out in the unlikeliest places? The communications revolution has enabled citizens of war-weary nations to see that many countries change their leaders through orderly elections instead of palace coups, nepotism, divine right, or military prowess. The United States has always professed to encourage the emergence of democracies, although its actual role has been decidedly mixed. The European Community has also put its oar in the water and barred entry to nations that have not progressed politically. The bright side of global communications is that people today are better educated, and their disgust with cronyism, official corruption, and regressive economic policies has encouraged them to force change—primarily through the ballot box.

But elections alone are not the answer. India prides itself on being a democratic nation, with a big, boisterous electoral system, a functioning legislature, and a free press. Yet violence unpunished by the law still occurs in cases of bride burning that go unprosecuted, as well as frequent and violent incidents between Hindus and Muslims. Nor is there a viable system of progressive taxation, judging from the extreme poverty suffered by a vast majority of its population. The former Soviet Union held elections, but the voters had no choice; how could they with only one candidate on the ballot? Even Japan, celebrated as one of the few functioning democracies in the Far East, still functions under one-party rule.

Elections have to be followed by fair treatment of minorities, the enforcement of laws, equitable redistribution of resources, and the guarantee of open channels of communication. As one Egyptian observed, referring to the Mubarak government's suppression of an opposition candidate: "We don't want democracy. The Muslim Brotherhood is the best-organized group in Egypt. If there are open elections, they will [eventually] win a majority of seats, and we will have another Iran or Afghanistan on our hands." The Muslim Brotherhood has already achieved dramatic electoral gains in Egypt, despite the government's efforts to curb its activities.

Phony Land Redistribution

LAND REFORM IN SOUTH AFRICA

Despite its recent successes, mounting frustration with its efforts at land reform may force the South African government to follow the lead of neighboring Zimbabwe and begin expropriating land from white farmers and handing it over to black owners. So far, only 3 percent of the land has been redistributed, breaking the government's promise of 30 percent. The land distribution was designed to relieve overcrowding in the nation's towns and cities and to offset the effects of South Africa's infamous Land Act of 1913, which reserved 87 percent of the land for the white minority.[13] This is also a good example of why the rule of law alone is no guarantee of good government: many laws, like the Land Act in South Africa, perpetuate racism, while others impede religious freedom, stifle free speech, limit representation, and curtail women's rights—the list goes on.

RAMPANT CORRUPTION

Corruption is at home everywhere in the Third World: Asia, Africa, Latin America, and the Middle East. Controlling corruption has proven virtually impossible, except in a couple of small, relatively insignificant cases. In Nigeria, for example, *bakshish* is a way of life; even some of the guidebooks spell out the cost (about a hundred dollars) to navigate the airport in Lagos and exit the country. Today, warning signs in U.S. airports alert travelers to the dangers of going through Nigeria's Murtala Muhammed Airport, in the hope of discouraging travelers from venturing there. American companies have long complained how the Foreign Corrupt Practices Act of 1977 has prevented them from competing for business against European and Japanese companies, whose governments have resisted imposing legal restrictions against bribery in international business.

Corruption spans continents. In Rio de Janeiro, a congressional investigation found that the governing Workers' Party paid dozens of deputies from other parties a $12,500 monthly stipend for their support.[14] In Turkey, the government has a hard time controlling police corruption, evidenced by a recent case involving the death in a car crash of a senior Turkish police officer, a mobster and his "lady friend," and a Kurdish legislator. Many believe that "graft" remains the biggest obstacle to Turkish membership in the European Union, and not—as usually thought—religious fundamentalism. Specifically, critics condemn the Turkish government's inability to eliminate bribery as a way of life in many quarters, despite the numerous promises of that nation's political leaders and their ironically named Justice and Development Party. They point to a proposed antigraft law that seems to have been permanently shelved. The party has also failed to lift the immunity of sixty members of parliament charged with corruption, which goes right to the top: Prime Minister Recep Tayyip Erdogan was forced after a public scandal to return a thirty-thousand-dollar necklace to the businessman who gave it to him for his wife, Emine.[15]

WARS AND GOVERNANCE

How different is the nature of war today than it was in the past? The battles, the armor, and the uniforms all may be different, but the causes remain the same. They all originate with geopolitical conflicts, cultural differences, or what can be called just plain "spin"—where clashes are escalated by leaders who then ride them to political victory. The insurgencies in Iraq and Vietnam, for example, strangely resembled the American Revolutionary War, where an indigenous army tried to boot out a foreign power with the advantage going to the native fighters, who knew the terrain and were willing to die for their cause.

The debate over whether wars are "clashes of civilizations," as political scientist Samuel Huntington has eloquently argued;[16] interethnic, as others believe; or intracivilizational, has become more than just an interesting academic exercise. It has forced national leaders to anticipate wars, rather than react to them. Recent history reveals examples of all three theories, and the eruption of all matter of wars has, unfortunately, proven them all correct. The war in Iraq is a good example of Huntington's clash of civilizations— the West against the Muslim world; the war in Iraq looks also like an intrareligious dispute, although most non-Muslims can't tell you what the difference is between Sunnis and Shiites. In Darfur, a region in western Sudan, Muslim troops are fighting Muslim villagers in a tragic example of intracivilizational war. Geopolitical factors propel China's ongoing war against Tibet, while interethnic issues occupy the long-standing fight between Greece and Turkey over Cyprus. Some interethnic conflicts have been blamed on irresponsible colonization by countries such as Belgium, which left the former Belgian Congo in such a shambles that the groundwork for the devastating war between the Hutus and Tutsis (resulting in the death of almost a million people) was inevitable. Iran, which calls itself an Islamic republic, sided with Christian Armenia, not Islamic Azerbaijan, in the war between Armenia and Azerbaijan. "All but five of the twenty-three wars being fought in 1994 [were] based on communal rivalries," wrote Ted Robert Gurr, a leading scholar of conflict. "About three-quarters of the world's refugees, estimated at nearly 27 million people, are in flight from or have been displaced by these and other ethnic conflicts. Eight of the United Nations' thirteen peacekeeping operations are aimed at separating the protagonists in ethnopolitical conflicts."[17]

At the heart of all of these conflicts is "governance," a word that means different things to different cultures. Many of the world's nations today function in a state of near anarchy, such as Pakistan, Colombia, Albania, the former Soviet republics, and much of Africa and South Asia. That means that their leaders cannot even provide what has been defined as the most basic function of government: "control of criminal violence."[18] Lesser roles of government include the allocation of resources, or feeding the people, which ranks as a higher priority in most societies than democratic government. Taking the place of the nation-state, to some degree, are other "governance" structures: the increased globalization of organized crime has weakened the police function of the state, the global economy has placed the market above other social considerations, and the thriving international business of exporting weapons has changed the nature of war. Even social welfare, once the exclusive purview of governments, has been replaced in some societies with private philanthropy. In the Arab world, for example, fundamentalist groups often provide welfare that secular governments have neglected; some of these "charities" have been revealed as fronts for terrorist activities.

How can the world assuage global anger to avoid future wars? Is conflict inevitable, and what should be the role of the world's only superpower? Few nation-states today are either homogeneous or strong enough to withstand the inevitable cultural clashes that arise with very little provocation. Some guidelines for avoiding conflict involve the following:

- A degree of modesty: knowing where and when to get involved.
- Anticipation: heading off conflict before it escalates into war. Creating systems for gathering information about "impending communal . . . and humanitarian crises."[19]
- Involving the international community: whenever possible. Or exercise patience until the major powers join the campaign.
- Soft-pedal the military: augment the military presence with civilian agencies and advisers, but make sure they coordinate with each other.
- Develop a new narrative about American foreign policy: talk about democracy, but respect indigenous cultures and their ability to transform their political system.
- Provide mediation services: in hopes of avoiding bloodshed.
- Try to develop an ideology of multiculturalism: inculcate the importance of tolerance, to head off intracivilizational conflicts.

NATION BUILDING, DOUBLE STANDARDS, AND U.S. HEGEMONY

After its elation at winning the Cold War, America stood alone as the world's only superpower: the richest nation, the nation with the lion's share of military might, and the nation responsible for addressing the world's problems. No one accused the United States of not having a vision—if only the rest of the world practiced democratic government, religious toleration, and the free market, harmony would prevail instead of conflict, and prosperity would soon take the place of poverty. Unfortunately, several obstacles emerged to block American goals and exacerbate world anger. The first is America's ambivalence about its own status as a hegemon. Does that mean the nation has to intervene militarily in every trouble spot around the globe? If so, why did the United States intervene twice in Iraq and in Rwanda not at all, where the death toll was greater and the problems far worse? The nation used to intervene quietly, with less bloodshed; unquestionably, a bloodless coup d'état engineered by U.S. intelligence agents in retrospect looks a whole lot better than the bloody insurgency in Iraq, where thousands of Iraqis and Americans have been killed, or Rwanda, where close to one million have died. Unfortunately, U.S. leaders did not always pick the right allies, and, as in the case of Iran, the people have long memories. Since the 1970s, Congress has prohibited the CIA from overthrowing foreign governments, leaving the nation with a much blunter weapon: the military option.

As evident in Iraq, military solutions to nation building have been found wanting. The U.S. military is not prepared and is ill equipped to take on the task of resurrecting a country fraught with religious strife, economic devastation, and a political legacy of dictatorship and misrule. Air power supported by ground troops easily conquered Iraq, but the question asked by the winning candidate played by Robert Redford in the movie of the same name (*The Candidate*), "What do I do now?" plagued the winners, who had neglected to plan for the period after the victory. The United States has the most powerful and competent military machine in the world, but through no fault of its own, it just happens to be the wrong vehicle for nation building. Closing a newspaper in a town in Iraq might have been a viable solution for a military leader unaccustomed to freedom of the press; to Iraqis, that action precipitated a revolt.

Because of Iraq, America suffered a significant loss in its international reputation. And to its added consternation, the nation now finds itself in the company of imperial powers in the minds of former colonies, even though the United States had very little to do with the current problems inflicted by colonialism.

Arrogance was the operative word—at least to the rest of the world, and to many U.S. citizens as well. For the fifth time since World War II, America has engaged in a full-fledged war without a declaration of war from

Congress, in violation of its own Constitution. The United States also waged war without UN Security Council approval, although it is doubtful that the Security Council would have permitted a war, no matter what nation was invaded. Still, the United States regards itself as the world's leader, insisting that other nations relinquish their nuclear weapons while it continues to keep its own—the premise being that America can be trusted, while other nations, particularly "nations of concern," cannot. Perhaps not quite a double standard, but that is the way it is perceived by the rest of the world. Also, although the idea of nation building is sound, it sounds too much like "the white man's burden" of colonial times, with the United States in the position of pressing democracy on nations who have neither the experience nor the appreciation for it. Today, America finds itself isolated: "Toughness, credibility, and military prowess will only get us so far; the purpose of . . . [military action] has become self-defeating."[20]

THE POLLS AND THE "POLS"

Polls have become the lifeblood of politicians everywhere. Originated in the United States, America's political pollsters now ply their trade abroad, with many of them developing lucrative international practices. David Garth, one of the first and most successful political consultants, broke into the Israeli market early on, campaigning for Menachem Begin with the slogan, "Rock 'em, sock 'em, hit 'em again Menachem." Other consultants have penetrated South America, Europe, Asia, and Africa with their skills at measuring public sentiment and their ability to win elections. The importance of polls cannot be underestimated, since they now color life in many fields other than politics: focus groups in advertising, market research for products, and ratings taken every seven seconds for television networks to gauge audience share and demographics.

The polls not only reveal the world's hostility to the United States, but they also show how out of sync Americans are with world opinion—although they are catching up. Iraq, for example, has been a sore point in America as well as the rest of the world since the start of the war. A CNN/ *USA Today* poll taken in May 2005 found that a majority of Americans (57 percent) thought the war was not worth it, compared with 73 percent who supported the war two years earlier.[21] But a leader need not be a slave to polls. Most Americans opposed U.S. preparations for World War II, for example, but President Franklin Roosevelt had the foresight to begin to arm both the nation and its allies.

Nevertheless, many of America's allies and friends suspect its motives for going to war in the Middle East, particularly after no weapons of mass destruction were found in Iraq. They are more likely to believe that the U.S.-led war on terror is more about "controlling Mideast oil and dominating the world" than about "America's stated objectives of self-defense and global democratization." But ambivalence also accompanies cynicism, more so after the London bombings: "While [our allies] chafe at the U.S. role as the world's supercop, they're also relieved that no one else is walking the beat."[22]

Then, too, ignoring the polls can create peril at the ballot box, as the government in power learned after the bombings of four crowded commuter trains in Madrid in March 2004. Outrage at the government of Prime Minister Jose Maria Aznar followed the attacks that killed 200 people and wounded 1,500 more, and after eight years in power, Aznar and his party were ousted in favor of the Spanish Socialists, led by Jose Luis Rodriguez Zapatero. The reason? Over 90 percent of the Spanish people opposed the war as unjust, with tens of thousands taking to the streets the year before to protest Aznar's support of the U.S. effort. Many voters believed that Al Qaeda had orchestrated the attacks to punish Aznar.

Prior to the election, polls indicated strong support for Aznar and his Popular Party. The bombings changed public opinion overnight and led Zapatero to promise to withdraw Spain's 1,300 troops from Iraq and restore good relations with France and Germany, both of whom had opposed the war.[23] After the election—with two million young people voting for the first time—the Aznar government issued a statement through its foreign policy spokesman complaining that the terrorists had "achieved their objectives . . . and transformed [themselves] into political actors."[24]

THE DEFEAT COMPLEX

The most politically successful ruse that leaders use to whip up sentiment against an internal or outside challenger is to recall an ancient insult or defeat. It doesn't matter if it happened ten centuries ago—as in the Crusades—or yesterday; the sting of defeat remains. The reason it stays so long is that defeat means humiliation: fortifications weren't strong enough, the soldiers not brave enough, or the peoples' faith in God had weakened.

The stigma of defeat also argues for a change in leaders, especially when those leaders are associated with defeat. The death of Yasir Arafat, who ignored the Oslo Peace Accords, gave the Palestinian people a new opportunity to negotiate with their longtime Israeli enemies.

According to some scholars of conflict, anger is a learned behavior; people more naturally gravitate toward peaceful coexistence. The great archaeologist Richard Leakey wrote that "the fossil record is more compatible with a peaceable than with a violent scenario of early hominid emergence." Anthropologist Margaret Mead concluded that "a violent approach to solving problems is learned behavior that can be unlearned."[25]

But long-term defeat leads to anger and to the aggressive behavior that is associated with war and revolution. The Japanese still refer to the "black ships," their way of expressing the humiliation they felt at having their culture that went back centuries invaded by the barbaric West. Similarly, the Chinese weathered long years of collective humiliation, as European nations carved up "spheres of influence" before they threw off the shackles of colonialism and struggled toward independence.

If the major problems today are psychosocial problems, perhaps the worst way to address them is through military might. Rather, some suggest that the best way to deal with them entails a "broad-based effort to address the psychological roots of radicalism and terrorism in the Islamic world . . . [and] taking seriously the character . . . of radical Islam." Policy, said political scientist and Middle East expert Fouad Ajami, can "never speak to wrath."[26]

ADDRESSING ANGER:
IMPLEMENTING TOLERANCE

The first step to peace in a conflict-ridden world is to recognize the major sources of world anger and, if possible, to address them. Some are obvious; others are not. Some anger is healthy, while some is not; too often, the results and the writers of history (which many claim is written by the victors) determine which is which. Was Menachem Begin, who spent years in the Irgun, the Jewish underground organization that bombed British targets, a terrorist or a freedom fighter? It depends on whom you ask.

Military solutions may last for a while, but they cannot alone compensate for diplomatic, economic, political, and cultural approaches to problems that may go back hundreds of years. Some problems seem so immediate—

like Saddam Hussein's misgovernance in Iraq—that the temptation to address them quickly trumps other solutions that might be more durable. Before jumping into the fray, world leaders would do well to remind themselves of journalist H. L. Mencken's warning that "for every problem, there is a solution: neat, simple and wrong." Nevertheless, even heeding Mencken, some modest suggestions for dealing with current world anger and hopefully heading off conflict are the following:

Addressing Religious Fundamentalism

For what it is, not what leaders interpret it to be, religion is a two-edged sword, with both edges cutting into politics. Many religious fundamentalists look toward religion to compensate for a grim present and ever bleaker future. It comforts them to believe in a glorious hereafter, especially since their present world promises so little in terms of regime change, an improved standard of living, or a genuine role in society.

Still others manipulate religion for their own purposes: to acquire power and then to keep old feuds alive to maintain their power. In many of these cases, a clash of interests occurs, as the rigidity with which fundamentalists interpret religion is bound to conflict with how others live their lives. When in power, the Taliban exercised such rigid control over women that women were prohibited from receiving either an education or medical treatment. In contrast, the "new constitution in Afghanistan requires that 30 percent of the members of parliament be women," said the Afghan ambassador jubilantly.[27]

Religion also can be a force for positive change, as witnessed by the many social movements linked to democracy and led by courageous religious leaders such as Martin Luther King Jr. in the United States, Bishop Desmond Tutu in South Africa, and the Dalai Lama in Tibet.

The real problem with religion lies in the clash of cultures, with nations like the United States and Western Europe preferring that religion and the state be kept separate, while other states, primarily Islamic states, consider their religion an inherent part of government. Clashes over these diverse interpretations occur most often when large groups of immigrants seek to impose their own culture on countries that resist those changes, or when groups within nations oppose the imposition of fundamentalist religious law. The head scarf debate in France is a prime example, while the stakes of other conflicts have risen much higher. What does the rule of law mean in Iran, for example, when nine-year-olds can be married against their will just because the law—religious law—says so?

Recognize the Defeat Complex and Keep That in Mind When Negotiating

As Anwar Sadat proved in his quest for peace with Israel, cultures that have experienced defeat—or feel defeated—need to experience victory in order to feel generous toward their oppressors. Even after a ten-year war and the loss of over three million lives, the Vietnamese do not hate the United States; on the contrary, bilateral business deals are brisk between the two countries, and tourism is flourishing. Why? Largely because the Vietnamese defeated the United States and can afford to be generous, while America "spun" the defeat as a stalemate, in the same year and very much the same way that Sadat spun the Yom Kippur War. Nations and cultures need a way to save face, a fact that only the most sophisticated leaders realize.

Recognize the Difference between a Real Tribal War and a Clash of Resources

As in Sierra Leone, when leaders (both internal and external) exploited minor conflicts between the Mende, Limba, and Temne tribes to extend a civil war into a brutal ten-year conflict perpetuated by illegal gunrunning, all paid for by the illegal export of diamonds, in Afghanistan, the United States and other countries ensured the flow of arms to fight the Soviets: "Instead of traditional leaders, guns were introduced as factors," said former Afghan ambassador to the United States Said Tayeb Jawad. "Millions of dollars in weapons were sent to Afghanistan to fight Communism." The illegal arms flow exacerbates conflict in many other places as well; there is too much money to be made, and nations are either reluctant to stop the arms merchants or are unable to stop them. The dark side of the global economy involves the ugly secret that while industrialized nations benefit from its fruits, they turn a blind eye to some of its worst practices. What it amounts to is the internationalization of the economy without a corresponding global governing force.

Enforce Embargoes

Again, witness the sad recent history of Sierra Leone. The ten-year civil war would not have endured for so long without the full-fledged complicity of Western nations. The Belgian diamond merchants continued to receive and pay for smuggled diamonds, the Belgian government neglected to regulate or prosecute them, the government of Sierra Leone and the United Nations were impotent to stop either the war or the trade that paid for it, and the rest of the world remained content to ignore the situation.

Would Saddam Hussein's government have survived if the UN had been able to enforce the Food for Oil embargo in Iraq? Would the war have been necessary? Avoided? Who knows, but it was worth a try. Long after the war started, in 2004, investigators revealed that the embargo was violated by many countries eager to do business with Iraq, with France the worst offender. Global solutions require a loss of sovereignty, something the United States was quite willing to do when it entered and promoted the World Trade Organization. But on a political level, sovereignty becomes more problematic, with individual nations too mistrustful of each other to enforce an embargo, or stop the world arms trade that fuels ongoing and, all too often, bloody conflicts.

Damage Control Is Not Enough

Public relations solutions no longer work to solve long-term problems that grow worse with each passing day. The nation–state is rapidly becoming irrelevant in the face of world anger, terrorism, and increasing violence. New groupings that have shown sensitivity to regional needs, ethnic auton-omy, and the recognition of plural interests can stem future conflicts before they escalate into open rebellions.[28] In 1980, for example, the Spanish gov-ernment negotiated regional autonomy for the Basque, Catalan, and Gali-cian regions. Independence for the Kurds has plagued Iraq and Turkey for decades, but both countries remain very reluctant to relinquish any regional autonomy for them. Mediating structures for "preventive diplomacy"[29] are sorely needed in many areas of the world, but without real guidelines or consensus, they are a long way off from realization.

Inclusion

"You don't get harmony when everyone sings the same note," reads a T-shirt from the Unitarian Universalist Fellowship. It is important to recog-nize past conflicts that have engendered anger that might breed future vio-lence. At the same time, it is also important to develop new political systems that envelop warring parties, attempt to get them to work together, and govern with an eye toward progress that will not satisfy everyone but that will at least leave the door open for future negotiations. "Our approach is not to antagonize tribal chiefs, but to bring them into the fold," said an Afghan diplomat from the Karzai government.

Implement Tolerance

Just as leaders can manipulate anger into wars, antisocial behaviors, and draconian budget cuts, they can also try to exercise positive leadership—even using the anger tool. Americans retell the Boston Tea Party as a memorable event in their history when a group of angry colonists jettisoned a shipment of tea into Boston Harbor to protest British rule. This led to the overthrow of the British and the establishment of America as an independent nation. Similarly, the leadership of Nelson Mandela, in South Africa, and Mahatma Gandhi, in India, also led to independence, primarily because those leaders were able to channel public anger against colonial rule in their countries into positive channels that led to political change. In America, the efforts of Martin Luther King Jr. and his followers effectively tapped into the anger of African Americans to bring about a revolution in the nation's civil rights policies. True, none of those regions remain free of problems, but there is no doubt that political anger that is mobilized by enlightened leadership can lead to genuine progress on many fronts.

The theme of an important OSCE conference in Belgium in September 2004 emphasized the importance of leadership in implementing tolerance. In fact, a small footnote to history should include President George W. Bush's successful efforts to hold the conference in the face of vigorous opposition from European leaders, who tried to cancel the meeting and sweep their problems under the rug. Bush and his then national security advisor, Condoleezza Rice, exercised their own vigorous leadership and ultimately persuaded the European leaders to support the conference.

At the meeting, one speaker after another spoke of the concept of the "Other," and how important it was to recognize it, identify it, and replace it with newer ideas, including multiculturalism, power sharing, and the benefits of diversity. The biggest problem confronting the fifty-two European nations represented at the conference was "Islamophobia," identified as the intense prejudice against Muslim immigrants in their countries. To defend themselves against public manifestations of Islamophobia, Muslims were beginning to form powerful voting blocs in France, Germany, and Great Britain. Turkey, which hopes to become the first Muslim country to join the European Community, has accused the EC of holding up its candidacy because of Islamophobia in many of its member countries. Although Turkey is a secular country, it still struggles with many of its Muslim citizens, who seek to introduce more of their religion into government.

The suggestions for implementing tolerance were plentiful, and it remained to be seen whether conferees would be able to convince the folks back home to put their lofty ideals into practice. "I prefer the word respect to tolerance," said Prince Hassan of Jordan, emphasizing how the three Abrahamic religions all stressed love, not hate. "We need to work FOR something, not AGAINST xenophobia and racism. . . . Muslims and Jews have been victims since the Inquisition in Spain. The killing still continues in Darfur, Palestine, Afghanistan and Iraq." Hassan stressed the importance of anticipating crises and heading them off, a strategy he called "crisis avoidance."

The president of the OSCE, Dr. Solomon Passy, proudly recalled how his own small country, Bulgaria, saved fifty thousand Jews from the Nazis in World War II—including his own family. Passy, now the foreign minister of Bulgaria, spoke of enlisting society in these efforts: "The entire country was involved. Bulgaria was the only country whose Jewish population increased in World War II." And in contrast to leaders who manipulate anger for their own nefarious purposes, "We have to take a stand against violent means of conflict resolution. We have to incorporate Islam into the OSCE agenda."

"Governments have the tools to combat intolerance," added Guy Verhofstadt, the prime minister of Belgium, who wanted his country to share its experience with conflict with other nations.[30] "These [laws and edicts] must be enforced by the courts. We set up a dialogue with immigrants. In 1945 [referring to World War II] we said, 'never again.' It is up to us sixty years later to make sure that is true."

The Belgian prime minister reflected Europe's willingness to regulate anger before it accelerated into antisocial behavior. European countries, for example, regulate the Internet, which Americans—more wedded to absolute First Amendment freedoms—do not. As a result, many hate groups abroad register their sites in the United States, from where they feel free to disseminate their messages around the world.

Another example of a proactive government—according to its representative—is Latvia, where there are few extremists but many ethnicities. Fearing ethnic conflict, the government has taken the initiative to prevent xenophobia, targeting Muslims, Russian refugees, and other immigrants for government protection. Their other ideas of "proactive policies" seemed weak in view of current challenges: an educational program to promote tolerance, as well as increased Holocaust education.

Religious leaders weighed in heavily in support of the role of religion in fostering tolerance, without admitting the divisive role that religion has also played throughout history. Representing the Holy See, Cardinal William Keeler of Baltimore blamed the media for much of the world's conflict. "The history of the world," he argued, "has shown long periods of peace between the wars. The media exacerbates conflict . . . the media should report interethnic peace." He also added that the "Catholic Church has played a very active role on the ground. It has used schools as an example of how successfully it can work with a multicultural population," pointing to education as the key to adding a "spiritual dimension that is important to civil society." Disagreeing with him, Gert Weisskirchen, vice president of the OSCE, delivered an impassioned speech in German, saying that the problem was not religion itself, but its context.

No one raised the issue of racism until the end of the conference, when Doudou Diene, an African representing an agency of the United Nations,[31] argued strongly for multicultural societies to take root in places where current realities reveal the opposite. We have to "affirm the history of the victims," he insisted. "Present conflicts are a dangerous mix of race, religion and culture. In multicultural Bosnia you have 'multicultural proximity.' The neighbor of today becomes tomorrow's enemy. The answer is a real multicultural society." Critiquing the clash of civilizations theory of political scientist Samuel Huntington, he added that Huntington was doing the world a disservice by emphasizing the difference in cultures: "Huntington gives a central argument that the presence of Latinos in the United States is a great threat to the U.S. identity. These are the kind of perceptions and images that lead to individual and national acts of genocide."[32]

The most positive approach to negative anger was the advocacy of strong government programs to combat "hate crimes." "If you're a Bangladeshi or a Sikh, you live with an everyday fear," explained Michael McClintock, a Scotsman representing a group called Human Rights First. "They are regularly beaten up. The violence in the south of England is going up. What gets on the books is minimal. There were two Sikhs killed recently. Only one murder was reported. In the United States, the Federal Housing Act has a hate crimes section. Officials are discouraged from reporting those crimes. They don't want it on their watch. The FBI also underreports and underrecords hate crimes."

Most European nations ban hate speech, which Americans are loathe to do. We prize our freedom of speech, and would rather see hateful speech defeated in the marketplace of ideas rather than supressed. Singapore has achieved ethnic harmony by severely punishing such speech and promoting diversity, but at the cost of liberty.

These, then, are the lessons of the last turbulent century. Use all force necessary to end genocidal conflicts and punish those most responsible for these crimes. The United States cannot act alone but in concert with like-minded nations. But then, as the United States did after World War II, and as some African nations are doing today, offer the hand of reconciliation and friendship to the vanquished, including some of the most vicious and brutal foes. As the United States turned Germany and Japan into allies, so nations torn by civil wars can unite behind the goals of conquering poverty and disease, and condemn ancient hatreds to their rightful place in the dustbin of history.

NOTES

1. Kevin Harris, *Collected Quotes from Albert Einstein*, 1995, http://rescomp.stanford.edu/~cheshire/EinsteinQuotes.html (accessed February 13, 2006).

2. Marc Lacey, "Victims of Uganda Atrocities Choose a Path of Forgiveness," *New York Times*, April 18, 2004.

3. Ibid.

4. Ibid. Also see appendix C.

5. Daniel Jonah Goldhagen, *Hitler's Willing Executioners: Ordinary Germans and the Holocaust* (New York: Alfred A. Knopf, 1996).

6. Richard W. Stevenson, "8 Leaders Hail Steps on Africa and Warming," *The New York Times*, July 9, 2005.

7. Edward Cody, "A Chronicle of Deaths Foretold," *The Economist*, July 11, 2005. 18–20.

8. Ibid.

9. James Traub, "The Congo Case," *New York Times Magazine*, July 3, 2005. See also Adam Hochschild, *King Leopold's Ghost: A Story of Greed, Terror and Heroism in Colonial Africa* (Boston: Houghton Mifflin, 1998).

10. Susan J. Tolchin, *The Angry American: How Voter Rage Is Changing the Nation* (Boulder, CO: Westview Press, 1998) 22.

11. Edward Cody, "A Chinese Riot Rooted in Confusion," *Washington Post*, July 18, 2005, 38.

12. www.whitehouse.gov/infocus/europe/2005/may/index.html (accessed February 13, 2006).

13. Cody, "A Chronicle of Deaths Foretold," *The Economist*.

14. Larry Rohter and Juan Forero, "Unending Graft Is Threatening Latin America," *New York Times*, July 30, 2005, 1.

15. Cody, "A Chronicle of Deaths Foretold," *The Economist*, 44.

16. See Samuel P. Huntington, *The Clash of Civilizations and the Remaking of World Order* (New York: Touchstone, 1997).

17. Ted Robert Gurr, "Peoples against States: Ethnopolitical Conflict and the Changing World System," *International Studies Quarterly* 38 (1994).

18. Ibid., 357.

19. Ibid., 367.

20. Michael Mazarr, "The Psychological Sources of Islamic Terrorism," *Policy Review* 125 (2004): 55.

21. www.reuters.com/newsArticle.jhtml.

22. Ibid.

23. Elaine Sciolino, "Following Attacks, Spain's Governing Power Is Beaten," *New York Times*, March 15, 2004.

24. Keith Richburg, "Spanish Socialists Oust Party of U.S. War Ally," *Washington Post*, March 15, 2004.

25. David W. Augsburger, *Conflict Mediation across Cultures: Pathways and Patterns* (Louisville, KY: Westminster/John Knox Press, 1992).

26. Mazarr, "The Psychological Sources of Islamic Terrorism."

27. Ambassador Said Tayel Jawad, in a speech to the University Club, Washington, DC, January 26, 2004.

28. Gurr, "Peoples against States."

29. Ibid.

30. Belgium has long tangled with the problem in integrating two cultures: Flemish and Walloon. They have partially solved this conflict by creating a bicultural society. Street signs and restaurant menus, for example, are in French as well as Flemish.

31. UN Special Rapporteur for Contemporary Forms of Racism, Racial Discrimination, Xenophobia and Related Intolerance.

32. See Huntington, *The Clash of Civilizations and the Remaking of World Order.*

Appendix A

GLOBAL ANTI-SEMITISM

Global anti-Semitism between July 2003 and December 2004, as reported by the U.S. Department of State in January 2005.

EUROPE AND EURASIA

Armenia—The director of ALM-TV frequently made anti-Semitic remarks on the air, and the Union of Armenian Aryans, a small ultranationalist group, called for the country to be "purified" of Jews and Yezidis. In Yerevan, vandals damaged a memorial to victims of the Holocaust.

Austria—Thirteen physical attacks on Jews during this period, among 122 anti-Semitic incidents in the first eleven months of 2004, and 134 in 2003.

Azerbaijan—Only one reported incident. When such incidents were threatened, the government was quick to respond, sometimes having police block and secure houses of worship.

Belarus—Memorials in Minsk, Brest, and Lida vandalized, as were cemeteries in Bobruisk and Tcherven.

Belgium—Thirty incidents between 2000 and 2003, compared with four a year in previous years.

Bosnia-Herzegovina—Despite a Jewish population estimated at five hundred to one thousand persons, tombstones in the Jewish cemetery in Sarajevo were vandalized.

Bulgaria—About 3 percent of 2,162 newspaper and magazine articles on Jewish-Israeli subjects were found to be anti-Semitic.

Croatia—A member of the municipal council in Dubrovnik commented that, "choosing between Serbs and Jews, Jews were still a greater evil."

Czech Republic—A small but persistent and fairly well-organized extreme right-wing movement with anti-Semitic views exists in the country. Vandals toppled eighty tombstones at a Jewish cemetery in Hranice, and damaged a memorial to victims of the Holocaust in Bohumin.

Denmark—Five incidents of anti-Semitic vandalism, primarily graffiti, and one anti-Semitic mailing were reported between January and June 2004.

Finland—A few reports of anti-Semitic activity, chiefly graffiti, such as swastikas with anti-Semitic slogans spray painted in public places.

France—The government reported 510 anti-Semitic incidents (both actions and threats) in the first six months of 2004, compared with 593 for all of 2003, and 932 for 2002. There were 160 attacks against persons or property in the first seven months of 2004 versus 75 during the same period in 2003.

Germany—A total of 1,199 anti-Semitic crimes reported in 2003, down from 1,515 in 2002.

Greece—Vandalism continued to be a problem in 2004.

Hungary—Fewer acts of vandalism in Jewish cemeteries in 2004 than in 2003.

Iceland—Harassment of the Jewish community was infrequent and not organized. Iceland has no synagogue, no Jewish community center, and no Jewish religious services.

Ireland—A 2003 study by the European Commission's European Monitoring Center on Racism and Xenophobia described the country as having "relatively little reported in the way of a problem with anti-Semitism."

Italy—Anti-Semitism is a growing problem because of widespread opposition to Israeli policies.

Kazakhstan—No reports of anti-Semitic incitement or acts during this period.

Latvia—Several incidents of desecration of cemeteries, vandalism, and anti-Semitic graffiti.

Lithuania—Desecration of a Jewish cemetery in the Kaisadorys region, and publication of anti-Semitic articles in the media.

Macedonia—Several spectators hung banners with swastikas at a handball match near the city of Bitola. Police officers who watched and did nothing were later disciplined.

Moldavia—More than seventy tombstones desecrated in the Jewish cemetery in Tiraspol, and Molotov cocktail thrown into synagogue.

Netherlands—The National Expertise Center for Discrimination found 204 cases in 2003, compared with 242 in 2002. About a quarter of the cases involved anti-Semitism.

Norway—Members of the Jewish community reported a doubling of anti-Semitic activity in the last two years. Forty incidents were reported in 2003.

Poland—Surveys show a decline in anti-Semitism. In April 2004, the pastor of St. Brigid Church in Gdansk said during services that "Jews killed Jesus and the prophets" and displayed posters asserting that only Christians could be true citizens. The archbishop of Gdansk subsequently removed the priest for this and other improprieties.

Romania—Extremist elements of the press continued to publish anti-Semitic articles.

Russia—Conditions for Jews improved in the absence of state-sanctioned anti-Semitism. However, anti-Semitic vandalism and other acts continued to occur.

Serbia and Montenegro—More than fifty acts of vandalism on religious property occurred during this period.

Slovak Republic—Anti-Semitism persisted, manifested by incidents of violence and vandalism.

Slovenia—With three to four hundred Jews, there was one incident involving desecration of a Jewish family grave. Jewish community representatives reported widespread prejudice, ignorance, and false stereotypes being spread within society.

Spain—The Jewish community reported incidents of verbal harassment, vandalism of synagogues and Jewish community institutions, and increasing anti-Semitic sentiment in newspaper commentary and sporting events.

Sweden—Police report an increase of anti-Semitic hate crimes. During 2003, 128 hate crimes were reported, of which three were bodily assaults.

Switzerland—The Swiss Observatory of Religions reported that anti-Semitic feelings increased during the last decade. Although physical violence was rare, most anti-Semitic remarks were fueled by extensive media reports over the Israeli-Palestinian conflict and the Holocaust assets issue.

Turkey—Suicide attacks against two of Istanbul's major synagogues killed twenty-three persons and injured more than three hundred others.

Ukraine—Vandalism and attacks on rabbis were among the anti-Semitic incidents during this period. A local court in Kiev ruled that publication of the newspaper *Silski Visti* be suspended for fomenting interethnic hatred in connection with the 2002 publication of an article, "Myth about Ukrainian Anti-Semitism," and a 2003 article, "Jews in Ukraine: Reality without Myths."

United Kingdom—Anti-Semitic incidents included physical attacks; harassment; desecration of property; vandalism; and hateful speech, letters, and publications. A total of 511 anti-Semitic incidents were recorded between June 2003 and June 2004.

Uzbekistan—Anti-Semitic fliers have been distributed throughout the country. However, these views were not representative of the feelings of the vast majority of the population. No reports of verbal harassment, physical abuse, or desecration have been made. Respected Jewish community members report that they feel very welcome in the country.

NEAR EAST AND NORTH AFRICA

Society and legislation in nations in the region, except for Israel and Lebanon, reflect the views of an overwhelmingly Muslim population and a strong Islamic tradition. At times, both social behavior and legislation discriminated against members of minority religions.

Egypt—Anti-Semitic articles and opinion pieces in the print media and editorial cartoons appeared in the press and electronic media.

Iran—Media disseminated anti-Semitic content, including articles and editorial cartoons.

Iraq—Former Governing Council announced that Jewish expatriates would be allowed to vote in 2005 elections and would be treated like any other expatriate group. Government also denied unfounded rumors that Jewish expatriates were buying up real estate in an attempt to reassert their influence in the country.

Lebanon—The TV series *Ash-Shatat*, "The Diaspora," which centered on the alleged conspiracy of *The Protocols of the Elders of Zion* to dominate the world, was aired in October and November 2003 by the Lebanese satellite television network Al-Manar, which is owned by the terrorist organization Hezbollah.

Morocco—The centuries-old Jewish minority generally lived in safety. However, terrorist attacks targeted a Jewish community center in Casablanca, and a Jewish merchant was murdered in an apparently religiously motivated killing.

Occupied Territories—Palestinian terrorist groups carried out attacks against Israeli civilians. While these attacks were usually carried out in the name of Palestinian nationalism, the rhetoric used by these organizations sometimes included expressions of anti-Semitism.

Saudi Arabia—There were frequent instances in which mosque preachers, whose salaries are paid by the government, used strongly anti-Jewish language in their sermons. Prayers for the death of Jews were made from mosques, including the Grand Mosque in Mecca and Prophet's Mosque in Medina.

Syria—The government barred Jewish citizens from government employment and exempted them from military service due to tense relations with Israel. Jews also were the only religious minority group whose passports and identity cards noted their religion. The press and electronic media spewed anti-Semitic material.

Tunisia—The government took a wide range of security measures to protect synagogues, particularly during the High Holy Days.

United Arab Emirates—The government closed the Zayed Centre for Coordination and Follow-Up, a local think tank that published some anti-Jewish propaganda and hosted anti-Jewish speakers.

Yemen—All non-Muslims are barred from running for Parliament.

WESTERN HEMISPHERE

Overall, anti-Semitism was not a widespread problem. Countries such as Brazil, Uruguay, Colombia, and Bolivia reported isolated acts of anti-Semitic graffiti and anti-Semitic material on Internet sites, mostly by small neo-Nazi skinhead organizations. But anti-Semitism remained a problem in Argentina, and Canada experienced an increasing number of anti-Semitic incidents.

EAST ASIA AND THE PACIFIC

Anti-Semitism was not a widespread problem in East Asian Pacific countries, where Jewish communities are small. But there were overt incidents in Australia and New Zealand, where the communities were somewhat larger.

SOUTH ASIA

Anti-Semitism is not an issue of any significance in India, nor in the smaller South Asian countries, specifically Bangladesh, Afghanistan, Sri Lanka, Nepal, and Bhutan. Pakistan is an exception. Although there are very few Jewish citizens in the country, anti-Semitic articles are common in the press. The Pakistani media sometimes refers to India as the "Zionist threat on our borders." But this attitude is not reflected by the government, which cooperated in the capture of those responsible for the 2002 murder of *Wall Street Journal* correspondent Daniel Pearl.

AFRICA

With the exception of the occasional report of an anti-Semitic article appearing in newspapers, anti-Semitism was not a problem throughout sub-Saharan Africa. Most African countries have very small Jewish populations. In South Africa, which has the largest population of Jews on the continent with an estimated eighty thousand, there were occasional reports of desecration and vandalism or verbal or written harassment, but no violent incidents.

Appendix B

GENOCIDE AND THE TWENTIETH CENTURY

Country/region/ethnic group	Victims of genocide (in millions, approx.)
Armenians	1.5
Ukranians	3.0
Jews	6.0
Gypsies	0.25
Slavs	6.0
Russians	25.0
Chinese	25.0
Ibos	1.0
Bengalis	1.5
Guatemalans	0.2
Cambodians	1.7
Indonesians	0.5
East Timorese	0.2
Burundis	0.25
Sudanese	2.0
Rwandans	0.8
North Koreans	2.0
Kosovars	0.01

Source: Genocide Watch, *The International Campaign to End Genocide*, 2004, www
.genocidewatch.org/internationalcampaign.htm (accessed February 13, 2006).

Appendix C

TRUTH COMMISSIONS: VARIETIES OF JUSTICE

Country & dates	Commission makeup, origin	Mandate	Outcomes
Argentina 1983–1984	Est. by president, 13 commission-ers (3 of them legislators), 60 staff.	Investigation restricted to disap-pearances by former military regime, 1976–1983.	Report *Nunca Mas* published 1985, report used for reparations and trials. Prosecutions later halted and pardons given.
Bolivia 1982–1984	Est. by president, 8 commission-ers, cross-section of society.	Limited to disappearances by for-mer military regime.	No report produced. Trials against former officials instigated in mid-1980s.
Burundi 1995–1996	Est. by UN at government request, 5 commissioners.	Report on human rights abuses, 1993–1995.	Report to UN in 1996. Interna-tional prosecution and new com-mission to investigate pre-1993 abuses. Action halted due to renewed violence.

Country & dates	Commission makeup, origin	Mandate	Outcomes
Chad 1991–1992	Est. by new president, 12–16 commissioners.	Investigate crimes and misappropriations by former regime.	Report in 1992 was first to name perpetrators; no purges or trials.
Chile 1990–1991	Est. by president, 8 commissioners, partisan balance, staff of 60.	Investigate disappearances, killings, torture, and kidnappings on both sides of 1973–1990 conflict.	Report issued 1991. Victims compensated, but Amnesty Law of 1978 barred prosecution. Report became basis for Pinochet extradition.
East Timor 2002–2004	Est. by UN Transitional Administration, public nomination of 36 commissioners.	Investigate human rights violations and deaths of 200,000, 1974–1999. Facilitate reconciliation and reintegration, recommend measures to prevent recurrence.	War crimes trials convicted 84 low- and mid-level military. New commission est. in August 2005 empowered to grant amnesty to those who apologize. No provision for prosecution.[1]
Ecuador 1996–1997	Est. by Ministry of Govt. and Police, 7 members from human rights organizations, Bishops' Conference, president's office.	Investigate human right violations 1979–1996.	Commission disbanded after 5 months due to insufficient financial support. No report.
El Salvador 1992–1993	Est. by UN as part of peace accord, 3-member commission of former Columbian president, former Venezuelan Foreign Minister, GWU law professor.	Human rights abuses committed by both sides of conflict 1980–1991.	Report released at UN in 1993 named perpetrators and mandated recommendations. Amnesty law was passed, but some perpetrators removed from positions; recommendations implemented with international pressure.

1. Ellen Nakashima, "For Survivors of E. Timor Massacre, Justice Still Elusive," *Washington Post*, September 16, 2005.

Germany 1992–1994	27-member body of political experts and specialists set up by Parliament.	Investigate human rights abuses in East Germany 1949–1989. Focus on historical analysis rather than individual human rights violations.	Academic papers commissioned and presented at hearings, 15,000-page report produced.
Ghana 2002–2004	Law passed by Parliament, est. 9-member commission appointed by president, broad investigative powers.	Investigate human rights abuses in times of instability and unconstitutional governments, 1957–1993, and recommend victim redress and institutional reform.	Report issued May 16, 2005.
Guatemala 1997–1999	Est. by UN as part of peace accord, 3 commissioners and staff of up to 200.	Investigate killings, disappearances, torture, and rape committed by both sides of conflict 1962–1996.	Report, *Memory of Silence*, turned over to UN and Guatemalan government, UN released. Documented involvement by "highest authorities." No naming of perpetrators.
Haiti 1995–1996	Est. by president, 7 commissioners, staff of 50–100.	Investigate human rights violations committed by former regime 1991–1994.	Report presented 1996, published 1997. Perpetrator names not released. Recommended international tribunal for trials.
Nepal 1990–1991	Est. by prime minister, 3-member commission.	Investigate human rights violations during the autocratic Panchayat system under which political parties were banned in 1962–1990.	Report completed 1991, released 2004. Perpetrators not named. Few recommendations implemented.

Country & dates	Commission makeup, origin	Mandate	Outcomes
Nigeria 1999–2001	President-appointed 7-member commission with limited powers and resources; public, televised hearings.	Investigate human rights abuses 1984–1999; identify perpetrators; recommend actions to redress past injustices and prevent future violations of human rights.	Report submitted to president in 2002, never released.
Panama 2001–2002	Est. by president, 6-member commission.	Investigate human rights violations during military dictatorships 1968–1989.	Report released April 2002.
Peru 2001–2003	Est. by government through legislation, originally 6-member commission, expanded later to 12.	Provide an official record of human rights violations 1980–2000; analyze causes, and recommend measures to strengthen human rights and democracy.	Final report released August 2003.
Philippines 1986	President gave broad powers to 7-member Commission on Human Rights.	Investigate human rights violations attributed to the military during the 1972–1986 rule of President Ferdinand Marcos.	No report issued.
Serbia and Montenegro 2002–2005	President est. 15-member commission with 3-year mandate.	Investigate war crimes committed in Slovenia, Croatia, Bosnia, and Kosovo over the previous decade.	Commission disbanded without reporting.

Sierra Leone 2002–2004	Mandated by peace agreement, enacted by president and parliament; 7 members, 3 selected by UN; operated in parallel for special UN tribunal for prosecution.	Report on human rights violations since 1991, make recommendations for reconciliation, prevent future violations. Included amnesty provisions, immunity from prosecution.	Report presented to president of Sierra Leone and then to UN Security Council in October 2004.
South Africa 1995–2001	Est. by Parliament, 17 commissioners and staff of 300.	Broad powers to investigate human rights violations by all sides during the apartheid era between 1960 and 1994. Public hearings, broadcasts. Amnesty upon disclosure.	Recommendations published in 1998. Named perpetrators and victims, recommended reparations policy (implemented) and prosecution (not implemented). Final report issued in 2003 recommended apology by head of state, actions to facilitate reconciliation, and education programs.
South Korea 2000–2004	Est. by act of Parliament, 9 commissioners.	Investigate the death of citizens opposed to past authoritarian regimes and report findings and recommendations to the president, and identify human rights perpetrators for prosecution.	Report of first phase implicated government authorities. Commission extended in 2002.

Country & dates	Commission makeup, origin	Mandate	Outcomes
Sri Lanka 1994–1997	President est. 3 regional commissions, each with 3 commissioners and staff.	Investigate disappearances 1988–1994, determine fate of disappeared, bring charges against those responsible.	Final report to president September 1997, released after international pressure. Recommended international tribunal to try perpetrators. Some reparations to victims, 400 eventually charged with human rights violations.
Uganda 1986–1995	Est. by president, 6 members with broad mandate.	Investigate human rights abuses by public officials 1962–1986, make recommendations to prevent recurrence.	After 9 years, findings and recommendations published in 1994. Some recommendations accepted, many ignored.
Uruguay 1985	Est. by Parliament, 6-member commission.	Investigate the fate of the disappeared during the military regime in power from 1973 to 1985.	Report forwarded to Supreme Court listed evidence of security force involvement. No prosecutions. In 1989, religious group SERPAJ released its report of 3-year study. Report ignored by government.
Zimbabwe 1985	Government est. commission led by Zimbabwean lawyer.	Investigate the killing of an estimated 1,500 political dissidents and other civilians in the Matabeleland region.	No report was released.

Sources: Hayner, *Unspeakable Truths*, Skaar et al., *Roads to Reconciliation*; United States Institute for Peace; International Center for Transitional Justice. Compiled by Carol Whitney, George Mason University.

BIBLIOGRAPHY

BOOKS

Abbas, Hassan. *Pakistan's Drift into Extremism: Allah, the Army, and America's War on Terror.* Armonk, NY: M. E. Sharpe, 2005.

Akbar, M. J. *The Shade of Swords: Jihad and the Conflict between Islam and Christianity.* Edited by NetLibrary Inc. Taylor & Francis e-Library ed. London: Routledge, 2002.

Anonymous. *Imperial Hubris.* Washington, DC: Brassey's Inc., 2004.

Aristotle. *Nicomachean Ethics.* Oxford: Clarendon Press, 1908.

Armstrong, Karen. *The Battle for God.* New York: Alfred A. Knopf, 2000.

Augsburger, David W. *Conflict Mediation across Cultures: Pathways and Patterns.* Louisville, KY: Westminster/John Knox Press, 1992.

Benjamin, Daniel, and Steven Simon. *The Age of Sacred Terror.* New York: Random House, 2002.

Bhagwati, Jagdish N. *In Defense of Globalization.* New York: Oxford University Press, 2004.

Blum, Howard. *The Eve of Destruction: The Untold Story of the Yom Kippur War.* New York: HarperCollins, 2003.

Brzezinski, Zbigniew. *The Choice: Global Domination or Global Leadership.* New York: Basic Books, 2004.

Buruma, Ian, and Avishai Margalit. *Occidentalism: The West in the Eyes of Its Enemies.* New York: Penguin Press, 2004.

Byrd, Robert C. *Losing America: Confronting a Reckless and Arrogant Presidency.* New York: W. W. Norton, 2004.

Campbell, Greg. *Blood Diamonds: Tracing the Deadly Path of the World's Most Precious Stones.* Boulder, CO: Westview Press, 2002.

Carr, Caleb. *The Lessons of Terror: A History of Warfare against Civilians: Why It Has Always Failed, and Why It Will Fail Again.* New York: Random House, 2002.

Carter, Dan T. *The Politics of Rage: George Wallace, the Origins of the New Conservatism, and the Transformation of American Politics.* New York: Simon & Schuster, 1995.

Chatterjee, Deen K., and Don E. Scheid. *Ethics and Foreign Intervention.* Cambridge Studies in Philosophy and Public Policy. Cambridge: Cambridge University Press, 2003.

Chesler, Phyllis. *The New Anti-Semitism: The Current Crisis and What We Must Do about It.* San Francisco: Jossey-Bass, 2003.

Chua, Amy. *World on Fire: How Exporting Free Market Democracy Breeds Ethnic Hatred and Global Instability.* New York: Doubleday, 2003.

The Compact Oxford English Dictionary. Oxford: Oxford University Press, 2000.

Conteh-Morgan, Earl, and Mac Dixon-Fyle. *Sierra Leone at the End of the Twentieth Century: History, Politics, and Society.* Society and Politics in Africa 8. New York: P. Lang, 1999.

Corn, David. *The Lies of George W. Bush: Mastering the Politics of Deception.* New York: Crown Publishers, 2003.

Diamond, Jared. *Guns, Germs, and Steel: The Fate of Human Societies.* New York: W.W. Norton, 1997.

Dobbs, Lou. *Exporting America: Why Corporate Greed Is Shipping American Jobs Overseas.* New York: Warner Books, 2004.

Esposito, John L. *The Islamic Threat: Myth or Reality?* 2nd ed. New York: Oxford University Press, 1995.

Featherstone, Mike. *Undoing Culture: Globalization, Postmodernism and Identity.* London: Sage Publications, 1995.

Ferme, Mariane C. *The Underneath of Things: Violence, History, and the Everyday in Sierra Leone.* Berkeley: University of California Press, 2001.

Fisher, Louis. *Presidential War Power.* 2nd ed. Lawrence: University Press of Kansas, 2004.

Fitzgerald, F. Scott, and Edmund Wilson. *The Crack-Up.* New York: New Directions, 1993.

Foxman, Abraham H. *Never Again?: The Threat of the New Anti-Semitism.* San Francisco: HarperSanFrancisco, 2003.

Friedman, Thomas L. *Longitudes and Attitudes: Exploring the World after September 11.* New York: Farrar, Straus, and Giroux, 2002.

———. *The Lexus and the Olive Tree.* Rev. ed. New York: Farrar, Straus, and Giroux, 2000.

Gaylin, Willard. *The Rage Within: Anger in Modern Life.* New York: Simon & Schuster, 1984.

———. *Hatred: The Psychological Descent into Violence.* New York: PublicAffairs, 2003.

Gopin, Marc. *Between Eden and Armageddon: The Future of World Religions, Violence, and Peacemaking.* Oxford: Oxford University Press, 2000.

Gray, John. *False Dawn: The Delusions of Global Capitalism.* London: Granta Books, 1998.

Greenberg, Stanley B. *The Two Americas.* New York: St. Martin's Press, 2004.

Grunberger, Michael W. *From Haven to Home: 350 Years of Jewish Life in America.* New York: George Braziller, 2004.

Gurr, Ted Robert, and Barbara Harff. *Ethnic Conflict in World Politics*. Dilemmas in World Politics. Boulder, CO: Westview Press, 1994.

Harris, Sam. *The End of Faith: Religion, Terror, and the Future of Reason*. New York: W.W. Norton, 2004.

Harris, William V. *Restraining Rage: The Ideology of Anger Control in Classical Antiquity*. Cambridge, MA: Harvard University Press, 2001.

Hira, Ron and Anil Hira. *Outstanding America*. New York: Amacom, 2005.

Hirsch, John L. *Sierra Leone: Diamonds and the Struggle for Democracy*. Boulder, CO: Lynne Reiner Publishers, and the International Peace Academy, 2001.

Hosseini, Khaled. *The Kite Runner*. New York: Riverhead Books, 2003.

Huntington, Samuel P. *The Clash of Civilizations and the Remaking of World Order*. New York: Simon & Schuster, 1996.

Jackson, Michael. *In Sierra Leone*. Durham, NC: Duke University Press, 2004.

Jergensmeyer, Mark. *Terror in the Mind of God: The Global Rise of Religious Violence*. Berkeley: University of California Press, 2000.

Johnson, Chalmers A. *Blowback: The Costs and Consequences of American Empire*. New York: Metropolitan Books, 2000.

Kaplan, Robert D. *Balkan Ghosts: A Journey through History*. 1st Vintage Departures ed. New York: Vintage Books, 1994.

———. *Soldiers of God: With Islamic Warriors in Afghanistan and Pakistan*. New York: Vintage Books, 2001.

Karnow, Stanley. *Vietnam: A History*. New York: Viking, 1983.

Kepel, Gilles. *The War for Muslim Minds: Islam and the West*. Cambridge, MA: Belknap Press, 2004.

Khadra, Yasmina. *The Swallows of Kabul*. New York: Doubleday, 2004.

Kinzer, Stephen. *All the Shah's Men: An American Coup and the Roots of Middle East Terror*. Hoboken, NJ: John Wiley & Sons, 2003.

Kirkpatrick, Jeane J., and the American Enterprise Institute for Public Policy Research. *Dictatorships and Double Standards: Rationalism and Reason in Politics*. New York: Simon & Schuster, 1982.

Kissinger, Henry. *Does America Need a Foreign Policy?: Towards a Diplomacy for the 21st Century*. New York: Simon & Schuster, 2001.

Knightley, Phillip. *The First Casualty: From the Crimea to Vietnam; The War Correspondent as Hero, Propagandist and Myth Maker*. New York: Harcourt Brace Jovanovich, 1975.

Lewis, Bernard. *What Went Wrong?: Western Impact and Middle Eastern Response*. Oxford: Oxford University Press, 2002.

Lifton, Robert J. *America's Apocalyptic Confrontation with the World*. New York: Nation Books, 2003.

Lincoln, Bruce. *Holy Terrors: Thinking about Religion after September 11*. Chicago: University of Chicago Press, 2003.

Lipset, Seymour Martin. *American Exceptionalism: A Double-Edged Sword*. New York: W. W. Norton, 1997.

Mamdani, Mahmood. *Good Muslim, Bad Muslim: America, the Cold War and the Roots of Terror.* New York: Pantheon, 2004.

Manchester, William. *American Caesar: Douglas MacArthur 1880–1964.* Boston: Little, Brown, 1978.

Mansfield, Stephen. *The Faith of George W. Bush.* New York: Jeremy P. Tarcher/Penguin, 2003.

Mencken, H. L. "The Divine Afflatus." In *A Mencken Chrestomathy,* xvi, 627. New York: Vintage Books, 1982.

Menocal, Maria Rosa. *The Ornament of the World: How Muslims, Jews, and Christians Created a Culture of Tolerance in Medieval Spain.* Boston: Little, Brown, 2002.

Merry, Robert W. *Sands of Empire: Missionary Zeal, American Foreign Policy and the Hazards of Global Ambition.* New York: Simon & Schuster, 2005.

Michael, George. *Confronting Right-Wing Extremism and Terrorism in the USA.* New York: Routledge, 2003.

Miles, Hugh. *Al-Jazeera: The Inside Story of the Arab News Channel That Is Challenging the West.* New York: Grove Press, 2005.

Nafisi, Azar. *Reading Lolita in Tehran: A Memoir in Books.* New York: Random House, 2003.

Nasr, Seyyed Hossein. *The Heart of Islam: Enduring Values for Humanity.* San Francisco: HarperSanFrancisco, 2002.

Neumann, Franz. "Anxiety and Politics." In *Identity and Anxiety: Survival of the Person in Mass Society,* edited by Maurice R. Stein, Arthur J. Vidich, and David Manning White, 658. Glencoe, IL: Free Press, 1960.

Nietzsche, Friedrich. *Human, All Too Human.* Cambridge: Cambridge University Press, 1986.

Nye, Joseph S. *Soft Power: The Means to Success in World Politics.* New York: PublicAffairs, 2004.

Palmer, Monte, and Princess Palmer. *At the Heart of Terror: Islam, Jihadists, and America's War on Terrorism.* Lanham, MD: Rowman & Littlefield, 2004.

Pape, Richard A. *Dying to Win—The Strategic Logic of Suicide Terrorism.* New York: Random House, 2005.

Pipes, Daniel. *Militant Islam Reaches America.* New York: W. W. Norton, 2002.

Plaut, W. Gunther, ed. *The Torah: A Modern Commentary.* New York: Union of American Hebrew Congregations, 1981.

Power, Samantha. *A Problem from Hell: America and the Age of Genocide.* New York: Perennial, 2003.

Rabinovich, Abraham. *The Yom Kippur War: The Epic Encounter That Transformed the Middle East.* New York: Schocken Books, 2004.

Randal, Jonathan. *Osama: The Making of a Terrorist.* New York: Alfred A. Knopf, 2004.

Random House Webster's. New York: Random House, 1997.

Redl, Fritz, and David Wineman. *Children Who Hate: The Disorganization and Breakdown of Behavior Controls.* New York: Free Press, 1965.

Reston, James. *Warriors of God: Richard the Lionheart and Saladin in the Third Crusade*. New York: Doubleday, 2001.

Robins, Robert S., and Jerrold M. Post. *Political Paranoia: The Psychopolitics of Hatred*. New Haven, CT: Yale University Press, 1997.

Rodinson, Maxime. "The Western Image and Western Studies of Islam." In *The Legacy of Islam*, edited by Joseph Schacht and C. E. Bosworth. New York: Oxford University Press, 1974.

Rosenbaum, Ron, ed. *Those Who Forget the Past: The Question of Anti-Semitism*. New York: Random House Trade Paperbacks, 2004.

Roy, Olivier. *Globalized Islam: The Search for a New Ummah*. The Ceri Series in Comparative Politics and International Studies. New York: Columbia University Press, 2004.

Rushdie, Salman. *The Satanic Verses*. New York: Viking, 1989.

Said, Edward W. *Orientalism*. New York: Pantheon Books, 1978.

Sardar, Ziauddin. *Orientalism: Concepts in the Social Sciences*. Buckingham, England: Open University Press, 1999.

Scheler, Max. *Ressentiment*. Trans. by Lewis B. Coser and William W. Holdheim. New York: Marquette University Press, 1994.

Schlesinger, Arthur Meier. *The Disuniting of America: Reflections on a Multicultural Society*. Rev. and enlarged ed. New York: W. W. Norton, 1998.

Schwartz, Stephen. *The Two Faces of Islam: The House of Sa'ud from Tradition to Terror*. New York: Doubleday, 2002.

Sciolino, Elaine. *Persian Mirrors: The Elusive Face of Iran*. New York: Free Press, 2000.

Shahak, Israel, and Norton Mezvinsky. *Jewish Fundamentalism in Israel*. London: Pluto Press, 2004.

Sharansky, Natan, and Ron Dermer. *The Case for Democracy: The Power of Freedom to Overcome Tyranny and Terror*. New York: PublicAffairs, 2004.

Smith, James M., and William C. Thomas, eds. *The Terrorism Threat and U.S. Government Response: Operational and Organizational Factors*. U.S. Air Force Academy, CO: USAF Institute for National Security Studies, 2001.

Soros, George. *The Bubble of American Supremacy: Correcting the Misuse of American Power*. New York: PublicAffairs, 2003.

Stearns, Peter N. *Global Outrage: The Impact of World Opinion on Contemporary History*. Oxford: Oneworld, 2005.

Stern, Jessica. *Terror in the Name of God: Why Religious Militants Kill*. New York: Ecco, 2003.

Strasser, Steven, ed. *The Abu Ghraib Investigations: The Official Reports of the Shocking Prisoner Abuse in Iraq*. New York: PublicAffairs, 2004.

Timberg, Robert. *The Nightingale's Song*. New York: Simon & Schuster, 1995.

Timmerman, Kenneth R. *Preachers of Hate: Islam and the War on America*. New York: Crown Forum, 2003.

Tolchin, Martin, and Susan J. Tolchin. *Selling Our Security: The Erosion of America's Assets*. 1st ed. New York: Alfred A. Knopf, 1992.

Tolchin, Susan J. *The Angry American: How Voter Rage Is Changing the Nation.* Boulder, CO: Westview Press, 1998.

Tolchin, Susan J., and Martin Tolchin. *Glass Houses: Congressional Ethics and the Politics of Venom.* Boulder, CO: Westview Press, 2001.

Tolchin, Susan, and Martin Tolchin. *Buying into America: How Foreign Money Is Changing the Face of Our Nation.* New York: Times Books, 1988.

Viorst, Milton. *In the Shadow of the Prophet: The Struggle for the Soul of Islam.* New York: Anchor Books/Doubleday, 1998.

———. *Sandcastles: The Arabs in Search of the Modern World.* New York: Alfred A. Knopf, 1994.

———. *What Shall I Do with This People?: Jews and the Fractious Politics of Judaism.* New York: Free Press, 2002.

Vollmann, William T. *Rising Up and Rising Down: Some Thoughts on Violence, Freedom and Urgent Means.* New York: Ecco, 2004.

Williams, Shirley. *God and Caesar: Personal Reflections on Politics and Religion.* Erasmus Institute Books. Notre Dame, IN: University of Notre Dame Press, 2003.

Woodward, Bob. *Plan of Attack.* New York: Simon & Schuster, 2004.

Wright, Robin B. *Sacred Rage: The Wrath of Militant Islam.* New York: Simon & Schuster, 2001.

York, Byron. *The Vast Left Wing Conspiracy: How Democratic Operatives, Eccentric Billionaires, Liberal Activists, and Assorted Celebrities Tried to Bring Down a President, and Why They'll Try Even Harder Next Time.* New York: Crown Forum, 2005.

Zayani, Mohamed. *The Al Jazeera Phenomenon: Critical Perspectives on New Arab Media.* Boulder, CO: Paradigm Publishers, 2005.

PAPERS AND CONFERENCE PROCEEDINGS

Alaikum, Ambassador As Salaam. "Address to Bd-Americans." Paper presented at the Reflecting Pool, Washington, DC, October 14, 2001.

Hira, Ron. "Implications of Offshore Oursourcing." George Mason University, 2004.

Levitte, Jean David. "Anti-Semitism on the Internet." U.S. Capitol Building, Hart 902, September 9, 2004.

"Relationship between Racist, Xenophobic and Anti-Semitic Propaganda on the Internet and Hate Crimes." Paris, France, June 16, 2004.

Snow, John. March 31, 2004.

Mendible, Myra. "A Woman's Place: Gender, Honor, and the Culture of Humiliation." 2004.

Tuna, Husnu. "The Scope and the Consequences of the Ban on Headscarf in Turkey." Paper presented at the OSCE Conference on Tolerance and the Fight against Racism, Xenophobia and Discrimination, Brussels, September 13–14, 2004.

Wolf, Christopher. "Needed: Diagnostic Tools to Gauge the Full Effect of Online Anti-

Semitism and Hate." Paper presented at the Conference of Organization of Security and Cooperation in Europe, Paris, France, June 16, 2004.

———. "Regulating Hate Speech Qua Speech Is Not the Solution to the Epidemic of Hate on the Internet." Paper presented at the OSCE Meeting on the Relationship between Racist, Xenophobic and Anti-Semitic Propaganda on the Internet and Hate Crimes, Paris, France, June 16–17, 2004.

ARTICLES, MONOGRAPHS, CASES, STATUTES, AND WEBSITES

Alvarez, Alex. "Ideology and Genocide." In, *Preventing Genocide: Threats and Responsibilities*. Stockholm, Sweden: 2004.

Ambrose, Soren, and Mara Vanderslice. *G7 Debt Relief Plan: More Grief Than Relief.* Jubilee USA Network, 2002. www.jubileeusa.org/jubilee.cgi?page = briefings.html (accessed February 13, 2006).

Anti-Defamation League. *Poisoning the Web: Hatred Online Internet Bigotry, Extremism and Violence.* 1999. www.adl.org/poisoning_web/poisoning_toc.asp (accessed February 13, 2006).

Anu-Masr, Donna. "Survivors Recount Terror of Campaign." *Dallas Morning News,* May 31, 2004, A21.

Backover, Andrew. "Hate Sets up Shop on the Internet." *Denver Post,* November 8, 1999, E1.

Barnes, Steve. "U.S. May Intervene in Head-Scarf Suit." *New York Times,* April 15, 2004.

Berger, Joseph. "Israel Sees a Surge in Immigration by French Jews, But Why?" *New York Times,* July 4, 2004, A3.

Berlinski, Claire. "The Hope of Marseille." *Azure* 19 (2005).

Bhagwati, Jagdish. "Why Your Job Isn't Moving to Bangalore." *New York Times,* February 15, 2004, A11.

Booth, Jenny, and Michael Theodoulou. "Bush: US Abusers of Iraqis Will Face Justice." *The Times, London,* May 5, 2004.

Boustany, Nora. "Arab Opinion Hits US and Hits Home." *Washington Post,* May 7, 2004, A24.

Bremer, Marie. "Daughters of France, Daughters of Allah." *Vanity Fair,* April 2004, 190–209.

Burch, Douglas. "Russian Jews Say Nationalists Rekindle Anti-Semitism." *Baltimore Sun,* June 29, 2005, A13.

Central Intelligence Agency. *Sierra Leone.* www.cia.gov/cia/publications/factbook/geos/sl.html (accessed February 13, 2006).

Chandrasekaran, Rajiv. "A Grand Mission Ends Quietly." *Wall Street Journal,* June 29, 2004, A1, A17.

Chandrasekaran, Rajiv, and Anthony Shadid. "U.S. Targeted Fiery Cleric in Risky Move." *Washington Post*, April 11, 2004, A1.

Cloud, David. "Red Cross Cited Detainee Abuse Over a Year Ago." *Wall Street Journal*, May 10, 2004.

Cohen, Roger. "What the World Wants from America." *New York Times*, January 6, 2005, 1, 4.

Dallmayr, Fred. "Lessons of September 11." *Theory, Culture and Society* 19, no. 4 (2002).

Dinmore, Guy. "Middle East Reform to Top G8 Summit Agenda." *Financial Times*, June 8, 2004, 5.

Donohue, John. "Mistranslations of God: Fundamentalism in the Twenty-First Century." *Islam and Christian-Muslim Relations* 15, no. 5 (2004).

Gosselin, Janie. "Businessmen Fight Anti-Semitism in Canada." *Barre-Montpelier Times Argus*. Associated Press. August 14, 2005.

Hoge, Warren. "UN Is Gradually Becoming More Hospitable to Israel." *New York Times*, October 11, 2005.

Jaffe, Greg, and David Cloud. "Officials in Iraq Knew Last Fall of Prison Abuse." *Wall Street Journal*, May 19, 2004, A1.

Jubilee USA Network. "Drop the Debt." Spring 2004. www.jubileeusa.org/dropthe debtspring04.pdf (accessed February 13, 2006).

Daily Mirror, "God Help America—The People Have Spoken." November 4, 2004.

Duncan, Benjamin. *US Muslims Condemn Brutality and Bigotry*. Al Jazeera, May 31, 2004. http://english.aljazeera.net/NR/exeres/F273E152-91F8-433C-8DCB-2353FE9D 535F.htm (accessed February 13, 2006).

Eggen, Dan, and Dana Priest. "Terror Suspect Alleges Torture." *Washington Post*, January 6, 2005, A1, A8.

Falk, Richard. "Stage of Siege: Will Globalization Win Out?" *International Affairs* 73, no. 1 (1997): 132.

Farah, Douglas. "Salving Deep Wounds, Sierra Leoneans Vote." *Washington Post*, May 15, 2002.

———. "A Protected Friend of Terrorism." *Washington Post*, April 25, 2005, A19.

Faruqui, Ahmad. "Splitting Egypt from the Arab World—Lessons of the October War." *CounterPunch*, 2003.

Farwell, Byron. "Five Days in Fallujah." *Atlantic Monthly*, 2004, 117.

Federal Research Division, U.S. Library of Congress. "The October 1973 War." In *Egypt: A Country Study*, ed. Helen Chapin Metz. Washington, DC: U.S. Library of Congress, 1991. http://countrystudies.us/egypt/41.htm (accessed February 13, 2006).

Fineman, Howard. "Apocalyptic Politics." *Newsweek*, May 24, 2004.

Forero, Juan. "Latin American Graft and Poverty Trying Patience with Democracy." *New York Times*, June 24, 2004, A1.

———. "Latin America Fails to Deliver on Basic Needs." *New York Times*, February 22, 2005, A1 and C2.

Friedman, Thomas L. "Axis of Appeasement." *New York Times*, March 18, 2003, A27.

Geneva Convention Relative to the Protection of Civilian Persons in Time of War. August 12, 1949.

Genocide Watch. *The International Campaign to End Genocide.* 2004. www.genocide watch.org/internationalcampaign.htm (accessed February 13, 2006).

Gerges, Fawaz A. "Islam and Muslims in the Mind of American Influences on the Making of U.S. Policy." *Journal of Palestine Studies* 2 (1997): 68–80.

Gettleman, Jeffrey. "4 from U.S. Killed in Ambush in Iraq; Mob Drags Bodies." *New York Times*, April 1, 2004.

Goodman, Amy, and Juan Gonzalez. *Diamonds Are a War's Best Friend: The Trade of Arms for Diamonds in Africa.* April 19, 2000. www.democracynow.org/index.pl?issue = 20000419 (accessed February 13, 2006).

Goodstein, Laurie, and William Yardley. "The 2004 Election: Faith Groups; President Benefits from Efforts to Build a Coalition of Religious Voters." *New York Times*, November 5, 2004, A22.

Graff, Peter. "Red Cross Was Told Iraq Abuse 'Part of Process.'" *Reuters*, May 10, 2004.

Graham, Patrick. "Beyond Fallujah: A Year with the Iraqi Resistance." *Harper's Magazine*, June 2004, 37–38.

Gray, John. "Global Utopias and Clashing Civilizations: Misunderstanding the Present." *International Affairs* 74, no. 1 (1998): 149–63.

Gurr, Ted. "Peoples against States: Ethnopolitical Conflict and the Changing World System." *International Studies Quarterly* 38 (1994): 347–77.

Hamdi v. Rumsfeld. 542 U.S. 507 (2004).

Haqqani, Husain. "The American Mongols." *Foreign Policy*, May–June 2003, 70.

Hersh, Seymour. "Chain of Command." *New Yorker*, May 17, 2004, 37–43.

Higgins, Andrew. "Could U.N. Fix Iraq? Word from Kosovo Isn't Encouraging." *Wall Street Journal*, August 2, 2004, A1, A8.

Hira, Ron. "Implications of Offshore Outsourcing." George Mason University, 2004.

Hoge, Warren. "Remove Wall, Israel Is Told by the U.N." *New York Times*, July 20, 2004, A10.

Hornaday, Bill W. "Outsourcing Didn't Pay Off for Conseco." *Indiana Star*, April 22, 2004. www.indystar.com/articles/5/140262-9565-092.html.

Hutzler, Charles. "Yuppies in China Protest Via the Web—and Get Away with It: Nationalistic Dissidents Press for Hard-Hitting Policies on Japan, Taiwan, U.S." *Wall Street Journal*, March 19, 2004.

International Network against Cyber Hate. "Anti-Semitism on the Internet." 2004. www.inach.net (accessed February 13, 2006).

Jehl, Douglas. "Some Abu Ghraib Abuses Are Traced to Afghanistan." *New York Times*, August 8, 2004, A11.

Kaiser, Robert. "A Foreign Policy Falling Apart." *Washington Post*, May 23, 2004, B1.

Kirkpatrick, David D. "Battle Cry of Faithful Pits Believers and Unbelievers." *New York Times*, October 31, 2004, 22.

———. "Bush Addresses Evangelicals on Prayer Day." *New York Times*, May 7, 2004, A21.

Krauthammer, Charles. "The Real Mideast 'Poison.'" *Washington Post*, April 30, 2004, A29.

Kristof, Nicholas. "Bush Points the Way." *New York Times*, May 29, 2004, A25.

Lacey, Marc. "Africa, Beyond the Bullets and Blades." *New York Times*, April 25, 2005.

Lewis, Bernard. "The Roots of Muslim Rage." *Atlantic Monthly* 266, no. 3 (1990): 47–60.

Lewis, Neil. "Justice Memos Explained How to Skip Prisoner Rights." *New York Times*, May 21, 2004, A21.

———. "US Judge Halts War-Crime Trial at Guantanamo." *New York Times*, November 9, 2004, A1, A14.

———. "US Spells out New Definitions Curbing Torture." *New York Times*, January 1, 2005, A1.

Liebman, Charles. "The Myth of Defeat: The Memory of the Yom Kippur War in Israeli Society." *Middle East Studies* 29 (July 1993): 412.

Lustick, Ian S. "Israel's Dangerous Fundamentalists." *Foreign Policy* 68 (1987).

Lyman, Rick. "As Legal Moves Dwindle in Schiavo Case, the Focus Returns to Governor Bush." *New York Times*, March 26, 2005, A16.

Mahr, Kris. "Next on the Outsourcing List." *Wall Street Journal*, February 2, 2004, B1, B8.

Marquis, Christopher. "U.S. Protests Broadcasts by Arab Channels." *New York Times*, April 29, 2004, A13.

Mazarr, Michael J. "The Psychological Sources of Islamic Terrorism." *Policy Review* 125 (June–July 2004): 39–60.

McDermott, Marcia L., and Alan W. Wallace. "Anwar Sadat and the 1973 Yom Kippur War Force: Sadat's Ultimate Instrument of Statecraft." National Defense University, 2000.

McNaught, Mark. "Secularism in France: The Banning of Religious Symbols in Public Schools." *Public Administration Times*, 2004, 9. *The Media Line*. 2004. www.themedialine.org (accessed February 13, 2006).

Moore, Molly. "France Beefs Up Response to Riots," *Washington Post*, November, 8, 2005, A1.

Moulton, J. C. *The 1973 War: The Egyptian Perspective*. GlobalSecurity.Org, 1997. www.globalsecurity.org/military/library/report/1997/moulton.htm (accessed June 2004).

Newsweek. "Bush Had Decided That Geneva Conventions Did Not Apply to Taliban, Al Qaeda by Jan. 2002." May 16, 2004.

New York Times. "General Said to Be Faulted over Speeches." August 20, 2004, A19.

Niva, Steve. "Between Clash and Co-Operation: US Foreign Policy and the Specter of Islam." *Middle East Report* 208 (Autumn 1998): 26–29.

Planned Parenthood of the Columbia/Willamette Inc. v. American Coalition of Life Activists. Civil No. 95-1671-JO (2004).

Poller, Nidra. "Betrayed by Europe: An Expatriate's Lament." *Commentary*, March 2004.

Radio Netherlands. *A Brief History.* January 28, 2000. www2.rnw.nl/rnw/en/ features/humanrights/historysl.html (accessed February 13, 2006).

Rasul v. Bush. 542 U.S. 466 (2004).

Reno v. American Civil Liberties Union. 521 U.S. 844 (1997).

Risen, James. "Secrets of History: The CIA in Iran." *New York Times*, April 16, 2000, 1.

Rivlin, Gary. "Hate Messages on Google Site Draw Concern." *New York Times*, February 7, 2005, C1.

Sciolino, Elaine. "On Bastille Day, France Buzzes over a Hoax and Racism." *New York Times*, July 15, 2004, A3.

———. "France Wants Sharon to Explain His Call for Jews to Flee." *New York Times*, July 20, 2004, A3.

Shadid, Anthony, and Sewell Chan. "Protests Unleashed by Cleric Mark a New Front in War." *Washington Post*, April 5, 2003, A12.

Slevin, Peter. "Ending a 'Deadly Hate' of Jews." *Washington Post*, April 29, 2004, A21.

Smillie, Ian, Lansana Gberie, and Ralph Hazleton. *The Heart of the Matter: Sierra Leone, Diamonds and Human Security.* Africa Nation, 2000. www.africaaction.org/docs00/ sl0001.htm (accessed February 13, 2006).

Smith, Craig S. "Europe's Jews Seek Solace on the Right." *New York Times*, February 20, 2005, 3.

Smith, Jeffrey, and Dan Eggen. "Gonzales Helped Set the Course for Detainees." *Washington Post*, January 5, 2005, A1, A8.

Smith, Martin. "Beyond Baghdad." *Frontline*, PBS, 2004. www.pbs.org/wgbh/pages/ frontline/shows/beyond/etc/script.html (accessed February 13, 2006).

Standard Minimum Rules for the Treatment of Prisoners. Resolution 663 C (XXIV) and 2076 (LXII). July 31, 1957.

State of Maine v. Thomas Belanger. 552 A.2d 27 (1988).

Suskind, Ron. "Without a Doubt." *New York Times*, October 17, 2004, 44.

Tessler, Mark, and Jodi Nachtwey. "Islam and Attitudes toward International Conflict: Evidence from Survey Research in the Arab World." *Journal of Conflict Resolution* 42, no. 5 (1998): 619–36.

Thottam, Jyoti. "The Master Builder." *Time*, June 7, 2004, 41.

Tolchin, Susan J. "Missiles to Plowshares." *Journal of Socio-Economics* 25, no. 4 (1996): 407–24.

Tolchin, Susan. "Mixed Feelings, Happy Trade-Offs." *Earth Times*, August 2, 1993, 16.

Tolchin, Susan, and Martin Tolchin. "The Feminist Revolution of Jihan Sadat." *New York Times Magazine*, March 16, 1980, 20–27.

Traub, James. "The Things They Carry." *New York Times Magazine*, January 4, 2004.

Tyler, Patrick E., and Don Van Natta. "Militants in Europe Openly Call for Jihad and the Rule of Islam." *New York Times*, April 26, 2004, A1, A10.

United States v. Richard Machado. 195 F.3d 454 (1999).

Vedantam, Shankar. "Gunman Found Haven on Nazi Web Site." *Washington Post*, March 23, 2003, A1.

Weil, Patrick. "Lifting the Veil of Ignorance." *Progressive Politics* 3, no. 1 (2004): 1.

White House. *Status of Detainees at Guantanamo*. 2002. www.whitehouse.gov/news/releases/2002/02/20020207-12.html (accessed February 7, 2002).

Wilgoren, Jodi. "Shadowed by Threats, Judge Finds New Horror." *New York Times*, March 2, 2005, A1.

Will, George. "The Perils of Protectionism." *Newsweek*, March 20, 2004.

Wills, Garry. "The Day the Enlightenment Went Out." *New York Times*, November 4, 2004, A31.

Wong, Edward. "Iraq Is a Hub for Terrorism, However You Define It." *New York Times*, June 20, 2004, 5.

———. "In Anger, Ordinary Iraqis Are Joining the Insurgency." *New York Times*, June 28, 2004.

Wright, Robin. "Desire for Nuclear Empowerment a Uniting Factor in Iran." *Washington Post*, November 14, 2004, A25.

———. "Will the Modern Era Come Undone in Iraq?" *Washington Post, Outlook*, May 16, 2004, B1, B4.

Zakaria, Fareed, "The Saudi Trap." *Newsweek*, June 28, 2004, 30–33.

REPORTS

Anti-Defamation League. "Anti-Semitism in Egypt: Media and Society; July 2003–February 2004." March 30, 2004.

Anti-Defamation League. "Anti-Semitism Worldwide, 2001–2002." Coauthored by Dina Porat and R. Stauber, and cosponsored by the world Jewish congress and the Stephen Roth Institute at Tel-Aviv University.

Anti-Defamation League. "Attitudes toward Jews, Israel and the Palestinian-Israeli Conflict in Ten European Countries." 2004.

Anti-Defamation League. "Jihad Online: Islamic Terrorists and the Internet." 2002.

Delahunty, Robert, and John Yoo. "Memorandum for William J. Hayes II, General Counsel, Department of Defense." Office of the Attorney General, January 9, 2002.

European Monitoring Centre on Racism and Xenophobia. "Manifestations of Anti-Semitism in the EU." 2002–2003.

Kaplan, James E., and Margaret P. Moss. "Investigating Hate Crimes on the Internet." Edited by Michael L. Lieberman and Stephen Wessler. Partners Against Hate/U.S. Department of Justice, 2003.

Kean, Thomas H., and Lee H. Hamilton. *The 9/11 Commission Report*. Edited by the

National Commission on Terrorist Attacks Upon the United States. Washington, DC, 2004.

Lustick, Ian S. "For the Land and the Lord: Jewish Fundamentalism in Israel." New York: Council on Foreign Relations, 1988.

NPR Online Newshour. "Background Report: The Hutu-Tutsi Conflict." 1999.

Rumsfeld, Donald. "The Geneva Convention Does Not Apply to Terrorist Organizations Such as Al-Qaeda." disinfopedia.org, 2004.

Tiven, Lorraine. "Hate on the Internet: A Response Guide for Educators and Families." Washington, DC: Anti-Defamation League/Partners Against Hate, 2003.

United Nations Development Programme. "Democracy in Latin America: Towards a Citizen's Democracy." 2004.

United Nations Development Programme. "Human Development Report." New York, 2002.

United Nations Development Programme. "Human Development Report." New York, 2003.

U.S. State Department. "Report on Global Anti-Semitism." Edited by the Bureau of Democracy, Human Rights, and Labor. Washington, DC: U.S. State Department, 2005.

Webman, Esther. "Al Aqsa Intifada and 11 September: Fertile Ground for Arab Anti-Semitism." In *AntiSemitism WorldWide*, Anti-Defamation League and the World Jewish Congress, in association with Tel Aviv University, Stephen Roth Institute for the Study of Contemporary Antisemitism and Racism, 2001–2002.

World Bank. "World Development Report: Attacking Poverty." Edited by Oxford University Press. New York: World Bank, 2000–2001.

FILM AND BROADCASTS

Dobbs, Lou. *The Dobbs Report.* CNN, 2004.

French Embassy. "France's Fight against Anti-Semitism." Washington, DC: French Embassy, 2004.

Frontline. "The Jesus Factor." United States: PBS, 2004.

Noujaim, Jehane. *Control Room.* Doha: Magnolia Pictures, 2004.

HEARINGS

Senate Foreign Relations Committee. *Testimony of Daniel S. Mariaschin, Executive Vice President, B'nai B'rith International,* April 8, 2004.

INDEX

1967 war, 7, 23, 45, 48, 52, 123, 126–28

abortion, 61–62, 171, 179–80
Abrahamic religions. *See* religion
Abu Ghraib prison, 9–10, 147–49, 151–53, 157, 160
Afghanistan, 43, 46, 48, 52, 72n9, 204; democraticization, 191; religion and state, 57, 58–59; war in, 61, 141. *See also* Taliban
Africa, 47, 54, 72n9, 81–82, 106, 115
and fundamentalism, 43, 51
and women, 59
African Americans, 23–24, 79, 97
Al Qaeda, 3, 9, 44, 52, 55, 83–84, 102; detainees, 147, 150, 151; and humiliation, 88; and the Internet, 174, 176–77; and terrorism, 89; U.S. war on, 136. *See also* Osama bin Laden
Albania, 20, 95, 107
Algeria, 91, 95; and fundamentalism, 48
Al-Jazeera, 32–33, 156, 165, 174
anger, 3, 71, 85–86, 88, 94–95, 97, 166; and children, 94, 96; and defeat, 6–7, 79–80, 199; military solutions, 199–200; political manipulation, 79, 89–92, 188; and tolerance, 199–206

Anglo-Iranian Oil Company (AIOC), 49, 158
anti-Semitism, 3, 10, 13–16, 21, 22, 48, 96; Eastern Europe, 30–31, 36; and Israel, 5, 15, 17–18; and scapegoating, 92; violent acts, 23, 26–30; Western Europe, 24–30, 36–37. *See also* hate websites
Arabs, and Islam, 72n9
Arafat, Yasir, 21, 45, 52, 199
Argentina, 107, 112
Armenia, 20, 79, 194
Asia, 33, 46–47, 72n9
Australia, 17, 19
Austria, 25, 26

Bangladesh, 52–53, 72n9, 80, 114, 205
banking, deregulation, 108, 109, 119
Bechtel, 10, 162
Begin, Menachem, 8, 127, 131, 197, 199
Belarus, and anti-Semitism, 30, 31
Belgium, 2, 4, 25–26, 29, 189, 194, 204; and anti-Semitism, 25, 26, 29; diamond trade, 100, 102, 120, 202; hate websites, 182; and Rwanda, 86
Berlin Wall, 83, 164

ABOUT THE AUTHORS

Martin Tolchin capped a forty-year career at the *New York Times*, where he reported on Congress and politics, by becoming founder, publisher, and editor-in-chief of *The Hill* newspaper.

Susan J. Tolchin is professor of public policy at George Mason University and author of *The Angry American: How Voter Rage Is Changing the Nation* (1996 and 1998).

Together, the Tolchins have written six other books—*Glass Houses: Congressional Ethics and the Politics of Venom* (2004); *Selling Our Security: The Erosion of America's Assets* (1992); *Buying into America: How Foreign Money Is Changing the Nation* (1988); *Dismantling America: The Rush to Deregulate* (1983); *Clout: Womanpower and Politics* (1974); and *To the Victor: Political Patronage from the Clubhouse to the White House* (1971).